Chester
No Limit!

Chester
No Limit!

From Educator to A's Scoreboard Operator
A Trip Down Memory Lane

Alive Book Publishing

Chester: No Limit!
From Educator to A's Scoreboard Operator
A Trip Down Memory Lane

Additional copies may be ordered from the publisher for educational, business, promotional or premium use.
For information, contact ALIVE Book Publishing at:
alivebookpublishing.com, or call (925) 837-7303.

Book Design by Alex Johnson

ISBN 13
978-1-63132-083-5 Hardcover
978-1-63132-078-1 Paperback

ISBN 10
1-63132-078-5

Library of Congress Control Number: 2019914770

Library of Congress Cataloging-in-Publication Data
is available upon request.

First Edition

Published in the United States of America by ALIVE Book Publishing and ALIVE Publishing Group, imprints of Advanced Publishing LLC
3200 A Danville Blvd., Suite 204, Alamo, California 94507
alivebookpublishing.com

PRINTED IN THE UNITED STATES OF AMERICA

10 9 8 7 6 5 4 3 2 1

Huey Lewis and Chester Farrow
at the 1985 Bay Area Music Awards (Bammies).
Photo by Pat Johnson

Table of Contents

Press Release - February 16, 1987

Glodow & Coats Publicity Service
4034 20th Street – San Francisco, CA 94114
(415) 864-2333

FOR IMMEDIATE RELEASE

February 16, 1987
Contact: John Glodow or Michael Coats

**Monte Vista High School Students
Produce Public Service Announcements
Airing on Bay Area TV and Radio Shows**

Student-Produced Weekly TV Show Enters 14th Year on the Air

For two decades, the electronics program at **Monte Vista High School** has been a source of pride for the **San Ramon Valley Unified School District**. Boasting a four-camera, full-color television studio and complete audio and video production and editing facilities, the program has sent literally hundreds of its graduates on to jobs in network television, teaching (including the prestigious broadcast programs at **UCLA** and **San Francisco State University**), and major video production facilities throughout the state.

Moreover, under the direction of electronics teacher **Chester Farrow** and with the support of technical education administrator **Stan Greenspan**, the Monte Vista students have produced a weekly magazine format TV show, *"Just for You,"* which has aired on area cable channels for fourteen consecutive years, a national cablecasting record for consistency and longevity. The show, which is done live, is run entirely by students, from on-air personalities to producers and directors to camera operators.

The class's latest project has been the production of public service announcements for **Vocational Education Week** (February 7-13), which were disseminated for airing on 68 television and radio stations throughout Northern California. Also brought into the project were the music department, one of whose students wrote and recorded the bass-line heard on the spot, and the school choir, which recorded the background vocals.

Farrow, who initiated the Monte Vista electronics program and has been its teacher and director for 21 years, firmly believes that a key factor in the program's success, and in the successful careers of its graduates, is the hands-on experience they receive at Monte Vista.

"When these kids leave Monte Vista," says Farrow, "they have production portfolios ten times the size of what's generated in most university-level broadcast programs. But even more important, they've had the experience of producing work that has been seen by the outside world, not just critiqued in a classroom."

This hands-on, real-world-based philosophy of education has been the keystone of Farrow's program since he began staging concerts to raise funds for **Rainbow Studio**, as the Monte Vista video and audio production facility is known. Using a combination of personal contacts and devoted determination, Farrow and his classes staged a series of remarkable concerts from 1970 through 1985, presenting in the school's 800-seat theater major acts such as **Huey Lewis & The News**, **Journey**, **Boz Scaggs**, **Greg Kihn**, and **Tom Johnston** of the **Doobie Brothers**. On each of these shows, all aspects of the production, from sound and lights to stage management to artists' relations, were handled by the students.

Stan Greenspan, administrator of technical education for the San Ramon Valley Unified School District, is a vocal proponent both of Farrow's electronics program and vocational education in general.

"At the bottom line," Greenspan points out, "vocational education means salable skills. Successful vocational education programs are those willing to let go of outdated programs and make the commitment to teaching the technologies of today and tomorrow. In the past few years alone, we at the San Ramon Valley Unified School District have moved from standard drafting to CAD (Computer-Assisted Drafting), from TV repair to computer and microprocessor repair, and from typing to word processing, to name but a few examples. Chester Farrow's electronics program, with its emphasis on video and its admirable record of job placements, is a perfect representation of vocational education at its best."

Press Coverage Through the Years

• On June 8, 1981, *Valley Times* reporter Rick Freeman penned an overview of my career for their "Lifestyle" section, entitled: "A's Scoreboard Man - Monte Vista's Farrow: Promoter of Words and Music." He wrote:

> *"He's promoted concerts for Boz Scaggs, The Greg Kihn Band, and Journey. But when mid-June approaches, Chester Farrow eases back and relaxes. He more or less has to. Most of his employees are on summer vacation. Farrow, an electronics instructor at Monte Vista High School since 1967, books rock 'n rollers at the Danville school and has succeeded in an area where others have fallen... Farrow insisted he was pushed into rock n' roll by his electronics students in 1968... it was only after his students' insistence that he get into rock after he put on a series of programs such as urban renewal. 'The kids wanted me to go in a different direction,' he said humbly. 'So, we did.' And through the high school theater (built seven years ago) have come some of the heavies of rock... And if rock promotion didn't take up enough of Farrow's time, he also began his 'career' as scoreboard operator at the Oakland Coliseum for the A's starting in 1969. 'I'll do it till I die,' said the IBM scoreboard computer operator at a recent A's contest. 'I love it. It's different.' Farrow has yet to miss a game since opening day of '69, a feat he is proud of... Farrow said he takes pride in his concerts, which have raised thousands of dollars for the school's*

> *electronics department and other needy organizations. He also concentrates on doing his scoreboard job well. 'I've had a million experiences here,' he said of his Coliseum work. 'And I've met everyone in the American League I've wanted to meet.'"*

• In March 1983, in the entertainment section of the *Valley Times,* reviewer Trine Gallegos wrote:

> *"Bay Area Music Award nominees Huey Lewis and the News gave an energetic show Thursday at Monte Vista High School in Danville. Lewis and his band performed excellent rock & roll for an hour and a half."*

• On Wednesday, June 8, 1983, Ted Johnson penned a story about "Just for You" for the *Valley Pioneer,* titled, "Studio Allows Rainbow Students to Shine." He wrote:

> *"(Chet) Farrow is a teacher at Monte Vista High School, and one of his classes consists of the production of 'Just for You,' a half-hour comedy-news show being taped for one of its 36 airings on Walnut Creek GE CableVision's Channel 4. 'Just for You' is conceived, produced and directed by Farrow's students, and shot right on campus. Farrow teaches five classes in electronics, but on Thursday his room becomes a viable television center known as Rainbow Studio. Farrow's role in the show is that of overseer. He allows freedom in the content and style but remains adamant about quality. Farrow likes a smooth, seamless package, and a missed cue draws his attention quickly. He makes sure everyone keeps their attention on the show... 'Just for You' is a 'pretty good show overall,' in the opinion of Chris Derdugo, program coordinator at CableVision. 'In comparing it to other shows from high schools, the*

production execution is good. They don't miss cues, their microphones are never down (off), and it has continuity. It's not hard to watch.' Tom Cusak, Program Manager at CableVision, admits that at one time he didn't like the show. 'I had to ask them to clean it up about a year ago. I leave it up to Chet to edit and gate-keep. I trust his judgment.' Both Cusak and Derdugo agree that students working in video production is a healthy activity. 'I think it's good to see students working in video, learning what they can and cannot say,' Cusak said. Through it all, Farrow remains teacher, with electronics in its many forms a primary consideration. Taking a friendly approach, the students call him Chet and liken him to a peer rather than a controller… Farrow stays in touch with many of his students, and many times has served as an employment counselor placing them in electronics jobs in the area. 'The thing I'm most proud of is my word is good. When a potential employer calls asking about needing a kid, I tell them what the kid can and cannot do, if he is trainable, what he can work and what he can't. When I say the kid can handle a piece of equipment, he can handle it.'"

• On March 19, 1984, the *San Ramon Valley Herald* wrote a story covering our fundraising efforts: "A Rock Auction to Roll in Funding." They reported:

"The Rock & Roll Sale and Auction is the latest brainchild of Monte Vista electronics teacher Chester Farrow, who has been bringing rock & roll to Monte Vista in one form or another since 1969. Proceeds from the fundraiser will be used to purchase color television equipment for the school's Rainbow Studio, which has produced community television

> *programming in black & white for the past ten years... Farrow and a former student, Michael Coats, have scoured the offices of Bay Area rock & roll stars and picked up posters, rock calendars, photos, T-shirts, sweatshirts, tour jackets, albums, cassettes, buttons, hats, and other assorted items. Bill Graham Productions has donated $400 worth of tickets to upcoming performances by Ozzy Osbourne, Van Halen, Huey Lewis and the News, and Jefferson Starship, Farrow says... Among the contributors to the auction are Jefferson Starship, the KMEL and KOME radio stations, rock critic Joel Selvin, Huey Lewis and the News, BAM magazine, Night Ranger, The Doobie Brothers, Journey, The Eric Martin Band, Greg Kihn, Hyts, Bill Graham Presents, Eddie Money, and Santana."*

• On Friday, March 24, 1984, *The Contra-Costa Times,* in their "Time Out" column, covered our fundraising efforts. In an article titled, "Monte Vista is the Site of a Rock 'n' Roll Auction," Clay Kallum wrote:

> *"Chester Farrow got caught between the rock and the roll, but luckily he's got some old friends who will help him out. Farrow, an electronics teacher at Monte Vista High School in Danville, brings rock 'n' roll bands to the school's theater to raise money for Rainbow Studio, a television project. Over the years, he's managed to raise nearly $10,000 so that the television program that Rainbow produces for Walnut Creek's Channel 6 can go full color. But his last show came up a bit short on the tickets-sales side and Farrow needed to recoup some losses. So he called some people he knew in the Bay Area music scene to get a few posters and records to sell around Monte Vista, and before he knew it, the Rock 'n' Roll*

Sale and Auction was born... Donors included people like Greg Kihn, Huey Lewis, The Jefferson Starship, Night Ranger, Journey, The Eric Martin Band, Joel Selvin, The Lizard King, The Doobie Brothers, and Bill Graham Presents, and some of the items will be one-of-a-kind Bay Area rock mementos that will never be available again. Farrow, who was just trying to make a couple of bucks back, has suddenly found himself in the middle of a genuine event. 'The really nice part about it,' he said, 'is that people in the Bay Area music scene, when you have a need, they help you.'"

• Dan Wood wrote a story about me for the *Herald* on Friday, April 17, 1987, entitled, "Scoreboard Operator A's '10th Man,'" where he said:

> *"The way the Oakland A's have been playing, the last thing the rest of the American League needs is the A's '10th Man.' But when the Seattle Mariners visit the Oakland Coliseum tonight for the A's 7:30 pm home opener, like every other team that comes to the Coliseum the Mariners will face the A's extra – scoreboard operator Chester Farrow. Farrow, 38, is a teacher at Monte Vista High and has been operating the scoreboard at the A's home games since 1969. While Farrow's job description doesn't exactly call for it, the Walnut Creek resident occasionally lends the home team a hand. 'Everyone gives credit to the manager for 8-10 wins a season,' Farrow said. 'Well, I would take credit for two or three wins a year. I would stand up to anybody and argue that point.' While Farrow's contributions will never be seen in a box-score, they can be felt at the Coliseum. With the touch of a button or a flip of a switch, the scoreboard operator can almost set the entire mood*

> *of the stadium. Certain scoreboard actions which get the fans pumped up may in turn lend juice to the A's or rattle the opposition enough to on occasion mean the difference between victory and defeat, Farrow said. 'I feel that no one knows the pulse of the A's and their fans better than I do. Part of my job is being a cheerleader, but the timing has to be right.' Farrow has been through thick and thin with the A's, from the three consecutive world championships in the early 1970s to the also-ran years of the later part of the decade and the burgeoning promise of last year… If Farrow has his way, tonight's game might even be one of the two or three he helps the A's win this season."*

• On Wednesday, February 24, 1988, Herb Michelson penned a story about "Just for You" for the *Sacramento Bee,* titled: "Students Bring Their Class to Screen." He wrote:

> *"There's only one weekly television program in this area ingenious—and ingenuous—enough to feature two mock punker-heavy-metalists as news anchors using the salutation, 'Good luck, good night, and go to hell.' 'Saturday Night Live?' Hardly. The 30-minute program is called 'Just for You.' It's had a cable system run of 14 consecutive seasons, is totally produced and cast by teenagers, in an advanced electronics course at Monte Vista High School here and, as far as any California vocational education maven knows, is the only publicly-aired high school TV program in the state… The show is not, however, the most significant product of veteran teacher Chet Farrow's course in video production. A visit to what in the old days of public schooling was called 'shop' and which Farrows dubs 'The Rainbow Studio,' illustrates the joy of both learning and teaching. The*

atmosphere is collegial. 'He makes this work fun,' says Eric Davis, a junior. 'He really gets you involved in what you're doing.' Farrow, 44, used to teach both math and electronics at a time when 'shop' was perceived as curricula for students unlikely to attend college. He was forever repairing students' electrical guitars and sound systems. Which exposed him to teenager 'garage bands' and led him into booking school concerts for such then-unknowns as Huey Lewis and Boz Scaggs. Which led him into videotaping band performances—with an old black and white Sony borrowed from a junior high—years before the invention of MTV. 'Just for You' and other video programming, including promotional spots for vocational education and special school presentations, naturally followed. Farrow's enthusiasm clearly stimulates student resourcefulness. You can find Farrow's furrows in a flock of Silicon Valley executive positions, at ABC-TV, at film post-production companies. 'He always knew how to make us feel comfortable, secure,' said alum Michael Coats. 'For many of us, he became a friend more than a teacher.'"

• Several major Bay Area newspapers covered my retirement party, including the *San Francisco Chronicle.* On Saturday, May 22, 1999, in an article titled, "A Hard Act to Follow – Popular Teacher Rocks Off into Retirement," Tanya Schevitz wrote:

"It was a curtain call that could only have worked for Chester Farrow. A rock show featuring a fourth-grader, a Raiderette, even the Mexican caterer performed on stage at Monte Vista High School in Danville with some rock's stars—Greg Kihn, guitarist Greg Douglass of The Steve Miller Band, Joe Satriani's drummer Jeff Campitelli—-plus the

local band Sy Klopps thrown in as the house band for good measure… After 32 years as an electronics and television production teacher, the 56-year-old Farrow, whose students call "Chet," is calling it quits. But he invited back some of his old friends on Thursday night to help him leave in proper rock & roll fashion—and 625 people showed up to watch.

"Farrow has organized more than 100 concerts at the school featuring some of Rock's biggest names—including Journey, Boz Scaggs, and Kihn—to give his students a chance to get a hands-on education running the sound and lighting systems… His past and present students say that he is always thinking of others. Hundreds of them showed up Thursday night to thank the teacher for the influence he had on their lives… 'Chet is responsible for launching my career,' said Andrew Haymen, 35, of Blackhawk, CA. 'I learned TV from him and I make television commercials now.' Farrow has helped several dozen students get into the broadcasting industry. He counts among his alumni executives at FM radio stations, LIVE 105, ABC television, FOX-TV's sports network, and the Oakland A's radio network as well as Michael Coats, who does public relations for the California Music Awards every year.

"Farrow will be a hard act for any teacher to follow, if a recent visit to his classroom is any indication. Dressed in tired corduroys and a moth-eaten surf T-shirt, he worked the class like a comedian, trading light-hearted insults and humorous anecdotes. 'I'll miss the kids, but how you see me interacting with the kids here, I am no different with my neighbors or with the kids who come and play in the creek behind my condo,' Farrow said. 'I talk and babble and have

fun. That's how I am.'"

• Clay Kallam of the *San Ramon Valley Times*, in an article titled, "Teacher Says Farewell with Rock 'n Roll Recital," wrote:

> *"When most teachers retire, they get a deli-tray luncheon in the faculty room and a cake from Lucky's. Chester Farrow is getting a rock concert… 'I would characterize him as my mentor,' said Michael Coats, who's now a partner in a public relations firm and a Sonoma farmer. 'I wouldn't be where I am today without him—and I could say that of 50 or 60 students. He gave us an alternative view of life that panned out for us. If you can make one kid a better kid, victory is achieved. Nobody bats 1,000—but if you look at his batting average, he's in the Hall of Fame.' Bob Gianinni, who was principal at Monte Vista during most of the 90's and is now an administrator with the Lafayette school district, said 'He's had such creative thoughts about how to fund-raise and about how to run his program that he drove us nuts trying to keep him in check on half the things he was doing,'*
>
> *"Some heavy hitters have come through Farrow's program. Mitch Riggin works for FOX and has been the technical director for baseball's All-Star Game and the World Series; Michael Baird handled the world audio feed for the 1996 Olympics and the 1998 World Cup; and John Moore has worked four Summer Olympics and three Winter Olympics for ABC. Moore has also done some work for the Oakland A's, which brings us to another chapter in Farrow's life. For the past 31 seasons, Farrow has operated the scoreboard for the A's. It's not something he plans to give up soon."*

• The *San Ramon Valley Times* published a piece titled "Electronics Teacher will get Musical Send-Off," where they said,

> *"Monte Vista High's Chet Farrow, who built the school's state-of-the-art technical program, will retire after 32 years. 'I know next year people aren't going to take this class,' said junior Sara Miramontes, as others around her nodded in agreement Friday. 'Because he's not there.' That Farrow is well-liked is an understatement. He's the charged-up ringmaster in a well-conducted show, somehow mixing together life stories, old jokes, compliments, and good-natured ribbing—and that's just while he takes attendance.*
>
> *"After 32 years, I asked myself, 'What else do I want to do,' Farrow said. 'How many times can you ask a kid to sit down? How many times can you ask a kid to take out a pencil?' Despite his feigned gruffness, it would be difficult to find a student who's been at the receiving end of a Farrow scolding. The wiry man constantly smiles and talks. He admitted to never failing a student because he finds the concept impossible. 'We all have flaws and we all do the best with what we can... I've never met a failure.' Principal Becky Smith said Farrow offers his students something other teachers don't. 'There's a certain amount of comfort with Chet,' Smith said. 'What you see is what you get. There's a certain loyalty between him and his students.' His students are already bracing for next year. 'It's going to be terrible without him next year,' said sophomore Kevin Repp, 16. 'He's not like a teacher. He's just there, you know. He'll support whatever you're doing.' Farrow said he has tried to give students a*

realistic view of what they are learning. Farrow's students raised enough money through the years to pay for most of the video and other electronic equipment. They make and sell videos of various school events. 'It took us a long time to build this up,' Farrow said, pointing around the multi-colored, carpeted rooms. 'This whole thing was done without special funds. Everything you see here was earned.'"

• In a letter to *The San Ramon Valley Times,* Peg LaRose from Diablo wrote,

> *"On May 25, I attended a 'Rainbow Reunion' concert at Monte Vista High School, produced by Chester Farrow and his former and present students... It was their way of saying, 'Thanks, Chet.' Farrow is no ordinary teacher, in fact, he is more of a 'real life' teacher. His style of teaching goes beyond the classroom, giving the students hands-on experience with video production, from start to finish. He really cares about his students, and they know it, and that's why they work hard for him, sometimes after school and on weekends... That's the uniqueness of Chet. He has played an important role in our son's already successful career. What Chester instilled in him during those three years at Monte Vista is being used today. Our son attends college related to his field and is already working in the broadcasting industry... Now it's my turn to say, 'Thanks Chet,' we're glad you came into our son's life."*

• In an article for a local paper entitled, "This Guy Can Really Light it up for Fans," Joshua Sense wrote:

> *"The game is less than an inning old, and things are looking dreary for the Oakland A's. The home team trails Baltimore 4-0, and scores of fans have started*

> *searching for more hot dogs and beer. But from his perch in a roof box behind home plate, Chester Farrow does not look away. For Farrow, a TV production teacher at Monte Vista High School in Danville, following every pitch isn't just a fascination or a passing fancy. As the senior scoreboard operator at the Oakland Coliseum, he has been keeping his eye on the ball at almost every home game for 27 years. Farrow started moonlighting at the ballpark in 1969, the year after former A's owner Charlie Finley moved his team to Oakland from Kansas City. Farrow was coaching football at Monte Vista when the father of one of his players—a Coliseum executive—dropped by the school to advertise the job. Selected for the position from 19 applicants, Farrow started that spring, earning $25 a game. 'It's tough sometimes working two jobs, especially around the time I am worn out from teaching,' Farrow says. 'But hey, if you have to work a night job, it doesn't get any better than this.'"*

• On Monday, October 9, 2006, in a front-page story entitled "The Good, Old Green and Gold: Longtime Employees Call McAfee Coliseum Home" for the *Tri-Valley Herald*, Angela Hill wrote:

> *"It may come as a surprise to many journalists who cover Oakland A's games at McAfee Coliseum, but 'Press Lounge Louie' does, in fact, have a last name. 'It's Pieraldi, Lou Pieraldi,' he said last week before Friday's home playoff game in which the A's finished off their sweep of the Minnesota Twins. Pieraldi is one of a handful of behind-the-scenes folks who have worked at the Coliseum for decades, and who are as much a part of the team as anyone, long-out-lasting players' careers, various owners' regimes, numerous*

> *Coliseum name changes, and enough mascots to start a small mascot zoo. People such as fellow long-timers Chester Farrow, who runs the scoreboard, and event supervisor Harold Miller aren't the ones who get the fame or sign any autographs, but that doesn't seem to matter to these fellas. They're happy having what they consider some of the greatest jobs in the world. Especially when the team is on a roll.*

"Farrow joined the A's in 1969, and until just a few years ago this was his moonlighting gig. In real life, Farrow taught electronics and TV production at Monte Vista High School in Danville from 1967 until he retired in 1999. He now sits in the DiamondVision booth during every home game, paying attention, punching buttons, root-root-rooting for the team and basically having a great old time. 'You're always in the game, watching every pitch,' he said. 'During a ballgame, there can be 300-350 pitches and you have to watch it all. Its three hours of drama that I get to be involved in, part of the American fabric of baseball. I sit up there eating sunflower seeds and watching the game, and they pay me for it. What a deal, eh?' Farrow says his first A's World Series win in 1972 was one of the best times of his life. '(Then-owner Charlie Finley) brought me to Detroit for the play-offs, and to Cincinnati for the Series. That was a thrill.'"

Inspiration

Around five, six years ago, I started to feel what we would call *signs of aging*. My hands kinda shook a little bit like I had tremors… then would go away.

My eyesight on the softball field would… there was an eye doctor that I played against in Concord.

"You're having… *something* optical, or *something* migraines… optical migraines. Sit in the shade, don't look at the sun, they'll go away in a half an hour."

And they usually did. But I never had that before. Now, we go from the tremors to adding these ocular migraines… Knees wobbled. Balance not so good. Kinda needed help getting up if I fell on the softball field.

While this was happening, I'm thinking, "Well, you're aging Chester. That's the way it goes."

I went to the hospital for a couple of tests. Nothing conclusive… maybe it was just age. Not sure.

Well, this progressed. While it was progressing, I went, "Whoa. I've got a lot of videos that we did at Monte Vista High School *Rainbow Studio* that I'm sure students would like to see. You didn't have to be a student to want to see it." But I mean, this is what we did.

I went to a guy named "Les" at *Action Video* in Walnut Creek and had him transfer all my VHS and three-quarter inch videotapes to DVD. Then he posted all of those on YouTube. If you'd like to see what I'm talking about, all of the videos are available if you'll go to *YouTube.com,* and then search for "Chester Farrow Videos."

I posted everything because I felt it was like a responsibility:

all these wonderful things that we did. They're going to be thrown away in the dumpster? I just couldn't do that. All of them are posted for eternity, as long as YouTube is around. I did that. I was very glad that I did it.

I started thinking immediately, maybe a movie should be done. Not sure. Something should be done, because some of the things that we did at Rainbow Studio at Monte Vista High School in Danville were unique, to this day. The world should know.

I did other things while teaching and also working for the Oakland A's as their scoreboard operator. Had wonderful experiences that I've never shared with anyone.

Most of my students — the core students, the very essence of why this book exists — don't know about these stories.

So the easiest thing to do was to write a book.

But I had already tried doing that before, going through the big publishers, big publishing houses… sent out a hundred and five little booklets, little thirty-nine-page-long booklets called "*The ABCs of VCRs*." Those were in the days when people were confused, in the '70s… they wanted to watch one thing and record another. This booklet simplified it. But I was rejected by a hundred and four of the hundred and five — for various reasons. I didn't really follow their rules. They only wanted you to send the first chapter and the Table of Contents. They'd take a look and see if it was interesting from there.

Well, the booklet was only thirty-nine pages long. I just sent the whole booklet. They immediately rejected it everywhere — except, a company in Canada. They showed some interest. Then that interest waned. Going with the big ones: tough.

Self-publishing?

I don't even know if I have enough time. What are you gonna do? Diagnosed now with rectal cancer… surgery and such… but it often returns — *eh*. So I'm running out of time.

I've always wanted to write a book.

One day, I go and see my attorney for a trust that I'm setting up for my children. Should have done this before but, well, I finally got to it.

While waiting for him, I picked up a free issue called *"Alive Magazine."* It's all about publishing. You could *self-publish*. You can go to the big guys, or you can go to the smaller guys, of which *Alive Media* is. Alive Media is the name of the company. Then, of course, they have Alive Magazine and a bunch of other "Alive" things. So anyway, I read maybe about a third of the article and then my attorney was ready to see me. So I put it down.

But it was in the back of my mind. Like, I want to go to a *small* publishing house. Sounds good. Maybe I'll contact those guys, because they had a number in there. Maybe I could find that magazine again somewhere. Didn't know.

When I was done with the lawyer, I came home. It was around one-thirty in the afternoon. I was hungry. I wanted to go get some bacon and eggs at the *Hick'ry Pit* in Walnut Creek. It's a couple of blocks from my house.

So I go in and what do I see at the front door inside, for free, the February issue of... Alive Magazine. So I grabbed the magazine, sat down, made my order and continued to read. I finished the article with my breakfast. I was determined to give this guy a call and see what happened. I called him and we set up a meeting and all that good stuff. That's basically how it all came together.

He recommended someone to ghostwrite and I used that person because time is very important to me now.

I used Larry Goldman, who used to be my engineer at the A's for the scoreboard for about seven years, eight years. He could type, like, *really fast*. I used him as a transcriber because what I do is, I talk into a tape machine like I'm doing now. Then it goes through the Internet to Larry Goldman up in Oregon. He types it and sends it to the ghostwriter, Steve Wagner.

Like that.

So, that's where we are on this. That's kinda why I wrote the book. Everything kinda dovetailed from the lawyer's office to the Hick'ry Pit in Walnut Creek. This thing said call this number. I did. We arranged everything. Just… perfect harmony.

I've been writing this book since April[1]. I was actually done at the end of April. But I had a few complications with my health. Doing this part — the Inspiration, the Forward, the other things that I'm going to do here — were the hardest part. Why? Because I had to think. When you're recounting stories — forty-something stories — okay, it's just reality. This is what happened. It's easy. Easy to do an autobiography.

To now create a thank you, to create these kinds of things: Why'd I do it? Ay! That takes more thought. I'm a back burner type of guy. I go like, "Hey. The book is done."

"Yeah, but Chet, you're *not* quite done…"

Well. All right. I'll get to it. I'm getting to it today. What is today? Yikes! Saturday, June 29th.

So I kinda finished it at the end of April. You blow by May. What'd I do in May? Not too much. What'd you do the rest of the June? I dunno. *Dealt* with my *issues*.

But I feel like finishing it up. It's only fair to get it going and take it to the press.

It's funny. I've always wanted to write a book. But I don't want to sit down and write it longhand. I want to do exactly what I'm doing now, which is looking out at my plants on the deck. No one's in the room. Just me and you.

---

[1] April, 2019

Dedication

This book is dedicated to the core students of Rainbow Studio.

There's nine individuals who have been with me from the beginning of their high school years, until the present time.

If I've got a function to put on, they're there.

If they were students at the time, they led the way.

Bands loved coming to play at Monte Vista. They were welcomed by one of the core and myself. They didn't have to touch a thing. We would take care of everything.

There's a whole chapter of the book you're reading now that is dedicated to the core — Rainbow Studio, The Core. It details what each individual did while they were in school for me.

At any time that I needed help, I could call them. Whether it's getting equipment for Rainbow Studio... what's the best thing out there at a price I could afford? Whether it's rewiring the entire studio so that the patch bay was professional. They would come back and they would work.

They would come back and teach my students how to read the 'scopes, how to read the meters, how to align the cameras just properly so.

These were things that they were professional in, that they had gotten jobs in, had careers in... They were at any time willing to come back to help us out. In fact, I think their eyes kinda lit up when I said, "I'm redoing the studio! The main control room is going to be *here,* and — ay!" They'd get excited. Why? We'll upgrade! We'll make it better.

That's basically what my core students did for all the projects that I've ever worked on: they made it better. So I thank them, and I dedicate this book to them.

Chapter 1

The Beginning

I'm from Pittsburg, California. I was born in 1943, but there was no hospital in Pittsburg — at that time — that delivered babies. So in reality, I was born in Antioch, California. Spent three or four days, I guess, in the hospital there and then moved on into Pittsburg, California.

My dad was "John", and was Irish and Welch. He was from West Virginia. My mom was "Mary" and she was 100% Sicilian from Pittsburg, CA. My sister, Madeline, is five years older than me.

Dad worked at Fibreboard Paper Products as an operator in the bleach plant. Mom was a 35-year waitress at The Riverview Lodge restaurant.

We lived on what's called "Oak Place," in Pittsburg. It was, like, ahead of its time. It was a cul-de-sac with about thirteen homes and a nice turnaround down at the end. Had some nice homes in there. Most of 'em were, like, three-bedroom, one bath. Some added another and had two baths, but most were three-one. A lot of times, they'd convert the garage. We never did. We used it as a garage, at all times.

It was very neighborly. Lot of fun. There were two kids in the first house, two kids in the second house, two kids in the third house — and so forth. Two kids in our house… one or two next door… that's the way it was.

We'd play "Kick the Can," and "Hide 'n Seek," and all those wonderful things that you hear about, that you kinda can't do on the streets these days.

Everything was family, back then. Everyone watched out for

one another. It was a different time. It was a wonderful time.

As I grew up — what'd I do? — I participated in the "Boys Club of Pittsburg." Now it's called the "Boys and Girls Club," and that's good. I think Ken Hoffman[1] put some money into it. I don't know if the Boys Club and Girls Club is still going. But I know it was an integral part of my life while growing up in the '40s and early '50s. That's what ya did.

Usually, someone would pick us up in the car, on Railroad Avenue, which would take you all the way down… you'd go to 8th Street, and then there'd be the Boys Club.

It had an indoor facility, and an outdoor facility for sports and such. It had a woodshop — and you could put some things together. It had a billiard room and a little library, and… soda machine — everything that an energetic, somewhat athletic young guy would just appreciate and have fun.

We'd have baseball games, football games, movie nights… Friday nights, they'd have movies… popcorn… All wonderful activities to keep young people off the street, and keep 'em busy, and help 'em to learn to socialize, and so forth.

Wonderful experience. Wonderful.

Oak Place, where I lived, was one street away from School Street. On School Street, was the elementary school, the junior high and the high school. I could walk to all three of my schools — and did — all the way through high school.

There were shortcuts, too. You could go over the fence and just cut… and you're right in the high school. So there was no reason that I couldn't go to the high school.

What did we do at the high school, even though I wasn't a high schooler? Well, there's basketball games. There might be football games. You know, there's a lot of grass out there on the football area at Pittsburg High School. A lot of asphalt with basketball things… tennis… those kind of activities.

It was a wonderful situation. It was just pick-up games. There

---

[1] Former owner of the Oakland A's.

was no involvement, in terms of heavy organization. We'd play each other, we'd choose up sides, and play. Have fun.

However, the Boys Club did have organized sports. They were divided up into — they'd call them "exponents." Some of you from Pittsburg, California, may remember that.

The exponent had to do with your age, your height, your weight — and so forth — as to what level you should compete at. They tried to make sure that people were sized — the little guys were called "midgets." The next level was called "juniors." The last group was called "seniors."

But it's not politically correct to use the word "midget," anymore. There were a lot of politically incorrect things, in those days. Much of that has changed. And that's a very, very good thing — that it's changed.

Just before junior high, by the way, I had a paper route. It was the *Oakland Tribune*, an afternoon paper. The route number was "X-S-17". I had thirty-two papers. You made 'bout a dollar a month off each paper. They had contests and things, and I won a trip to Disneyland. I went down there — kinda, the first year that Disneyland was open. I wouldn't recognize it now. We went down there — there were no people. There were — I don't know — I'm guessing, a thousand people in the park... fifteen hundred. They were all delivery boys. It was a special day for delivery boys and girls, I mean... whoever delivered papers. You did that by selling subscriptions to magazines, and such. I made up my mind that I was going to Disneyland — never been there, kinda heard about it. It was a Walt Disney thing... why not? I won the contest. I got to go. It was the first time for me in an airplane.

I did the cars — the "*Autopia*" — I think was what it was called in those days. You rode the cars around. You don't really race, but you got to drive 'em and steer 'em, and so forth, yeah? For a twelve-year-old kid delivering papers... what a thrill!

What was nice in those days — try it now — was that I didn't have to get out! "I'm staying in! I'm ridin' some more!" Okay. Next person, they'd help 'em out, next... You don't gotta leave! So I rode it for a couple hours. Try doing that at Disneyland! I did! I never got off! Why? It's the most fun thing they had back then. And, "back then", we're talking about... I don't know... '55? '56? You know, when Disneyland opened up.

That's the first time I'd ever heard about something called "Knotts Berry Farm" — wow! I didn't know they had all those attractions. But that was a nice experience.

Junior high was right there, Pittsburg Junior High School. Nice experiences, that I recall. I didn't play much for the junior high. Coach Caviglia — one of the coaches — wanted me to play... and for some reason, I didn't feel inspired. So I didn't play baseball there, for a couple of years. Played a lot of baseball in the Boys Club, and then I got kinda old for the Boys Club; got involved with junior high, but I didn't like their team. I didn't want to be a part of it.

I played baseball in high school, and I did pretty good. I made all-league all three years that I played. I remember my very first year, as a sophomore, I made all-league, along with Frankie Cardinalli. It turns out that I'd end up going and staying in college with Frankie Cardinalli. He was a little older than me, a couple years older than me.

We made the all-league team. Then I played some football. And I did... all right. I was an okay football player, but a better baseball player.

I liked basketball. I was a scrappy guy and could get rebounds... but I had no *shot*. I mean, I'd be twelve feet away...

"C'mon. Can you hit that shot?"

No. Clank! Clank! Clank!... you know.

So, I knew that I'd be like the twelfth man on the team, maybe getting in a game that we're losing big or winning big. I'd only play sparingly. I didn't want to put in all that work not to play. So I passed on basketball.

Track and field? I was very fast… for the first twenty-five yards. I could almost beat anyone in high school. Kinda did… kinda did it on a regular basis, even while hangin' around at the *Lucky's* parking lot. You know, you're cruising up and down… then you kinda park for a while… you get a little bored, and you go, "Let's race, from here to there." For twenty-five yards, you're not going to beat me. After that, I don't have anything. But twenty-five yards is enough to help get you down the first base line… twenty-five yards is enough to sprint out of the backfield of a play in football, and so forth. That was enough.

I tried to go on to college. It's funny. I'll just relate this real quick. Rod Dadieux was the famous baseball coach for USC. That's where I wanted to go play baseball when I graduated from high school. I sent him a letter. Told him, "I'll fly down" — which people didn't do in those days, at all. "I'll fly down. I'll bring my equipment with me. I'll walk on… have someone who's a pitcher throw batting practice to me. Lefty or righty? I don't care. In a half-hour, I'll demonstrate what I could do for your program."

He called me back.

"Chester! I can't do this. The number of people who would like to walk on, would like to have me watch their batting practices… is enumerable. It just can't be done."

"I'm making an offer you can't refuse, here. Cost you nothing. I fly down. I'll find where you are. I'll take a taxi to where you are. I'll hit. I'll field for you. Then you'll see… that you'll want me on your team."

"I'll make *you* an offer *you* can't refuse."

"What's that?"

"You go to Harvey Mudd School right next to us, at USC. They play about sixty to seventy games a year, almost as big a schedule as USC."

Maybe I'm exaggerating. Maybe it's only… fifty games a year — I'm not sure. But a lot of games. Way more than high school.

"That gives us one full year to observe you. We'll have a scout at each game. Then, we can make a decision as to whether or not you're ready for USC."

"Who's going to pay for Harvey Mudd?"

"Well, it's not that expensive…"

"If you pay for Harvey Mudd, I'll do it."

"Chester, you're asking too much of me. Just come down, enroll… It's not too expensive to live here…"

It wasn't very expensive to go to college in those days. USC was private. It was more expensive, but still… not exorbitant, like it is today.

Well, anyway — to make a long story short — I did not go. I did not accept his offer.

And, as they say, "the rest is history."

But, nonetheless, then I go to San Francisco State College…

Oh, meanwhile — while in high school, I started dating a gal named Sharon Clawson. We started going steady. It was like a regular thing. I knew, "this is the gal I'm going to marry."

So, anyway, I go off to college now. But I didn't know where I was going to go. Here's where Frank Cardinalli comes in again. He comes down one day. We were bowling during summer. I had graduated from high school. He comes down to watch his future brother-in-law, Louie Salvetti, bowl. Frank was dating Louie Salvetti's sister.

"Where're you going to college?" — no… "*Are* you going to college?"

"I dunno. I wanted to go to USC, but they don't want me there, and… *whatever*."

Crazy how you think in those days. *They don't want you there.* The man made me a clean offer. Today, you would jump all over it. But in those days, and at that time, I went, "Eh, he don't want me." End of story.

"Come live with me! We'll go to San Francisco State. I've been going there two years. It's a great school. You'll have fun. You'll get an education."

I hadn't thought about anything.

"Sounds good."

This is July of 1961. School starts in a couple months. *These* days, you've got to be registered... pre-done. It's a complicated process. In *those* days, you could walk-in off the street... long as you had an ID... "I'd like to take some units"... You'd pay for 'em. By the way, it was like thirty-six dollars for the whole semester. You want fifteen, eighteen, twenty-one units?... whatever you want. It was relatively inexpensive.

I completed six years at San Francisco State, very nicely. In my third year... we become pregnant.

Well now, Sharon and I, we planned our marriage. We got married in November. I played two years of baseball at San Francisco State. Then in my — I'll never forget this — in my junior year, now I'm married.

It's November — maybe it's December — of 1963.

I get a phone call from Bob Rodrigo, who used to be the football coach at San Francisco State College, assistant, and now was the head baseball coach at San Francisco State College.

"Chester, I want you to play baseball for us."

"Coach, I can't do it. I'm married now. I have a child on the way. I got to get responsible and buckle down. Baseball life is not responsible. It's fun, it's enjoyable, but not for a married man."

"Chester! No, no! We can find work for you. You won't even have to work and..."

I had that same thing for two years — you don't work. They pay you seven dollars an hour, I think, in those days, to an athlete. It's pretty good money. You had to rake leaves... This was down in what's called "Cox Stadium" at San Francisco State College. There's eucalyptus trees all the way around. They dropped leaves all year round. I used to go and rake 'em — seriously — and I'd come back and they'd go, "Wha— Chester!

Wadda you doin'?"

"I'm gonna clock out."

"For what!?"

"I raked all the leaves! They're all right —"

Oh, my! They laughed.

"What are you doing? You don't gotta rake… just… get lost out there… go down to the high jump pit and have fun…"

That's how you made your money. That was pretty good.

But when I decided not to play baseball because I'm married now and I had to get responsible, then I had to find work.

I was very fortunate to find work at a place called "Home Yardage." It was on Geary Street. It was a fabric store. It was owned by a guy named Ted Corn. He wanted me to be a salesman there, forever. He says — he used this phrase: "I'll have you farting through silk."

"Ted. Uh, I don't know. I mean…"

"Chet! You're good at this. The ladies like you. You find the fabrics that they need, and they rely on you. They bring you the samples. You're the only one who knows where they're located, 'cause we have so many rolls of fabric."

It was an unbelievable store. It had everything. Stuff from Bergdorf Goodman. Stuff from… you name it. We had it from everyone. The finest of silks, the finest of… *whatever*. But that just wasn't for me, to make a career out of it. But I did a few years there, and that was very nice.

Then, I worked at a liquor store called "The Loyal Liquor Store." It was on the corner of Haight and Masonic. I lived on the corner of Page and Masonic, one step, one street down, from Haight. I was right in the middle of all the action[2]. Made good money at the liquor store. Flexible hours. The guy who owned it was a guy named Ted Soulis. Ted is no longer with us anymore.

I almost went to work for him. He owned a mortgage

---

[2] In the Haight-Ashbury district in San Francisco, in the 1960s.

company, something like that, providing capital to buy houses. I saw him at the racetrack one time.

"Chester, you gotta come work for me. The little pittance you make as a teacher… can't compare to what you can make with us. We'd have a good time…"

It was very tempting. But I passed on it, like I have a lot of things… I just pass on it.

"Thank you for the offer. But I'm goin' in another direction…"

I graduated from college in '65. I got my General Secondary credential in '66. Why? Why then? You see, I had planned to get my Master's right after I had graduated. *Then* I was going to get my credential. Graduate… Masters… credential to teach.

Why do I want a General Secondary? Because you're allowed to teach any grade from K through 14 — second year of junior college. Any subject. Now, I don't know German or French. But if it was anything that I did in my background — I do have a math background, I do have a physics background, electronics… there's a lot of things you could teach with a credential. The last year they were going to offer one in California, was 1966. So I changed plans, got the credential.

By the way, I don't think they teach teaching the way they used to. They've shortened it, and the experiences are not as rewarding. First, in order to do your student teaching, you had to *observe*, for the first semester, someone in your major, and someone in your minor. Then, you took over their classroom, for the second semester. You're the teacher now, for your major and for your minor.

One of the classes I taught — one of the ones I observed — was physics, and one of the classes I observed was electricity class. It was really like, electric *shop*. In electric shop, I learned what I *didn't* want to do in electronics. In physics, I learned how to teach physics. I actually did teach physics one year with another teacher at Monte Vista, named Brian Young. That was when *PSSC Physics* came out. That was a high-powered physics that concentrated way more on electricity and electronics. For your classic physics teacher, it was a bit much. So, I taught the electronics part of it, which was basically the second semester: magnetism, optics… He taught the mechanics part, called "Classical Physics": weights and measures, pressure, and so forth. It was a fun experience. It was wonderful.

But anyway, I graduated from college, I got my credential, I got my Master's degree. I wrote my Master's thesis in Urban Studies. I had a chance to work with a guy named Justin Herman. In fact, Justin Herman offered me a job. The job paid a little over a hundred-thousand dollars, I think $103,000, to be a deputy *something* in the Urban Renewal Department[3], to work with him. I passed. The reason I passed was that I didn't like the way he did urban renewal in the Western Addition in San Francisco. His method was: post that you have to be out of your place by a certain time… gave people maybe six months leeway. Got rid of everybody. Tore the stuff down that was there… and then rebuilt. Hopefully the people'd come back. He raped the Western Addition. He just… oh, my!

For a lot of reasons, I couldn't work for him. It's not my method. I wanna know what the people want. What do you want in your neighborhood? And you know what's funny? They want the same things you want: safety… well lit, broad sidewalks… Yeah, landscaping… those kind of things. They wanted safe, first. They wanted the basics, like you would want, like I would want.

Then you just provide it for 'em. C'mon. You don't boot anyone out, unless you need to go to their place. You gotta help them find a relocation place. That's your responsibility as a re-developer. What are you gonna do with these people? I'm going to put them here for now. How long is it going to take to renovate or build their unit? I don't know, six months. Then they can move back in. You kinda make arrangements. You help them out.

---

[3] For the city of San Francisco.

Justin Herman did not believe in those things. So I passed.

So now it's time to actually get a job and get serious. I set up interviews with San Francisco's Unified School District. Why? I student-taught at George Washington High School in San Francisco. I did my observations there. I did my student teaching there. I liked the school. I liked the weather: kind of foggy out there in the Richmond, but not bad. I said, "Hey, San Francisco."

I also said, "I'm gonna do Oakland."

Now, why did I pick those districts? I don't know. One, San Francisco, 'cause I taught there. Oakland, because — I don't know. They might have a job for me, I dunno. Oakland sounds good. I also put in Pittsburg, California. I thought I'd go back and help out my alma mater and teach there.

San Francisco says, "I got a job. Part-time, two periods. You can —" Eh, no good.

Oakland says... same kind of thing, "We could do this, but we can't do that."

So I go to Pittsburg figuring like, you know, c'mon: prodigal son comes home... that type of thing. Nah. "... We got part-time this, and maybe that, but that's all we got... and maybe next year..."

So I set up an interview with the San Ramon Valley Unified School District. You set up these interviews at San Francisco State. They'd come to your school and interview you there. If they liked what they heard, and you looked like a possible candidate, then they'd turn that in to the Powers-That-Be... and those Powers-That-Be would get a hold of you.

So the San Ramon Valley Unified set up an interview with me.

Chapter 2

The Journey Begins

I went and interviewed for jobs in San Francisco, Oakland, Pittsburg — all in California — and was offered part-time work, but *that* I couldn't take. I couldn't make ends meet. It'd be impossible. All I'm looking for is *full-time* work. The only requirement I ever had was, "Gimme some full-time work. I'd love to have it in electronics. I'd love to start my own program. I have my own ideas, but I just need a start."

So an interview was set up with the San Ramon Valley Unified School District, with a guy named Dick Foster. Dick Foster was the superintendent, at that time.

The San Ramon Valley Unified School District — now located at 699 Old Orchard Road, in Danville — was at that time in *downtown* Danville, next to San Ramon Valley High. The facilities were small, probably converted from something else… that's the way districts did it then, in those days. The *new* district office — new to me, but it's been there for many years, now — is well built, designed for executive offices. Done absolutely correct. That's where the School Board meetings are held, and so forth.

So anyway, I go to the old facility next to San Ramon Valley High. I interview for the job. I'm dressed best I can. I have a tie, a sport jacket, and a pair of decent slacks. I didn't have much to choose from, but at least it had gone to the cleaners. I looked and smelled presentable.

"We have an opening at Monte Vista High School, in Danville. Just what you're looking for."

"Wow! That sounds wonderful!"

"There's something I want to tell you, though, about Monte Vista."

"What's that?"

"It's an *experimental* high school. They do things a little differently there. It's an educational experiment happening, as we speak."

"It sounds terrific!"

"Well, I don't do the hiring. I sign-off on you, but the way we do it, here in this district, is you're going to go interview with the principal and the teacher..."

The principal's name was Ray... *something*. It's funny. I had four different principals in my first four years. I was hired by a guy named Ray. He never even worked a day there that I was there. He was their first principal, I guess, but he moved on. I think he went to teach at Cal, or something. Then another one. Another one got fired, and so forth. It doesn't matter. A lot of flux, a lot of change. But, anyway.

I had to go talk to the principal of Monte Vista High School. I didn't know where it was located. They gave me good directions. It was easy to get to. I'm driving on Stone Valley Road...you climb Stone Valley Road... you go over a little hill... you come down... and there's, like, a little valley... there's *fifty-four acres* dedicated to Monte Vista High School.

Each classroom is its own little pod, so to speak. Re-sawn redwood on the outside. It just looked gorgeous, something that you'd find in Big Sur amongst the redwoods. All the siding was re-sawn redwood. Every year, the colors would change. It just was gorgeous, as the time went on.

So, I go do my interview. I'm interviewing with the principal.

"We're an experimental high school... Our teacher of electronics, right now..." His first name was Rick. I forget his last name, the fellow I replaced. "...he's going back to school. He's going to medical school. He's going to be a medical doctor."

"Wow! Sounds like it's wide open." I'm saying to myself in my mind, "That sounds wonderful!"

"You'll probably have around four classes of electronics, maybe an advanced class. You might have to teach some pre-algebra — to get some of the slower kids ready to take algebra."

"Sounds fantastic."

"But, I don't do the last of the hiring. I just kind of sign-off. You have to go visit the instructor. You have to make a time. I want you to go down there now, and make a time to be with — then come back and tell me what that time is, so we can have an interview after you've observed his class, find out what he has, what he does…"

And I did.

I discovered that he taught, at that time — Morse code… for shortwave radios, and such: uh… dit… dah… Those kind of things. He devoted about the first ten minutes of class. He says he did five, but it took more like eleven or twelve for them to set up and get ready and then… y'know, he'd read something, and they got to go ahead and type it out, you know, *whatever…* which is nothing that I wanted to do. But he's leaving, so it doesn't matter.

We're going to change that right away. We're going to go into stereos, music, amplifiers, speakers. That's what we're going to do. The basis is going to be *music*. All kids like music. I like music.

And I was hired.

It turned out that the guy I was replacing said, "He looks fine to me."

He never saw me teach; he doesn't know. But he seemed to like me, and that was fine. He was just glad to get someone to replace him. The principal was like, "No problem. You're hired."

Then, I had to go to the district and file papers. I had a job.

I go down the district office. One of the first offices I had to visit, after I talked with the superintendent, and he just kinda rubber stamped their approval process, like, "*They* like you, *I* like you… end of story — you're hired." He says, "The first office you got to go to…"

The secretaries were just great — always were, in the San Ramon Valley Unified School District. Without secretaries doing the job that they do at each school, schools would collapse. Absolutely collapse. The secretaries keep the offices humming. They know the rules. They know the regulations. They know what decision you made last time, when this came up, and so forth. They know where it's located in the file cabinet. They know everything. Your secretaries are the backbone of your school. If you ever do anything as an administrator, make sure you hire great secretaries. You'll be glad you did. Very, very important. But, anyway…

The secretary said, "You have to go to this office, here, and sign up for the State Teacher Retirement Plan."

"State Teacher Retirement Plan? Do I have to contribute?"

"Yeah…"

"Well, I don't want to. I'm making less than twenty-thousand to get hired here." I think it was sixteen-thousand in those days when I got hired, in '67. Might have been fifteen. It was barely enough to get by on. Even then, you don't get by, you better have a second job. But anyway…

I told the gal in the office, "I don't wanna sign up right now. Maybe in a few years, when I get rolling, I could afford to put money in for my retirement. I can't afford it right now."

"Chester, let me make it very easy for you. You *have* to. It's a requirement. You can't get around it."

You know, I never challenged that, but it's like — I don't know, maybe you can't. Why do you have to contribute to your own retirement? If you don't want to, don't contribute.

Maybe they changed the rules, now.

It was over a hundred dollars out of your paycheck, that went to your retirement. Money I could have used badly. Now, thank God I did. Thank God they forced me to pay into retirement. Otherwise, I'd probably have nothing.

I have a little more than nothing. (Heh-heh.)

So I started the program, and we changed everything around. In the first year, they had built a bunch of testing equipment: oscilloscope, audio generator, ohmmeters… those kinds of things. They were *Heathkit*. Heathkit made good stuff. You can see he kept the kids busy, teaching them how to solder, how to follow directions… they'd build it slowly… you installed three or four parts a day. You keep doing it. You could take a whole semester to build one of those pieces of equipment. You had lots of equipment. You could keep your kids busy.

But I was wondering, you can't just do Morse code and shortwave radio for electronics… He was gone anyway, so it didn't matter. I had decent equipment to start with, and we added a lot more. I had to have 'em all calibrated. They were all off. It's very expensive to have equipment calibrated.

In the early days before Prop. 13, we had lots of money in education. After that, not too good.

<Student, inquiring> "Chet! Did the lottery help?"

No.

"Yeah, but they raised it for education…"

Good. Then, they'd reduce the amount that was raised from your budget. Oh, yeah. Absolutely. Sure, the money went for education, kinda… but not directly. There you have it.

So, I start the program. We start with the basis that "FM Stereo is beautiful." It had just come out… isn't that crazy? Here we are, in 2019, and we're talking about FM Stereo. We still listen to it… still wonderful, if it comes in clear. But it was a new technology in 1967. I think I heard my first stereo broadcast on K-FOG. I was hooked from *then*.

So while at Monte Vista, I taught electronics… I taught pre-algebra… I taught physics. I taught pre-algebra for about three or four years. I taught physics for one year, along with Brian Young. We team-taught. The team-teaching thing is a good thing because then I, as part of the audience — especially while he's going over the fundamentals of mechanics and physics — if the key question isn't asked by one of the students, then I raised my hand. I would ask a key question, like I didn't know the answer. That helped spur the learning process along.

I'm not against team-teaching… at all. We had twice as many students, but it was easy to handle. It's hard on lab days, though. Then, when you try to put stuff out for forty, fifty students, it's like, wow, we have to double- and triple-up. You can't have your own little area there so you could do your experiment. It was tough.

I also taught studio recording. We had a great little studio there. We operated it, probably for about ten years, as an active recording studio. We were listed in *Mix Magazine*, one of the magazines that was a spinoff of *BAM Magazine*… that was Dennis Erokan, as the publisher. We were listed, "Monte Vista High School." Ours was four-track, four different channels. Rental for a four-track was generally fifty to sixty dollars an hour at the professional studios. That's not even talking about Wally Heider's, and like that — *they* were over a hundred an hour, you know, the big professional studios… where the musicians who are signed to big contracts, go. Over a hundred an hour.

We were *free*. We were the only free studio in the entire Bay Area. *Rainbow Studio.*

One of the first bands we recorded was with Jeff Campitelli. Jeff Campitelli came to my retirement party and played, in 1999, when we had our first *Rock and Roll Recital*. He was the drummer for many, many years, for Joe Satriani. Now, I don't know if Joe Satriani came to Monte Vista with his band, at that time.

But I do know that he'll never forget: that was his first recording experience, Jeff Campanelli, at Rainbow Studio, at Monte Vista.

We had all the bands that played all the nightclubs come through. Why? You wanna put a demo tape together, you came to Rainbow Studio.

We had all the same microphones that all the best studios had. We had the same studio monitors. We had the same *Auratones*. Those are small five-inch speakers that you did your final mix on, to make sure it sounded good on the radio, that it sounded good if it came through the TV. Not the big speakers with fifteen-inch woofers — no no no, no, no, no. You do your *pre-mix* there, with the big speakers. You do your *final* mix with the small Auratones. We had 'em.

There was no reason to even go anywhere, other than Monte Vista High School. We were backlogged, five months.

There are a lot changes in five months: bands dissolve... bands get formed... it doesn't matter. We had more than enough recording to do.

Our Rainbow Studio students did all the recording themselves.

On occasion, I would do some recording myself. But then, I usually just turned it over. Why? It's hard work. If I'm tied down mixing, if I'm tied down recording, then I'm not producing and making sure that I'm around everywhere, to make sure everything is humming along. I can't be tied down in the control room. So I turned it over to one of the better students. You might get me for one song... and that's it. I would circulate around, never to come back in there... except to hear a final mix, or something of that nature.

I did television production for about twenty, twenty-five

years. We had a show called, *"Just for You."* If you go to *YouTube.com,* and search for "Chester Farrow Videos", you'll see plenty of our television shows called "j4u". It means, "Just for You."

"Chet! The kids are dressed kind of like — it looks like a dress rehearsal."

We didn't have a wardrobe. Later on, we started to get a wardrobe. We started to put it together... Then you can wear this jacket or you can wear this shirt. It was nice. Sometimes we even had kids dress up: suit and tie... sport jacket and tie, or sport jacket and — no tie. But... nice.

It was a little magazine-format show. We had reviews of concerts, albums, and movies... we had a little cooking segment, with a camera overhead so you can watch the guys cook — or the gals. We did the Nightly News, just like they do on *"Saturday Night Live"* — tongue-in-cheek. Sometimes a bit sacrilegious, but generally pretty clean.

I was also doing concerts and other things, all to raise funds. We started doing the video Yearbook in 1993. That made a ton of money, like nine- or ten-thousand, maybe twelve-thousand a year. All the seniors would buy their Yearbook, and then they'd get a *video* Yearbook. You'd be silly not to. Those who didn't buy, wish they had it now. I tried to get 'em all on Chester Farrow Videos, but I don't have year 1993. It's the only year that we're missing, I'm pretty sure. We did it all the way through '99.

That's essentially what I did for thirty-two years.

I started at an experimental school. The experiment lasted about five years — from '67 through '72, maybe '73. Then the district started to hire more conservative, little bit older, more established teachers... and it started to change to a traditional high school.

Was it ever announced that they're changing? No. Those plans never are. Those are done behind closed doors, those decisions. The decision was made to change Monte Vista High School to a traditional high school.

What was so experimental about Monte Vista? Well, we had things like "Open Wednesday Afternoon." Once a week, on Wednesday afternoon — I think they changed it, later, to every two weeks, every couple of weeks — we'd have the afternoon off after lunch. You'd put on special seminars, educational seminars. I brought in State Senator Phil Burton... I brought in senators, congresspeople. I brought Justin Herman once... let him speak, let 'em hear what his technique was.

These were going on all throughout the school. The Black Panthers came to the library. They had their say, and they drew a lotta people... In those days, we were helping people sign up to avoid the draft[1], to go to Canada, to get out. We were one of the most active schools around, helping out. You want to get out? We'll help you get out.

These were all things that didn't necessarily take favor to the school board. It was, like, too edgy. Too different. I don't know what they were scared of. I've never understood fear in education, but I'll explain it as best I can.

"Follow the law... keep your mouth shut... you'll keep your job."

<Chester, inquiring> "Wow. I mean, that's the basic requirement for the administrator?"

"Yep! Show up on time. Do what we ask. And do it well. Don't get into trouble."

Wow. Not too heavy a requirement to be an administrator. It's kind of sad. You can't think outside the box.

No wonder so many charter schools have popped up over the years. There's thousands of teachers in America that wish

---

[1] Military conscription to serve in the USA's Vietnam War was mandatory for men 18-years old then. https://thevietnamwar.info/vietnam-war-draft/

they could just get eight or ten of the best teachers around — twenty of 'em — to start their own school. The charter schools are fought by the standard situation all the time. All the time. You read about investigations into the charter school. Investigations of misuse of funds. I don't know. Misuse of funds goes on everywhere. It's not a charter thing. It's just a thing.

You don't make much money in education; it's very tempting to put your fingers in the pie.

But anyway, that was my experience of teaching. It was 1967 through '99. Had a nice retirement party. Everything was great.

I retired from teaching, but I went right into the guitar recitals, for the next *seventeen years*.

That's my experience at Monte Vista High School.

Chapter 3

… And Down the Stretch, They Come!

A lot of times people ask me, like, what kind of childhood I had, and I will go into all of that and explain it in detail. But, one of the things that's kind of different from most people in Pittsburg, California, where I grew up, is that there was always horse racing in the household.

We didn't *own* horses, but my mother kinda fell in love with *betting* the horses. She felt strongly that she could find nuggets that the daily racing form didn't provide. She would keep individual sheets for each day's races, because you couldn't find those statistics in the daily racing form. All *it* showed was that your horse came in sixth in the last race… and it didn't do so well.

But it didn't show where they were at the quarter, where they were at the half, at the turn, in the stretch. There's a lot of information that my mother tried to glean from the newspapers that weren't available in the daily racing form.

My father on the other hand, was a long-shot kind of better. He would bet two dollars to win, let's say—used to be the minimum bet: two dollars; now, I think, you can bet a dime; I'm not sure, fifty cents, a dollar… cheap, now. I know you can bet a dime on all your exotic bets, you know, like Trifecta, and Exactas — very cheap.

They're trying to get you involved and take your money. They hope you might win, and you'll come again. As so often happens to people — and it did happen to my family, my mother and father — they were hooked.

<Student> "Chet! What does it mean to be hooked on horse

racing?"

Every day: five o'clock, five-thirty, Sam Spear would come on the radio with the re-creations of races from Bay Meadows, Golden Gate Fields, Tanforan[1]... Bay Meadows and Tanforan aren't around anymore. I think there's a Tanforan shopping center complex, but there's no racetrack.

The popularity is waning. Of course, in the '40s, '50s, '60s, '70s, even the '80s, attendance was growing. There's a lot of tracks around the United States. You could gamble at those tracks if you were in Las Vegas or Reno[2]; You place a bet, no problem.

But every day, we listened to the recreations of Sam Spear. Every day, they'd come *down the stretch*, and we'd be listening... And my mother's horse — let's say she'd bet it to place — would come in *third*. "Place" means you come in second or better. The horse would "show," or in other words, come in third.

"Eh! Close! Lost by a nose... but you lost your bet."

To make things happen, so my parents could always have a bet on the races, they had *bookies*. The bookies went by the name of — here we go — "Blackie" and "Brownie." The least creative names I think I've ever heard. Ever.

All right. Blackie. Blackie is holding your tag. He's got your bet. You owe the man six dollars. They had a little black book. Blackie had a black book. I don't know, Brownie maybe had a brown book. What do I know? But he had a book. They all kept the book.

You were allowed a certain amount of credit. If you could show that you'd pay any bill up to fifty dollars in a timely manner, then the credit extended to you is fifty dollars.

So you got thirty-eight dollars bet so far that you owe? Go

---

[1] Amazingly, there were horse racing tracks located throughout the San Francisco Bay Area.

[2] Nevada casinos often had a "Race Book" where you could legally bet on professional sports and horse racing.

ahead! You've got another twelve dollars.

"No, I just want to put two-dollars on..."

Yeah, sure.

All the way up to fifty. Then you stop.

"Okay, we need repayment before we can continue."

A lot of people just paid down. They owed fifty; they gave twenty. Whatever it took. They would call the bookie every day with bets.

My mother thought she could beat the horses. My father knew he couldn't — doesn't matter. They both tried.

Now, what did I learn from all this?

Well, I learned to read the racing form. I could read the racing form as good as anyone around. In fact, the last two *Breeders' Cups,* I picked the upset winner. The heavy favorites, the one down in *Del Mar*[3] and the one just recently at *Churchill Downs*[4], Breeders' Cup races, best horses in the world? I said, "The favorite is not going to come in," each time. The favorite came in fourth each time. I hit the Exacta and Trifecta, both times — yeah, for a few hundred dollars.

It's funny how that goes. I can do all right.

"Chet! Do you go gamble a lot on the horses?"

Never. Once a year. Maybe twice, if there's a Breeders' Cup thing. We're kind of used to it now. If the Breeders' Cup is in California, Wendi — my longtime companion — and I go. If the Breeders' Cup is not in California, now we go to Pleasanton on that day, sit outside on the patio. They serve you breakfast, lunch, drinks, whatever you want. Nice and shady on the patio... with the umbrellas. Very relaxed. It's a wonderful day out.

Wendi and I went to Pleasanton this past year. Like I already said, I hit the Exacta and Trifecta[5] in the big race, the six million

---

[3] Del Mar Thoroughbred Club, Del Mar, California

[4] Churchill Downs, home of the Kentucky Derby, Louisville, Kentucky

[5] To win the Exacta, you have to pick the horses that come in first

dollar mile, mile and a quarter — whatever the big race is.

So Wendi, I had given her some money to enjoy herself on that day. Specifically, that money was for her to gamble on the horses that she liked. You liked a certain horse's name? Take it. You liked a certain horses colors? Bet it.

But whatever you do, make sure you bet the Exacta and the Trifecta in each one of them. You could bet a dollar Trifecta. A normal fifty-cent bet usually makes you… seventy-five dollars. So betting a dollar, that's a hundred and fifty dollars.

If you hit the Exacta, for a dollar… I don't know, thirty, forty dollars… at least? Especially, if you're going to go for the upset.

So, she asked me — just before the big race, "Who you playin'?"

"One, five and ten."

I gave her the names of the horses — but you really only needed the numbers to make the bet.

"All right."

Then she left, and she made her bets.

About five minutes later, I got up to make my bets. Then we came back and sat down and… continued to enjoy ourselves and… here comes the race!

So they came in. Who won? One, five, ten.

It doesn't matter what order I had 'em in. I'd boxed 'em all.[6]

She had the money to box. That's exactly what I told her, "You box it all the way."

In an Exacta, you had to pick the top two horses: first and second.

All right, let's say it's one, two.

My mother used to do this all the time: bet one, two — but

---

and second, in that exact order. The Trifecta is picking the first, second and third… in that exact order. You can see that selecting more horses gets harder and therefore pays more money if you do.

[6] When you "box" the Exacta, you reverse the numbers so that you've got it both ways. When you box the Trifecta, you cover all the combinations. I win no matter the order.

not two, one. What she'd do? Lose.

Later on in life, when I would go to the track with her, she'd give me five dollars to go bet the Exacta, because that's what it was at that time: five dollars… and I'd box it.

She'd go, "Oh, darn! I lost! It came in two, one."

"No, no… You won, Ma. I got you covered. Here."

"Oh! I'll buy you a drink!"

"Well, thanks!"

But, she always seemed to never box anything. Why don't people box stuff? Costs twice as much to bet. You were going to bet a dollar, now you gotta bet two. If it's a Trifecta, okay, that's six times as much, to box 'em all. Not a dollar; six dollars. You have the combination one-two-three, one-three-two, two-one-three, two-three-one… all the combinations. That's called "boxing it."

So the race was over, *budda-bum*.

"Wendi! We're in the chips! We're in the chips! Twice in a row now! We nailed them! Nailed 'em!"

"I didn't bet it."

Ay, ay, yai!

"What? You didn't bet it? But the money was to… bet!"

"Well, I just — I thought it was a waste of money…"

Whatever.

It doesn't matter. When you give someone a gift, then you give them a gift. If they don't use it exactly how you wanted, that's not a problem. Why? Gift is a gift.

Now, you don't want to see him take your money or take your gift and just throw it away or step on it or burn it. But in reality, it is theirs to make a decision on, and she passed.

We'll continue to go to the races a couple times a year… long as I'm around. We'll have fun. We go to Pleasanton once a year. If you've never been to Pleasanton, it gets very hot there, Pleasanton, California. It's called the "Oak Tree Program." That's what they call it, "Oak Tree." They have about eleven days of racing… usually Thursday through Sunday – maybe a little more. Very inexpensive: it's like free, unless you want to sit in some better seats, which we always do. I like to be near the finish line. I don't want to be down by the rail. I don't want to hang around the bar. I want to sit in the shade in my chair and just people-watch, horse-watch. That's all I want to do. Just enjoy myself.

I set aside five-hundred when I go. When I go to the Breeders' Cup, I carry a thousand. Okay, why? C'mon! Special vacation. Just in case I want to really push my luck.

By the way, when I set aside a certain amount of money, that's it. It doesn't matter. If I lose it all, I lose it all. Budda-bum! Done. Twice a year.

But anything like Breeders' Cup at Pleasanton, or Breeders' Cup or just the Pleasanton races during the summer – five-hundred, and that's it.

I grew up in a household in which there was gambling every day, even when we used to go on vacations. Where'd we go on vacation? *Del Mar*.

"Chester! You went all the way to Del Mar in Southern California because it's beautiful?… And it's a nice coastal town?"

"No! Went down there 'cause they got a racetrack!"

"Chet! The race track's closed on Sunday. What did you do?"

"We went to Tijuana… to go to the races at Agua Caliente, in Mexico."

"And, Chester, when the races were over in Mexico – 5:00-5:30 – did you then go back to your motel and kind of lick your wounds?"

"No! We went to a jai alai and gambled on jai alai." That's a crazy game. Kind of like handball, only they have baskets at the end of their hands. They grab that ball while it's flying, and they whip it around and – oh, my! You better be careful: that thing'll kill you. I've seen some people be hit, (heh) and you're out for a while… my, my.

I had gambling all around me. I still play some poker today, usually once a year with the family. Nice little game. Fun. That's good. Win a dollar, lose a dollar — it doesn't matter. It's family. It's fun. I like to gamble a little bit.

"Chet! Do you go to the Indian casinos?"

No.

I used to like Tahoe. I used to like *Harrah's*. Kinda dead up there now. You don't even want to make eye contact with the dealers. There's no one to deal to. No one at the table, especially, for example, eleven in the morning.

Now don't get me wrong. In the old days — back in the '70s, and such, '60s — okay, the tables were pretty much taken up already, especially in the summertime, on a Saturday. An' they're adding more dealers, and so forth. Now you go: it's pretty empty. Kind of sad. But — things evolve.

Anyway, that's it for horse racing in the Farrow family.

Chapter 4

Second Jobs

If you're going to be a public school teacher, you start out awful low in terms of what your net is each month that your check comes out. By the way, teachers do not get paid by the week, or the two weeks. In my case, the money was divided up evenly into twelve months. So, every month, it'd be the same check — within a penny or two. And… not much money.

<Student, again> "Uh, but, Chester… You're a professional. You're a teacher. You went to college."

I know, but the process is very slow, and not very incentivized for young people to make good money early in their career. It's kind of built in a reverse order: the longer you stay, the more money you get… until you go beyond the limit. Then they give you a bump and raise. That means you've reached the highest of the scale, you got a Master's degree all that extra stuff. I think it was a BA[1] plus seventy-five units, what our district had. Then you were at the top. You try to get there as soon as you can, get your educational things out of the way, start teaching, start making good money.

But it takes a while. A second job is kinda necessary. Absolutely.

If you have someone in your household who's a teacher in their first ten years of teaching, then the other person's gotta be working… part-time, something — Or, in my case, my wife, Sharon, was a stay-at-home mom. So, *I* took the second jobs.

I took anything the district had.

For example, I coached at Monte Vista High School. I coached

---

[1] An undergraduate Bachelor of Arts degree

JV[2] baseball. It was a great experience. You got the kids that are called "tweeners." They're in-between making the varsity. Maybe they should be cut. They need some place to play, and that's JV baseball. They're not very intense at the JV-level. At the varsity-level, it's a little more intense. But the wins are still important. Success is still important. Making a great play is always wonderful. You like to leave each game — if you can, as a ballplayer — with something in your mind that you can recall from that day, that you did something well.

You gloved the ball — there was a short hop in front of you that could have taken off, but you gloved it and made a nice toss to second, to force out the runner coming from first. Very good. Very good.

There's a pop-up! — especially for seniors. Yikes! Hit a ball over your head. Pop-up. You're not catching it. You'll go in circles. The ball might hit you on the head! I used to be great at pop-ups: straight up, over my head, behind my back — didn't matter. Now, it's got to be in front of me. I got to be able to see it all the way, for me to actually make the catch. Things change.

At the JV level, you get a lot of in-between… some ability, some not so good… but it's a great time.

I'll tell you a quick story: I was a JV coach for about three years, in baseball. We needed a pitcher on that year's team. Well, we didn't have anybody. We had a really good kid, but they brought him up to the varsity. That happens in JV. Sometimes, it even happens at the freshman level. "Bring him up!" Wow! They didn't have that when I was in high school. We only had ten, eleven and twelve… freshman is the norm now, at high school.

But anyway, I'm looking for a pitcher. There's this kid named Gary Rafatto. His name kept coming up when I was asking, "Isn't there anyone around here, in this gym, that used to play Little League, and now just doesn't do it anymore?"

---

[2] Junior Varsity

"Yeah. Gary Rafatto's pretty good. Gary Rafatto could throw strikes. Gary Rafatto —" You know what I mean.

Well, Gary Rafatto was on my football team, that I'll talk about in a minute. So I go to him.

"Gary, you used to play in Little League?"

"Yeah."

"Well, what position did you play?"

"I pitched. I played some shortstop. But, mainly, I pitched."

"Were you any good?"

"Eh, I'm all right. I could throw strikes. I have no breaking ball."

"Gary. You don't need a breaking ball. You come and play on the JV's? You're gonna succeed here.

<Sounds of Chester's deliberate tapping.>

"They said you throw strikes? We're going to have you keep it *low*... all the time. Let 'em *pound* it into the ground. Let our defense do the job. We don't need a changeup. We don't need a breaking ball. We don't need any of that. Keep it down: around the knees. Batters hate that."

A left-handed batter is different. But the number of lefties that you see — when I was coaching — are few and far between. Maybe there are more left-handers now, around, than used to be. But, y'know what's funny? Quickest way to the majors, relief pitcher or starter? Left-handed. You don't gotta throw ninety-five. You got to throw at least eighty-five, eighty-four. Keep it down, break it low and away, low and in... Keep it down.

To underscore that, I'll just tell you about one game that we played against Los Lomas — *at* Los Lomas.

This is approximately — I don't know, 1970? I'm just guessing... '69...'70. Gary's pitching for us.

We have this little meeting ahead of time. I told the infielders and outfielders, "This is going to be your game. Our success depends on your defense, and nothing else. Sure, we need to score a few runs — and we can do that — but we're going to concentrate, today, on *defense*. Gary, your job is just: keep the ball low."

And he did. He threw a *no-hitter*, on that day. The ball is in the trophy case at Monte Vista… probably long gone now; it doesn't matter.

But it was a wonderful example of a young man capable of throwing the ball, at a reasonable speed, JV-level. No overpower, no pop the mitt… none of that. But just keep it down. Make it uncomfortable for the hitters. Let 'em pound it into the ground… and let your defense do the job. It worked.

At Monte Vista, I also coached varsity *football*. This all started in '67 when I first was hired. I was responsible for the defensive backs and the receivers. We had a great time. In 1967, when I was hired, that season there was no varsity. There was just JV's. Because our first class started in '65, we hadn't been a school long enough to have anything higher than juniors.

Well, when you have a class that's all together for all these couple of years, and now you're playing at the JV-level… a lot of them are juniors, waiting to be a senior, to be fully-grown.

At the JV-level, we *dominated*. I believe the record was 10-0-1. We tied our very first game against a team from Santa Cruz, in football. But we knocked off everybody's JV teams pretty handily.

We finally had the Varsity in '68. Of course, their graduating class would be in June of '69. So, we had our football team in '68 and it was at varsity-level.

Our rival was San Ramon. Let's see, I coached 4 years, 3 at varsity-level. In my varsity years — with seniors — we beat San Ramon 6-0, 16-0, and 6-0. That's kinda all I remember. Ay! Everybody celebrated…

It's funny: our team would fall apart, every year, after the San Ramon game.

"Wasn't the San Ramon game the last game of the year?"

No, they rotated it, like goofballs.

<Goofball Administrator> "Uh, this year, it's the, uh, sixth game of the year. Next year, it will be the fifth game of the year. And next year, it'll be the —"

What!?

We would go undefeated through San Ramon. I don't care who you were. When we played San Ramon, we'd beat 'em. Then we'd lose, lose, lose, lose.

We'd look real good in the stats — up to and including the defeat of San Ramon — so our record might look: 5-0. You end up 5-4. Badda-boom. That's it. I don't know why we collapsed, but it has a lot to do with — you know — gearing up, wanting to beat your rival… and we were successful. Then, they didn't care.

I taught summer school. C'mon, you gotta make money. You got the teacher job… we gotta augment that. So, I would teach summer school. The first year, I was kind of stupid in a way… naïve… you don't know. I taught electronics at San Ramon High, and — eh — it was all right. It was all right.

In fact, I taught even before I started teaching at Monte Vista. They offered me a job. I said, "Sure, I'll take it. Are you kidding me?" Make eighteen-hundred bucks for the summer, or something. Maybe less. I forget. But it was money. I'll take it.

Coaching's bad. Coaching's fifty cents an hour — and that's if you're being paid pretty well. I think our biggest paycheck that we ever got was five-hundred, for the year. They call it a "stipend". So my stipend was five hundred. Then they take out taxes. Come on, so you take home three-seventy-five, or something like that… four-hundred. C'mon. Get outta my face, for all the work you put in. It's crazy.

Summer school is fun after that.

Why? I taught Elementary. There you go. I taught classes like "Fins, Feathers and Furs." We learned about the animals.

There were four teachers, three ladies and me. My job was to build birdhouses for the kids. So, we'd build birdhouses.

Then I'd pile all the kids into my station wagon – probably fifteen… totally illegal – and go down to *Foster Freeze*. Everybody'd get a nice ice cream cone, come back…

Who wouldn't wanna be with Chester!? Y'know. C'mon! We're havin' fun.

They'd paint their little houses, and we'd put 'em up… see if they attracted any birds… have some fun. Summer school was fun.

I taught one year at night school. Oh, man! If there's anything you don't ever want to do is teach all day, come home, have a bite to eat, and go back and teach all night. Those of you that do that: my hat goes off to you, right now.

Now. How good a job did you do, in each of your jobs? I don't know. I'm not there to judge. Only *you* know how you did.

But, it burned me out. Too much teaching.

It's funny. I'll just say this very quickly: I went to A's *spring training* for about five years. It was too much baseball for me! I had eighty-one home games at the Coliseum! Now, I'm gonna go down and spend a lot of money in… *Arizona*? Hotel… car… all these things… watch more baseball? What, it's better… when it's hot!? I dunno. It's ball.

Now don't get me wrong. You go down, you're very relaxed, you enjoy yourself, you go out to eat, all of these things, but…

I had more fun watching the March Madness[3] – the NCAA's. One and done. So, I'd always make sure that I went down while that was in full swing. Games are on… all day Thursday… Friday… Saturday… Sunday. There you go. Otherwise, it would've drove me nuts.

You reach a point where it's too much, even *too* much of a good thing. In other words, how could going to spring training be bad? It's not! It's just a little too much for me. Ball is ball. So if I'm going to go watch ball, I'd rather get paid for it, and go to the Coliseum. It's as simple as that. Short little commute… I love

---

[3] College Basketball tournament

all the people there.

I go to spring training, eh, a few people know your name, and… *eh.*

I used to attend seminars. This is pre-Proposition 13, in the State of California. Pre-Proposition 13 was: lotta money for education. Lot!

I think I mentioned once before: thirty-six dollars, my first semester, in 1961, at San Francisco State College.

Prior to Proposition 13, a lot of monies were available to attend certain teaching seminars. They'd pay you. Attend conferences, they paid me. All of these things helped augment the salary that I got from teaching.

I even did some of these — like, I continued varsity football, maybe did one year of extra baseball — *while* I had the A's job, which started in 1969.

After a while, I started to make some decent money. And, so… I no longer had a need for a third, fourth, and a fifth job.

I'm retired now. I just have one job. It's working for the Oakland A's, as their scoreboard operator.

Life could not be any better.

Chapter 5

Sesame Street

Circa 1972-73, I was watching *Sesame Street* with my children, as we did often. A public service announcement came on the television. The public service announcement said, "if you have a black and white or color TV in working order, please call this number — KQED will come pick it up and make sure that the TV is distributed to the daycare center program," — kind of a national program, I think — so they could have TVs to watch Sesame Street and the other KQED programming.

So I watched that public service announcement a couple of times and I said to myself, "Self? This is crazy. I'm currently watching a *Zenith* 21-inch color TV, about 12 years old. The colors are still pretty good. The picture is okay." In those days, it cost five hundred to a thousand dollars to get a nice big TV set. Who's got five hundred to a thousand dollars when you're a teacher — when you're almost *anything*? I mean, you've got to have *money*.

I didn't, and a lot of people don't.

So, I called up KQED.

"You know, I've got this Zenith color TV. It works real good. I can't — in good conscience — donate it to your program, though I'd like to. However, I have an idea and I think you'll like it."

The lady said, "Yeah? Go ahead."

"Instead of the announcement, 'black and white, color, *working*', how about, 'black and white or color — working, *or not*'?"

Now, the ones that were not working, all right, people would donate it. It was up in their attic. In their garage.

So, we made an arrangement. It turned out that for about a three-year period, this group out of Oakland and San Francisco would come with a truck every other Friday with approximately ten TVs. We kind of agreed on that number. I can't take too many. I didn't have that much storage in my facility at the time. They would deliver ten. We were successful usually at about sixty per-cent. Every Friday when they would drop off ten, we would generally hand back six, on average, that now worked.

"Chester, good question: Are you a TV repairman?"

No.

"Have you ever repaired a television before?"

No. I changed tubes in the old days. They had tube testers. You'd go down to the drugstore, check and find out if it was a good one or bad one. That's all we had.

It turns out that in the electronics field, there were a lot of resources — especially booklets — that looked like a kind of calendar. You'd flip the pages over. Let's say the first page said, "You have no picture and you have no sound." Okay. So the TV you were working on that was broken, that was donated, we'd plug it in: no picture, no sound. It then would tell you, "Step one: check and see if there's a fuse or a circuit breaker. If there is, change or reset it. Step 2: check to see…" you know, and they'd have eight or nine things that could cause no picture and no sound. For many though, the repairs had to be at the *circuit board level*. That meant the parts were soldered and so forth and not something that you could replace like a vacuum tube. This was something you had to desolder, re-solder in the new part and so forth — but, I had lots of parts and I had capacitors, resistors — whatever was needed.

We were very fortunate.

We did this for about three years. They were very happy. At the end of the three-year period, everyone in the Oakland area that needed a television set for their daycare center had one. We were very proud of that.

One of the offshoots of that, was my students and I began to understand that everything was repairable — not like today. We have a disposable society — out the window, throw it away — but in those days, things were repairable.

We found that we got pretty good at it. Some of the students got very sharp at that. Not that they necessarily wanted to go into TV repair, but it's just logic: follow the guide and that's it.

One of the things that we started then in my electronics program was something called "Open Lab." In Open Lab, you could make *kits*. We would do this for a one-week period. Every day for an entire week, you could bring in kits to solder and put together and see if you could get something to work. Or you could bring in any appliance that you could carry in your hand. I didn't have room for washing machines and those things, so the heaviest thing that I let them bring in was a microwave.

By the way, while you're reading this, you probably didn't know this. Probably the only appliance in your home, that in fact has a fuse — an old-fashioned fuse, probably 10-, 12- or 15-amps, probably 10- — is a microwave.

The kids would bring in this microwave that had been put in the attic and of course replaced with something new.

I'd tell them it's got *Phillips* screws. That's like a four-sided little screw, as opposed to a regular slot screw. Here's a screwdriver. Take off these thirteen or fourteen screws on the back and in the bottom. Take the metal shrouding off of the microwave. Now, you're looking inside the guts. What do you see? The power cord comes in. The first thing that it goes to is a fuse. You take the fuse out. You could either look at it manually — you know, with your naked eye — and take a look; my eyesight wasn't that good. So I'd use what's called an *ohmmeter*. If the ohmmeter read zero resistance, that means, of course, the fuse is good. If the resistance is infinite — like many, many millions of ohms — okay, then there's an open circuit. It won't operate. So what did we generally find? The fuse is blown. We'd change the fuse and move on.

Now, what happens when they bring home an appliance that works, that they loved? Mom's got a new one. I don't know, maybe the kids put it in their own bedroom for popcorn or something — I don't know.

By the time Open Lab was really going — I could really be very helpful to all the students. One of the things that we taught in Open Lab, was how to solder. How to solder *well*. To follow directions. Identify parts and so forth. It was a wonderful experience. We did that for 30 years of my 32, Open Lab. We did the Open Lab probably once, sometimes twice, in a nine-week quarter. So we had between four and six, maybe as many as eight times a year.

It was a wonderful experience for the kids, opening up a transistor radio just to see what's going on. Some of those small transistor radios, they were meant to be tossed: Doesn't work? Put new batteries. Doesn't work? Throw it away. Well, my students learned, through the soldering techniques and their good eyesight, they could see where there was — what's called — a "cold solder joint," which means solder was put on by a machine or a person, but it didn't flow with nice heat, nice and shiny — kind of dull. OK, here: hit that with a solder pencil. Whew! How nice! Nice and smooth, the melted solder. Let's keep doing that. Okay, we think we've hit all the joints. Let's put a fresh battery in and let's check it out.

About seven out of ten times, it would be repaired, because that was kind of common. These transistor radios often came from Japan with no guarantee that they would continue to work. Sure, they'd check them when they came out of the manufacturing plant. But how long would it last, how long would that poor solder connection still allow electrical flow? The answer was maybe six weeks, maybe five years and it'd fail.

Then we would repair them at the circuit board level.

So my students were exposed to some wonderful experiences. They never had difficulty — no fear. There was just no fear. Like, let's open it up!

We always made sure the power was unplugged. We always made sure that the battery was disconnected. In this way, no little power might shock us in any way shape or form, especially that appliance that you plug into the wall. Careful, careful: unplug that guy and then check it out.

So that was our experience with KQED, how it expanded into Open Lab. We were very proud of those three years that we put in, the work that we did.

Oh, by the way, the ones that they brought to us in the truck, that we couldn't get to work, we were allowed to dispose of them in the dumpsters at Monte Vista High School. So, they got rid of their junk by bringing it to me. If myself and my students, we couldn't repair it, then off to the dumpster to goes. We repaired everything on the television set except the cathode ray tube. There's no room in my facility to store these big giant tubes, so if it needs a picture tube, it's out. But everything else, including power transformers, we had.

It was a great experience and I'm very proud of the kids.

Chapter 6

Up Close and Personal with Stevie Wonder

In the mid-'70s, I'm teaching television production, studio recordings... The program was launching very nicely. It took a long time to get equipment, but we just kept building.

In the midst of all this, one day — it was around April or May, kinda near the end of the school year, I think — I get a phone call. I forget who called me — it was somebody from Pittsburg, California.

"Chester! Stevie Wonder is going to be playing tomorrow at the Creative Arts Center, the theater, at Pittsburg High School. It's going to be an assembly. It's going to go from one to about two-thirty. They'll be a warm-up band, which is Tommy Nunnelly."

I think his band was called "Pacific Gas and Electric" — I'm not sure. But they had a nice backup band with horns and all these things, ready to go. A nice piano, and such.

"... and *Stevie Wonder* is going to play."

In fact, Stevie Wonder was coming back from the Grammy Awards. He was supporting a bunch of awards for "Superstitious" — I think. The following year, "Songs in the Key of Life", or maybe I have it reversed. I'm not sure. But he was rocketing to the heights of popularity. He was the man, for many, many years. Stevie Wonder. I mean, you didn't get much better. You could be different, and there were a lot of successful musicians and singers and bands in the '70s and '80s, y'know, but he was awfully unique.

"Let's see how we could work this out."

I got someone to cover my classes in the afternoon.

One of the guys who worked in the warehouse would help my program out all the time, whenever. One time, he gave us a switcher so that we could switch black-and-white cameras — up to four cameras. It was a Sony SEG-1A. "SEG" means: "Special Effects Generator", 1-A. That was the first model that Sony had ever come out with. Worked just very nice. He had it... *somehow*. He purchased it, or whatever, but he gave it to our program. So, many of these things that were in my program came from help from outside, as with this phone call.

"Chet! Tomorrow, let's go see Stevie Wonder. I want to take a lot of photos and stuff..."

And he did. But I don't have those photos to this day. I'm sorry. But anyway, so we go.

I know the people there...

"Oh, I'm glad you're coming. It's going to be a real treat and all of that."

"Wow! Very nice."

So I felt — in a way — like a special guest. You know, that's *my* alma mater. It felt good, like I belonged there. But I was just going as a fan. This guy from the warehouse was going to take his photos, of which he said he'd give me copies later, and he did, and I lost 'em. I was just going to be watching Stevie Wonder perform.

Oh! I got to see the warm-up band. They were from Pittsburg. I loved them and all of those guys, so I was in my element. I was just happy as a pup.

So, I'm on the side of the stage. I'm looking around checking out the PA[1] system. The opening band, now, was performing. Stevie Wonder was to perform in about forty minutes. Maybe thirty. Maybe the band warmed up for thirty, then he came on. He hadn't arrived yet, because there would be an entourage and so forth. So, he wasn't even on-campus — I don't think — when the show started.

---

[1] Public Address

I'm looking around at the PA and I go, "Whoa!" They've got a sixteen-channel unit. That means sixteen microphones. They've got a big band. They've got four horns, guitar, bass, all these things... vocals... taking up the majority. Stevie Wonder only needs one microphone. I looked, and there *was* no microphone for Stevie Wonder. I scratched my head. I looked around. I also saw that the wires connecting to the speakers were, like, twenty-two-gauge *telephone* wire — not made to carry power. The whole thing was kind of hokey. I could only say that because I had been putting on shows for several years by then, and I knew what good equipment looked like, how they're supposed to operate. I knew exactly how each piece operated. This wasn't right.

But, I guess they'll get by. I don't know. They put a wireless mic out for Stevie Wonder, prior to his coming on stage.

"Oh! That's what was missing. All right! We got a wireless mic!"

Except they had no open channels. The wireless mic went nowhere. Uh-oh.

Now Stevie Wonder's coming on stage. I don't know if he's totally blind, but he had one person who was helping him navigate the short walk from the back of the stage to the front — no problem. Then he goes to welcome the audience... there's nothing.

So I said, "Chet, you could stay here for forty-five minutes and watch all this confusion, or you can roll up your sleeves and solve this problem."

None of my other Rainbow Studio students were around, but I was young enough at the time to climb up and climb over stuff. We'll get it done.

So I told Stevie — in his ear — I hadn't met him...

"I'm Chester. Your mic is not working. I'm gonna make it work."

"All right, Chester. Do your thing!"

I thought it was kinda funny.

So we took that mic out, put it down, like that. I took a sax mic, told the sax player, "You share the mic with the other sax player."

Two saxes on one mic. Very common. Very, very common. We take the mic. There's no mic stand. No. There's a mic stand, no *boom*. The boom allows you to adjust the microphone, so it comes up to the mouth of the performer. Perfect at whatever angle they want. So it's not too high. They could look at the audience.

So I told Stevie — I mean, excuse me. I'm not — I don't know Mr. — I've never met him! We never formally said, "Hi. I'm Chester." "Hi, I'm Stevie Wonder." I don't know. We never did that.

"I have your mic. *I'm* your mic boom."

I took his hand. "Here's my arm… put it where you need it."

He laughed.

"This is a first."

He took my arm, and he pulled it near his face. I went, "Looks good to me."

He said, "Looks good to me."

This was off-mic. Now, he's going to go on-mic.

We don't know how the volume is for him. But, I was just praying that it was enough, so we didn't have to stop, then re-adjust. 'Cause I don't even know who's working the PA. I just know that they had a minimal PA, and certainly not a wealth of knowledge.

But anyway, it was pretty good! The volume was good enough. He smiled. I smiled.

They had a very crude monitor system. Eh-heh. It's really not a monitor system, it's just that the PA is actually behind you — the speakers — so that you can hear what's going to the house. That's your monitor. But it works, as long as there's no feedback. It works.

So, for forty minutes, I was the mic holder. Actually, it's called a "mic clip on a boom." I was all of those things for Stevie Wonder.

We made little jokes in between each song. I said, "That a boy."

"You like that one?"

"Yeah."

"You have a tin ear."

So the next song, "Wadda ya mean, tin ear?"

"That other song, I was flat."

Yeah. Oh, I'm sorry. I don't know. I don't know a flat from a sharp and anything...

But anyway, when it was all over, we hugged, heh, heh... It was a great experience. We never were formally introduced. But I'm sure, way back in the back of his mind, Stevie Wonder does remember the incident... simply because it's so unusual.

Chapter 7

The Concerts, from the Early Beginning From Garage Bands up to *Journey*

When I came to Monte Vista in 1967, the teacher who I was replacing — he was going to go on to medical school — was teaching Morse code for the first five to ten minutes of class. Morse code. Ham radio. Just wasn't my thing.

When I discovered stereo, in 1965, in San Francisco, K-FOG: <foghorn sound> MMMmnnnn. Oh, yeah. Oh, yeah. When I heard stereo for the first time, I was hooked. So, obviously, I wanted to go in a different direction than what the other teacher taught. One of the things that evolved was, what I called — actually, a former student of mine, Steve Martindell, coined them — he called them "mini-concerts."

It's funny. I had a club. The club changed names over the years, but it started out — Michael Baird kind of coined it — "Zap City." We were called that for about four or five years. Then for about three or four years we were called "Crapé," which was an acronym C-R-A-P-É with the accent over the E: Concert Recording and Production Enterprises.

We did concerts, recording, all the production — all my students did it. At first, we had to have someone to be in charge. That would be me. Then someone had to be a manager, an assistant to me to where I could trust them with the keys and make sure that things got set up. It's funny: kids rise or fall to their level of… confidence? How much heart they have… If they believe, "I could do this," that's half the battle. It's like a lot of kids go on to college and then "I don't know…" Eh! You just gotta believe: you could do this. Stick to it.

It finally turned into *Rainbow Studio*, probably the most

famous name of the three. That used to be at the top of all the concert posters: "Rainbow Studio Presents..."

We started out doing small little concerts. They were held in the English rooms, one whole half. The English rooms were divided up into eight separate rooms. They had accordion walls that could open and close. If you opened everything up and moved all the chairs out, there was a nice space.

We didn't yet at that time have our theater. We only had a gymnasium. Some of these small concerts didn't belong in a setting like the gym. Athletics were going on and there was only one gym. There's girls' sports and boys' sports and too many things going on to try to tie up the gym. There's not many sports on Saturday night though. If you take care of the floor, they didn't mind it – the PE people, physical education people. That's their building. They want to take care of it. They allowed me to put on some shows down there. But it wasn't intimate enough.

So we went to the English people.

"This is what we want to do."

Jan Worthington was one of the teachers at the time.

I made a proposal: We need to have your room between seven and ten on a Wednesday night. We used to do Wednesday nights. My bigger concerts were always on a Thursday. But anyway, Wednesday nights. The room was fully opened up, maybe eighty by twenty feet? thirty feet? Kind of a nice, big, open area. Our promise was, that we'd put it back in better shape than when we found it when we came in after school. If the place wasn't vacuumed, of course, we vacuumed. We vacuumed anyway, whether they had done it or not. If all the chairs needed to be up on the tables, all the chairs were back. All the tables back where they belonged, exactly marked, all the chairs back where they belonged. The reason is, no teacher wants to come in to their classroom to start the day and, ah my gosh, you've got to clean up a mess, rearrange, ask kids to help you. It's a lousy way to start the day.

I found that out in a lot of things that I did for other teachers and work that I did in their classroom. Neat, clean, looked better when I left then when I started. So, that's the situation there.

"Okay. We'll try it. No guarantee you could do this all the time. But a Wednesday night seems fair. If you'll put it back in better shape than the custodians left it — or would have left it, because we're using the rooms — Okay."

Then, because they might not have had time to do the vacuuming and picking up papers, we picked up everything. If there was a sink, we washed it. If there was a floor, we vacuumed it. You know, we took care of everything. We liked to be good neighbors. This was not my facility. I know it belonged to the school, but it was really the English people, the English teachers'. That was their room.

By the way, while we're on the topic of English teachers, they are the hardest working people in the public school today, as a group. The papers they have to read and correct, spellings and so forth. The amount of time that it takes, compared to maybe a math teacher… It's easy to correct tests and you're home with your family, doing what families do… not tied up and doing homework and so forth. But I digress.

So we held our first little concert. It's funny. The people that we started with were all garage bands. We're talking 1968, '69, '70, '71, like in there — '72.

What was nice: there wasn't much money. We only charged a dollar.

We started at seven, finished at ten. We always had three bands. The percentage breakdown went: headliner gets fifty percent; next band gets twenty percent; the third band — that opened the show — gets … I dunno. We'd end up with ten or twenty percent ourselves, you know, for "Rainbow Studio" — or "Zap City," in those days.

We made a few dollars. But most importantly, was the

experience that my students received in putting on a concert: setting up the stage if necessary, bringing in the PA, making sure there's no feedback, then recording off of that. We'd record what we did so the bands could have something — if they wanted it — and we'd work off that.

We discovered right away, that what you record and what you use in a PA are two different things. In other words, in a PA, the vocals need to be very loud in the room, so people could hear the words. But in the recording, therefore it comes through fairly loud. Now, the bass: there's no bass in your recording. Why? There's usually enough bass in the room that you don't even turn up the microphone on the bass. So what do you get in the record, if that's your direct feed — right off the mixer? Way low bass. Where's the bass? Drums, too. In a smaller room, drums and cymbals could be heard easily at the back of the room. Well then, how much do you have to turn the microphones up for that? Pffft, hardly at all. Therefore in the recording what do you get? No drums. So it's vocal-heavy and maybe lead-guitar-heavy and it's lacking bass and it's lacking drums. So you learn as you go that if you were going to take something straight off the mixer, that mix is not a good recording. Wow, so now we've got to have separate feeds.

And so forth. This requires a little bit more sophisticated equipment, but that's what we did. We kept building... got money anywhere we could... maybe a grant or two. We became the concert capital of the San Ramon Valley. No one held regular concerts. We did it every other Wednesday.

That's what we gave all these bands: the opportunity to play in front of an audience. Usually, the audience numbers were probably fifty, on average, probably twenty of them - my students, but everyone had to pay a dollar. Want to come, costs you a dollar. Then we stopped that, after which it was: my students paid nothing.

We did that for a little bit. Half the audience would be my

students. Then as it grew, then one-fifty to two-hundred. Boy, you got a party going on when you got two-hundred in one room.

Nobody smoked. They'd go outside to smoke — we had fifty-four acres on the campus. You could come and go. Got a little stamp on your hand? Perfect, come in - *badda, boom*. We didn't care.

A lot of bands got their first opportunity. In fact, a guy named Josh Harris — keyboard player/vocalist — I managed a band that he was in, based on his request, and my having seen him play at these "mini-concerts," two, three, maybe four shows. He'd always be with different people. He hadn't formed *his* band yet, but you could tell he was gonna be the center of the band. I took a liking to him, so I managed his band for five years. That all started from the mini-concerts.

The mini-concerts grew.

Then the theater was opened — an eight-hundred-seater. *Journey* happened. And the rest — as they say — is history.

But it all started with the little mini-concerts.

My kids, if there were lights, they ran the lights; PA? they ran the PA; tickets… They took the money, tickets, change… we had popcorn, then we'd have to vacuum a lot after, but didn't matter. In the morning, everything was vacuumed. It might have smelled like popcorn, but there are worse smells.

Chapter 8

Funding My Program

As a teacher of electronics — and eventually TV productions, concert recordings, and all of that — the program is very expensive by its very nature, to operate. The budgets that you're given — in the very early days when I was there, there was no Prop. 13 — much more generous. Then, after Prop. 13, boy, things got cut back severely. Raising money for a program — whether it's choir, sports, the French club — it doesn't matter. You want to go take a trip to France, you want to defer as many costs as possible, making it less expensive for the students to go — you've got to do fundraisers.

I hadn't thought it through, when we started. I started like anybody else would do. Okay, we'd tell the kids in our little electronics club, "What do you guys think? How are we going to raise some money?"

"Let's do a carwash," someone says.

All right. Carwash sounds good. We did one car wash. We worked our tails off. Everybody helped. They all had fun. It was a gorgeous day, playing in the water — the whole thing. I don't know, we profited about a hundred and eighty dollars, two-hundred and twenty maybe — maybe — to be generous? Come on!

What are you gonna do, hold a car wash every week?

<Students' voices> "No, uh, I can't do it next week, Chet." "No, I… I'll do…" "I didn't mind doing it, but…"

You got thirty-eight kids in the club and twenty-one show up for the car wash. I went, "Whoa! This is a lot of work." It's an all-day thing — longer than that. You gotta make arrangements.

You gotta soothe everybody's fears.

We had bake sales. We did a lot of things. But, nothing really generated a lot of money.

I like live music. And we were doing these little mini-concerts.

I said, "Let's put on a fashion show." We did several of them, over the years. They were so popular. It was unbelievable. We held 'em in the gym, and then when the theater was constructed, then we held them in the theater — gorgeous setting.

Who were the models? Ten boys, ten girls. Then, four female teachers, four male teachers.

Whose clothes are they wearing? At first, I went to *Smario's* in Pittsburg. Jack Smario, he was alive at the time, very generous guy… Boom! Outfitted us with clothes that these people hadn't seen. In other words, they knew they were coming to a golf course community area, Round Hill Country Club. So when doing so, they brought the clothes that those members — on a casual, to semi-dressy occasion — would look sharp in. He brought those. That's what the kids wore — cutting edge.

For the for the girls, it was a woman's shop in Walnut Creek — I forget the name. Oh, no! The woman's shop was Josh Harris' mother. She had a shop in Danville. She supplied the clothes. She's kind of a hippie gal…

Boy! What a show.

Believe me, when you put on something like a fashion show, you open up a can of worms. For example, heh, heh, heh…

<School PA voice> "… Anyone who's a female or a male who would like to be in the fashion show, please put your application in. Applications are available in our studio, Rainbow Studio… Come on down! Get the application and… everyone's eligible. Fill out the little basic thing: name, age, which class you're in, that's all. We don't care about anything else — and, eh, student ID number — something like that. That's about it." And, uh, that's it.

So each time — in the guys — we'd have, like, around fifteen to pick from. We needed ten or twelve. Now that's pretty easy.

For the girls, we'd have, like, *forty* or *fifty*. Yikes! We were only gonna do ten or twelve. What do we do? So I made this up on the spot, no big deal:

<Instructor Voice> "Everyone here must mark a ballot... where your name is, you put an 'X'. Do that right now. Find your name, put an 'X'.

"Now, vote for eight more."

Maybe the number was six — doesn't matter.

In order to do this, we're gonna go all the way around in a circle — it was a very large room where we did this — to select the models. You stand up and you tell them who you are and what activities you're involved in and why you wanna model.

Most of 'em are just like, "... I thought it'd be fun to dress up..." Whatever, I got you. Sure is. Always fun. Kids love dressing up. Mom and Dad out there — I'm telling you: dress your kids up more. They'd like it.

<Administrator voice> "But, Chet — Uh, no one does that anymore."

"I know, I know. Just do it."

Look sharp. Suspenders, maybe... eh? Li'l tie? Come on, now. Li'l sport jacket? Dress that little guy up. Nice dress for the little girls. They love that — love that.

But anyway, getting back to the selection, so that's how we'd do the process.

Then some people would ask, "Well, how come *I* didn't get picked?"

"I dunno. I mean, I don't know. How do I know? You picked yourself for sure, and then we added them all up and you came in like fourteenth or fifteenth. I mean, what am I gonna do?"

"But I really wanted to —"

I know. I know — it's tough. That was a part of the process that I didn't particularly like. I'm not exclusive in anything I do.

Totally *inclusive*. Everyone's welcome.

But, now, getting ready for the day of the show, boy, that's exciting. The truck arrives around — let's say the show starts at seven… The show included a fashion show — takes about an hour — a little break from the action, and the parents are requested to… *get out.*

<Announcer voice> "Thank you for coming! Thank you for buying a ticket! I hope you patronize these shops that brought their clothes, but now we're going to dance to live music."

The first show I did was a trio — maybe a quartet. Keyboard… I think it was Sal Mercurio and Frank Mercurio. They're cousins. In fact, I think the band even was called, "Cousins." They had a drummer, maybe a singer, I'm not sure. They played some of the jazzier hit songs and things… maybe a current song or two. But the kids had a nice time.

So the trucks arrive, they bring the clothes. They have all the racks and those kind of things like that. It's time for fittings. I mean they did the fittings at the store. All the kids had to go to the store, and their outfits, they tried them on… made decisions.

The store made the final decision: "This looks terrific on you."

"But my favorite color is" — whatever — "Peach," you know, "Violet." I don't know.

They go like — "No, this looks terrific." And that would be it.

Most of the people were thrilled with what they had. It's expensive, these clothes. We had to put tape on the bottom of the shoes so you didn't ruin the soles, so they could be sold as new. A lot of times when you put on a fashion show, you're not given the shoes. This had everything. Umbrellas. A hat. Oh, jeez, they went crazy. Very nice. We had a great time.

The attendance was around, um… four-hundred. Then, when the parents left, it was around, uh… three-hundred, two-seventy-five? We'd dance for a couple hours.

That was the first time I had hired security. I lined them all up when they were done, and I tipped 'em five dollars each. I thought it was appropriate, because I had asked them ahead of time, "Please don't hassle my students. They're here for a fashion show. They're going to be dancing and having a nice time. Having security," I told them, "makes me uncomfortable. But if you'll be welcoming, if you'll assist them if needed, if you'll give them direction if needed — then I would be highly appreciative."

And they did. They did for all my shows, all the different security.

That was the first and only time I tipped 'em. The reason is, because that's an added expense. You put down the expense. Then there are five or ten of them? Ay, eh! Where does it stop? An extra twenty dollars for the guy who mixed — you know — he made the band sound terrific in a gymnasium. Where do you stop? I stopped right then — that was it, the last time I did a tip for security personnel.

The kids had a terrific time. What's crazy — as you're reading this — understand this: It's one of the activities that the other students will attend. You don't gotta twist an arm to come and watch a play. You don't gotta twist an arm to come watch a choir. No arm twisting. They *want* to see it. Especially, some of the gals were — may I use the word — *stunning*. I mean they were cute gals, five-foot-seven, maybe, pick one out — hundred and twenty pounds to a hundred twenty-five, I don't know. But then all dressed up, and the hair done. I don't think we had the hair done. I'm not sure — we might have done one show — I forget. But that's another — you know — *bonus*. "This would look good in an updo..." — and whatever hairstyle they're talking about — and do it.

The kids looked great. The audience appreciated 'em — a lot of whistles, lot of clapping, lot of *whatever*. Some of the kids were very stiff, even though we told 'em to relax and have a good time. Some hammed it up as they went up and down the walkway. Some smiled to the audience and waved and laughed.

Others were very stoic — usually the boys. You know, it's weird. When you got a sixteen-, seventeen-year-old boy who was selected to go — he didn't have much competition, but anyway selected to go — he may not be outgoing and wave to the audience. So, he doesn't become a fan favorite, because he didn't interact with the audience. But nobody cares. There's enough kids to have a good time.

I was a model. Four, five of my fellow teachers: models. We all just had fun.

But — that was just the beginning. Live music was finally introduced in a setting that the parents could see — I kind of eased them in, for these concerts, these live music things. The impression when the parents left was excellent. Each year after that — we did about four, five years — was wonderful. It was a good moneymaker.

Along with doing concerts at the same time, that was fantastic. Also, we did a basketball game against —

It's funny. This was a fundraiser for athletics. Ray Crawford was going, "Yeah, we've got to get a game together." Ray Crawford was the athletic director and also the co-scoreboard operator with me. We both got the job together. He stayed with the A's for about five years. He's up in Oregon now.

So, Ray put together some basketball games against the Raiders[1], and the Raiders were very popular at the time. We paid 'em I think fifteen-hundred to come out. Like ten players would come. It's a hundred-fifty dollars if you split it evenly and don't pay any others. It's not very much money. What are world-class athletes doing on the floor with us? I don't know. So it'd be the teachers versus the Raiders. Those games drew some pretty large crowds.

Then I got an idea. I said, "Wait a minute."

---

[1] Oakland NFL Raiders, who shared the Coliseum with the A's.

So I picked up the phone — 'cause I came from San Francisco and I had been to the Playboy Club once. Ostentatious? I dunno... not so ostentatious. Revealing an' everything? Yeah. Yeah, they showed the cleavage and — bending over — you got to see the shape, and eh... it's, eh... *alluring*. It's a good thing; drinks are too expensive and watered down — doesn't matter to me.

Here we go. I make a phone call.

"I want to talk to the *mother*," it's called — I don't know. I don't think she's called "Mother Superior." That's like in the Catholic church, I think, but it was, like, the lady who took care of the ladies. Usually an older lady. Maybe a former Playboy bunny... who had aged a bit — you know, I dunno.

But anyway, we're talking on the phone.

"Listen, we're doing a fundraiser here at Monte Vista High School. It's for the athletic department. We need to buy this equipment — " or whatever it is we were doing — "and we've done these things... they're awfully popular — with the Raiders — but we'd like to change it up this year. Do you guys by chance — I thought I heard that it's possible — you got a basketball team... that travels?"

"We do."

"Oh, you do. Yikes! Are any of the girls that come... Playboy bunnies?"

"All of them."

Ayiiiii.

"Oh!... then... is it possible that I could hire you?"

"Well, sure, it's possible, but we don't come cheap."

All I have to go by is the fifteen-hundred that we paid the Raiders — that's all I had to go by.

"Well, we're prepared — we're taking a chance here — but we're prepared... to pay fifteen-hundred."

"That's our fee!"

"Well, then we have an agreement once we get a date?"

"What are you looking at?"

"Well, we're hoping for this date." It was a Thursday.

"We're open."

"Well, how do we consummate this contract?"

We did, and that's it. I sent her money — five-hundred for the deposit, but it had to go through the school. It took two days to write a check, and another five days to get — I dunno.

It's just schools, and doing business with rock bands... Playboy bunnies... Raiders... There's this cash delay *thing*.

The bunnies were fine with it. "No, no problem."

The Raiders wanted theirs in cash. We probably cashed their checks for 'em, which was a common practice. You have checks for them. They endorse 'em, they give it back to you, and you hand them cash.

We agreed on a date. We're all set. Publicity is up and around the school. The tickets are selling like hotcakes.

<Random student> "I can't believe the Playboy bunnies are coming here!"

Now, these are other things that I hadn't even thought about. You know, I'm so naive sometimes, it's unbelievable.

To help me out, for the sale of tickets, so that we're profitable and gladly pay the fifteen-hundred, Mother gives me a call — the mother bunny.

"One of the gals we're bringing is the 'Playmate of the Month,' for this particular month. So, you might mention that, and maybe they'd like, well..."

Pftttt, Hello! Of course, I want to mention that.

Ah! Feedback from the community!

I don't know and I don't care — don't matter. Just: "Playboy bunny is coming to play some basketball." 'Bout as innocent as it gets.

But to make the evening special I said, "You know, these tickets are selling so good, that we need to host — to have a dinner for the ladies." So I call Mother Bunny.

"They'll be twelve of us (bunnies), total."

"Well, they'll be twelve of us men, total."

It was men and some boys, you know, some students — probably students of mine that could play a little basketball, I don't know.

We went to — it was in San Ramon, a nice, nice dinner house, *The Brass Door.*

But anyway, so we go out to dinner. We went about... five o'clock. We were done, eh... six-thirty, quarter to seven, for a seven-thirty thing. The restaurant and Monte Vista High School were just right around — you know, I mean not right around the corner, but a few miles away.

Gym was packed. SRO. People had a wonderful time.

Couple of my students were on the basketball team. I had to call a timeout and talk to 'em...

"Take it easy, you know, like bumpin' the gals over to get a rebound. Come on! Ay ay ay, ay ay ay. We're having fun here. We're not trying to win here, heh, heh..."

But anyway, I think we netted eighteen-hundred after expenses.

So those are the kind of fundraisers and things we did, leading into concerts and stuff. But you need to know — you needed to know — to complete the picture, where we started, how we did it, things we tried. Then you realize that we did settle on concerts and, eventually, video yearbooks that we'll talk about.

First Annual Fashion Show and Dance (Spring of 1968) of six such events total, at the Monte Vists High School Gymnasium. The dance band "Cousins," featuring Sal and Frank Mercurio, from Pittsburg, California played. Photographer: Unknown.

Chapter 9

THE JOURNEY CONCERT

By 1976, I had put on eight to ten shows/concerts at Monte Vista High School – a couple in the gym. The theater was brand new. It had just opened, so we did a few there.

One of the bands that we booked was a band called "Yesterday and Today," who later became "Y&T." They had a great time, and the kids enjoyed them. There were maybe three hundred in attendance. Our theater held eight hundred, for a sellout.

No chairs. Everything was standing. The worst line of sight in the theater was fifty-five feet away from where center stage would be – like the lead singer – and you'd be in the farthest right- or left-hand corner of the theater. So all the sight lines were outstanding.

It was kind of sunken where you stood. At first, the theater was designed to be *in the round,* but we built a huge proscenium stage for the theater when it was erected. It was ready for big-time rock and roll.

I made a call to Walter Herbert, "Herbie." He was the manager of *Journey*. He also oversaw *Yesterday and Today.*

"I'd like to bring you guys out: Journey."

"Let me get back to you on that." And a couple of days later, Herbie called and said, "All right, let's cut a deal."

I don't have the original papers, but I think it was around fifteen-hundred that they charged us. We were charging somewhere between three and five dollars for every show at the time. Everybody made money and everyone had a good time, but let me tell you about the show.

First of all, the administration was very shaky, like, this band may be too big for what we're doing – too soon. They had a good point. Can you handle this? Let's find out.

I try not to overlook opportunities – though, there's a chapter on flubs later on in this book that tells you how I messed up and did not book some great bands. But anyway, the Journey thing was booked.

Administration was nervous. We went over the plans. Let's put two more police officers – I mean rent-a-cops, two more rent-a-cops – down in the parking lot. Let's go two more rent-a-cops down in the bathroom areas, and so forth. Let's have our best chaperones, for all my concerts.

This is how the chaperoning worked: I needed someone to watch a door on one side of the theater and another door on the other side of the theater so people could exit only but could not come in that way. So that was a couple of chaperones. Then, you needed a couple at the door taking tickets and stamping hands as the kids or the audience came in.

Usually, I hired between four and eight chaperones. For this one, we had eight. What I did was I'd pay 'em $50 each – in cash. The bookkeeper at Monte Vista would make out the checks to the chaperones and at the end of the evening, every chaperone got their $50 check and we would cash it for them. If they wanted to go somewhere and maybe have a drink or something, they had money in their pocket immediately. One of the things I didn't like about doing extra work for the school or school district – even though they might pay you – is you did the work and maybe a month later you got a check. It's like there's no impact in your life. I like to make impacts in people's lives, so they remember. Did they have a good experience as a chaperone? You need some help? We've got regular cops. We've got rent-a-cops. We've got chaperones – we've got everything. Administrators? It's a team.

The administration wasn't necessarily on board. You have to

understand.

"How are ticket sales, Chet?"

"Uh, they're going well."

"What do you mean by 'well'?"

"I think we might have a sellout."

"Oh my God, a sellout?!" Rather than reveling in the idea, which is, "How nice: you put on a show, it's almost already a sellout, congratulations! Let's roll up our sleeves and do a good job." That was never the attitude of any administrator that I worked with, except a man named Jerry Grandhoffer, who was principal at the time, and a man named John Morrison, who was vice-principal at the time.

The administration was not quite on board. All right.

So now comes the day of the show. We're going to load in.

My students helped the PA company load in, they helped the band load in, they broke down the cases, they set up the microphones, mic stands. We'd plug 'em in if you wanted us to, we'd leave the connector there at the mixer or at the "snake" — a big mic snake, maybe had twenty-four channels, so you could plug in your microphones and send them in from many different directions going to the mixing console. My students did a lot of work and helped.

The theater was prepared. All the chairs were removed. Everything was vacuumed. The stage was clear. Now the equipment was being loaded in.

One of the first things we'd do at all of our shows was as soon as the trucks arrived, we'd take their order.

"We're going to Burger King. What would you like? There's no charge."

That was just part of the expense of doing a show. But it was highly appreciated by roadies, whether it's a PA company or the band itself; they sure did appreciate it. We always had food backstage for all the bands. So everything was taken care of.

Now they started sound checking… just fooling around and

testing. "Test: one, two, three..." that type of thing. This was when I would visit, to see how things were going and chat with the headlining band.

The headlining band always checked first. Then the last one to do a sound check would be the opening band, whoever that might be. Then you'd be ready to go. You'd leave it set up for them. You knew where the settings were for the headliners so you were ready to do the show. The soundcheck was usually about an hour long — I've seen shorter; I've seen longer — but usually within an hour, everything was ready to go. The band was well-balanced.

In the band at that time, Walter Herbert was the manager. I had met him and liked him — and to this day, I love that guy. Neal Schon was on guitar, Aynsley Dunbar on drums, Gregg Rollie on keyboards/Hammond B3 organ I think, and I forget who the bassist was — I thought it was someone from Lafayette, but it doesn't matter. It was the early Journey. They were writing their latest album that they had put out, "Look into the Future" or something — I forget. But anyway, we were very blessed to have such a big band to come play at a high school. Of course, over the years, I did over a hundred and fifty shows. We had some huge bands. Journey was definitely the biggest at the time.

While I'm wandering around, I thought I'd go see Gregg Rollie, simply because he was in a band with a guy named Coke Escovedo[1]. They had an album out and it was a wonderful album. They only put out one; the name of the album was "Coke." They had performed in the fall of 1975 for me, October — great show, 'bout three, four-hundred in attendance; real danceable music, great time. It turns out that Gregg Rollie and Coke Escovedo were in the same band. Now what band would it be? I don't know, maybe Santana? Maybe Malo? — I don't know, and it really doesn't matter — but they were in the same

---

[1] Coke Escovedo was the brother of Pete Escovedo and the uncle of Sheila E.

band. So I just figured, hey, I'll go chat Gregg Rollie up a little bit and we'll talk about Coke Escovedo as a common denominator and go from there. Perfect.

So I walked up to him.

"Gregg Rollie, my name is Chester Farrow. I'm the promoter here. I'm a teacher at Monte Vista High School. We're so proud to have your band here. Oh, we're going to do a great show for you. You're going to love this.

"Greg, uh, you know, Coke Escovedo performed in October of this past year..."

I told him about it, what that they played, what a great show and so forth.

He looked me square in the eyes.

"I'll *kill* that son of a bitch if I ever see him again."

Wow, where do we go from there? I don't know. Something had gone awry between them. That was the end of our conversation.

- - -

All right: now it's showtime — not quite yet. We were going to let the people in. We had seven-hundred-forty pre-sold; the room holds eight. So I was praying that no more than sixty came to fill it up.

The doors opened at seven o'clock. At 6:30, there were two hundred and something people lined up in a separate line — those without tickets.

Yikes! That's going to put us at a thousand and six, if I count pretty good. That was the final attendance: a thousand-six, in a room that holds eight-hundred. Where'd they all go? Well, we know there are approximately eight-hundred in the theater on the floor, approximately another two-hundred up in the catwalks, on the spiral staircase that leads to the catwalk. If a fire marshal had come in, he would have shut us down immediately.

So with the line out there, I went to Jerry Grundhofer, who was vice-principal at the time; a man named Sam Zacheim was the principal at the time. He was blown away. No, no public school does what I did over all those years. But anyway, he was pretty scared.

Jerry Grundhofer was the administrator in charge.

"Jerry, what are we going to do?"

"We can't turn all these people away. That's money, Chet."

"Yes it is."

"We're going to have more trouble if we turn 'em away then if we let 'em in."

"That's true. But there'll be some things we can't control, like someone firing up a joint in the middle of the thing, and we can't even reach 'em. But don't worry about it. Everything cleans up pretty good and vacuums real good and we'll make it look good when it's all done, Jerry."

He said, "Let 'em in."

And we did. They were crawling up and around and… my gosh. It was jammed. They performed. It was a great show. Kids kind of went wild. It's not the *best* show we've ever had; it was the *biggest* show that we ever had. The best show was Huey Lewis and the News, and we'll talk about that in a separate chapter.

It was really out of control. No one was punching and things like that. But, when you're in control, that means if somebody were to light up a cigarette, you go, "Excuse me, pardon me, excuse me…" work your way into the crowd, grab the cigarette — I did it all the time — with your bare hand, crush it… because you don't want to put it out in the carpet.

So I'd take it, crush it, "No smoking in here. Thank you." That's it. I would take it away.

"Oh, oh, I'm sorry—"

"No smoking in the theater."

That's called having control. This, I couldn't even reach 'em;

it was *out* of control.

Everyone had a great time. I think there was one fight down in the parking lot: somebody got a bloody nose.

We evaluated the concert the next day, Friday. The only thing they could talk about was: couldn't get to certain things, we had to let slide, and somebody got punched in the nose, had a bloody nose. Let's get serious. You finished a concert and all you have is some cigarette butts on the floor — that you can clean. A broken nose. For a sold-out jammed concert. Come on, now. That's a bit over reactive.

So from then on, we talked on *Monday*. Why?

What did we talk about on Friday? Broken nose, this and that, we need more cops, out of control… that's Friday.

What did we talk about on Monday, now that the parents have had a chance to talk to their kids and ask them about the show? We had a chance to ask the kids if they enjoyed the show.

By the way, that's something I always did: I would always walk around…

"Hey, uh, Chet! Good show!"

"Are you enjoying yourself?"

"Yes!"

"Is the band a good band for you?"

"Yes!"

"Okay. It's all I wanted to know, you're having a good time."

How about this? I'd ask this one:

"Are you getting your money's worth?"

"Oh, man! Yeah, Chet, really! Thanks for bringing!"

"Okay."

What did we talk about on Monday? Ah. "Well, a Mrs. so-and-so called and said it was a little bit loud." All right: concerts are loud. All the doors are closed. No one asked you to move here. When we built our school, there were no houses anywhere near us. Cameo was the closest place and that was up and around the bend, on Stone Valley Road. All we had were cows, horsies. We were there first. People used to complain about the PA system on Friday night football. Well, come on, we established that school in '65. I came there in '67, but they established in '65; you guys came much later. Sorry, we were here first. Precedent had been set. Friday night football would be announced and that's the way that goes. The crowds would cheer. And so forth.

On Monday, then, we discussed also how the kids really enjoyed the show; how the kids really felt that they got their money's worth; how the kids were very proud of Monte Vista High School hosting what was to be a major band — they were up-and-coming at the time.

The kids had pride. I had pride. Parents had pride.

Administration did not. Administration had worries, letter of the law. Come on. Give me a break.

This was territory that was new, different. Had been tried before and failed. I think in 1965, Campolindo High School or one of those schools in the Moraga area had The Grateful Dead. Lots of dope-smoking, lots of whatever, swaying, people kind of messed up. Administration said, "No more."

Why?

Don't book The Grateful Dead anymore. Why? They're going to do LSD and marijuana. Come on. That's what you got — alcohol way down.

Oh, by the way, speaking of that, I just want to tell you one thing.

Who did we love to come into the concerts? People smoking dope — you bet. I'd look 'em square in the eyes and tell 'em, "You're not going to give us any trouble today, are you?"

"Oh, no, Chet! Oh, no! —"

"Good, because it looks like you've been kinda smoking and… you know, you're cool? You sure you're cool?"

"Ah, I'm cool, Chet. No trouble from me."

"All right."

Now, who *don't* you want? The drinkers. Oh, yeah. Yeah, very loud. Push, shove. "Get out of my concert." Although, of course, we'd let 'em in, but you'd know where the trouble lies: it's in the alcohol. They'd get fueled up and away we'd go.

That was just a little aside. I'd take dope smokers at my concerts, any, any time. Leave the alcohol at home. I don't need it.

Just to finish off — on the little Monday's, what we talked about, it was way calmer. Then, the broken nose becomes "just part of the overall picture," you know, it's just what happened.

"Gee, only one broken nose? Only one punch in the nose? All right, not so bad." That kind of thing. Remember now, these were testosterone-fueled guys, drinking or whatever — some of them came to punch.

There was one guy from San Ramon. I forget his name, but I knew he was trouble. He punched one of my former students, Michael Baird, who was trying to break up the fight. I told him, "Michael, we have cops for that. Don't ever do that again." And he didn't. But that guy came for trouble and he found it. Punched a couple of guys, the cops found him, took him off-campus and we were done with him.

But anyway, it was a great show.

They wanted to suspend concerts for a while. I had The Tubes already lined up. That hurt. The next time I tried to get them, they were too big. Too big to bring The Tubes.

<Doubting Administrator> "Chet, aren't The Tubes too wild for Monte Vista?"

"It's a concert! Anything could go on."

Everyone, please, keep your pants on; it's all we ask. Come on, people. It's no big deal. The Tubes would have been great.

Instead, we had a band called "The Med Flies." That concert[2] — outstanding audio, great visuals. They were like, "Tubes, Junior," if you want to know what The Tubes were like. It was a

---

[2] At *YouTube.com*, search for "The Med Flies 2/84 40"

great show. At one point, even our chaperones were, like, a little bit embarrassed, because there's a flogging scene and there were a few other things and… Great show. Very entertaining. No, foul language. Nothing stupid.

Chapter 10

The Greg Kihn Concert

Circa 1982…'83 – right in there – Greg Kihn came and played for me, I think for the fourth time. We had Greg Kihn and his band in the late 70's, maybe early, early 80's, then we had him again another time and another time… He always put on great shows.

The very first time that Greg performed for me, the attendance was two-eighty, if I recall, and that's kind of a thin crowd. The next time was four-hundred. And the next time – so anyway…

This being the fifth show that Greg did, the audience was well, well aware of how well he was doing. The song "Jeopardy" had not come out yet. But in a very surprising thing for me, they debuted "Jeopardy" at Monte Vista High School. It wowed the crowd, but I'll get to it in a minute.

We put tickets on sale, put the signs out. For all my concerts, I'd buy orange craft paper, fifty-yard rolls of bright orange, shiny on one side, which was the side we printed the stencils on. We'd make 'em eight feet long.

The reason was, Monte Vista High School was essentially built all redwood. In the theater, all re-sawn redwood, very expensive. On the exterior, re-sawn redwood with little two-by-twos – three-inch by two-inch – by twelve-feet tall slats that kind of covered the seams… very tasteful. Monte Vista essentially looked how I envisioned an Eastern private university. Fifty-four acres. Wonderful layout. They spared no expense in the materials. The reason I bring up those slats – two by three, by ten feet high I guess, whatever the walls were – is that they allowed us to use thumbtacks for an eight-foot-long sign that was easily readable. The headliner's lettering would be six-inches high, in stencil, and all the detail information would be four inches high or three inches high.

So, we put up our "Greg Kihn Concert" posters. I think the band, "Tickets," was the opening act — I forget. The concerts are all on YouTube — you go to *YouTube.com* and search for "Chester Farrow Videos Greg Kihn Band" and there will be all the concerts from Greg Kihn right there.

This particular concert sold quickly. In fact, I didn't put tickets on sale until Friday morning, which was two weeks before the concert. By 12:30, noon…

"Uh, Chet! Didn't you teach class? You sold tickets?"

Well, the rush was so heavy that people were cutting class, they didn't care. They wanted to buy tickets. It was a red hot ticket. It sold out by 12:30 in the afternoon. At one o'clock — after I had a little lunch, I called Victor Rocke, who was the manager for The Greg Kihn Band. He worked for Matthew Kaufman, the President of Beserkley Records. Matthew never came to any of our concerts, but he came to this one. So I knew it was special.

So anyway, I give him a call.

"Victor, I got some good news."

"What would that be, Chet?"

"We're sold out. All eight-hundred: gone."

"Wow!"

"Now, Victor, you wanna do a second show? They're clamoring for more tickets. Second show: we'll start the first one at six instead of seven, and we'll go to eleven instead of quitting at ten… on a Thursday night, of which we had already scheduled."

"Let me talk to Matthew and the band."

He calls me back.

"No, we don't want to do a second show."

"Okay. I have another proposal for you: I'd like to book you at the Concord Pavilion[1]. We'll sell it out. Let's pick a date, kind of like an October evening, September — be fabulous."

"Let me get back to you on that."

About four or five days later, he got back to me.

"Uh, Chet, we're doing a concert at the Concord Pavilion — but not with you."

It was with a guy who owned a nightclub in Berkeley. I forget the name of it. But he had booked Greg since the beginning, kind of like a house band. He did deserve to have that show.

As Victor Rocke said later on at the Concord show — 'cause I was there — he said, "Chester, this is your concert."

"I know."

That happens sometimes — just the way it goes; no regrets. No regrets. Just, "Okay."

I knew I was onto something, and *they* knew that I knew that I was on — and so forth. They wanted to spread the word — the wealth — elsewhere. We'll talk about spreading the wealth elsewhere in a chapter on Flint's Ribs.

But anyway, now is the day of the show.

Everyone knows it's sold-out. Do not come if you don't have a ticket. That makes it easy. There's no separate line for those of you without tickets — they're all gone. All the kids knew. The sold-out signs were stenciled over… in big six-inch letters, all throughout campus: "Sold Out," Sold out.

So the trucks load in, as they usually do. My kids are helping, getting hamburgers, setting things up. But I could tell there were a lot of things different. One: Sound-on-Stage, Jerry Fieffer's PA company — they brought a bigger mixer. They brought different and better amplifiers.

Something's up. Something's up tonight.

So, they do the sound check. At the backstage, we have food as we always did. Everyone's eating, enjoying themselves…

Now it's *showtime*.

---

[1] https://en.wikipedia.org/wiki/Concord_Pavilion

So, it's funny: Greg, he liked to smoke his pot. You have to provide a place for him. How do you provide a place at a public school for bands to smoke a joint before they go on? Well, my studios, my classroom — all of that — were located right next door to the wood shop. If you exited the wood shop the *back* way — you know, from the classroom — you could exit and go down. You come to a little landing outside the door, not big enough to actually be called a patio or loft or something, but eight-by-eight, top landing area, about twelve stairs down to the school... At that location, you can't be seen by anyone on campus — period. You're going to have a cold beer? Help yourself. You're going to do shots before you go on? Do it here. You're going to smoke your marijuana? Right here.

No hurry, except we're looking at the clock. You're going on, let's say at eight-thirty. You've got an hour and a half set. We finish at ten.

By the way, I never pulled the cord on anybody. I never would.

But everyone — every band, every manager — cooperated one-hundred percent.

When all they wanted was a ten-minute "high sign" — ten — I flashed my two hands spread open. I showed them and they'd see it. I'd be standing on the side of the stage. I'd walk onto the stage a little bit if needed. There it is: ten, and we're sticking to it.

If maybe they'd finish up a song, start another — almost everyone, I think everyone, stopped at ten. They'd like to get home and get going.

They finished up the smoking and so forth, and I'd lead them onto the stage. My introduction was always the same.

"Monte Vista... you ready to *rock*? Please welcome, THE GREG KIHN BAND!" *Phoom!* That's it.

I might go, "Monte Vista, you ready to rock? Please welcome, Huey Lewis and the News" — although, I didn't introduce that one. The guy who introduced it, he says, "What kind of intro do you give?" I told him, and he used that exact intro. Because it's clean, it's simple, respectful. You don't go, "Hey, kids!" Don't use words of kids. Sixteen-, seventeen-, eighteen-year-old people… kids? These are adults doing adult things. It's amazing. Your children can act very nicely at a campus, with rock and roll.

Will any high school ever do it again? No? Might there be someone who tries it once? Yeah, sure, go ahead. We did thirty years of it, three shows a year minimum. Not a bad track record. Not a bad track record.

We lead the band onto the stage. But I kind-of split off to the side. I liked to see the intro. I liked to see how they'd start.

The kids — I call them kids, but I'm saying the *audience* — all kinds of signs. "We came for you, Greg Kihn!" — Uh, I don't know — "Greg, we love you!" People were on shoulders already, the girls on top so they got a better view. The electricity was high in the air.

As I looked across the stage on the other side, I saw Matthew Kaufman. Heh, heh, heh… Matthew Kaufman. Well, Matthew doesn't go to shows, you know, another gig another thing. Come on.

This night was going to be special.

Greg started performing. He had all these great tunes and great covers that he had, and an original or two, but — what a show! He does put on a great show. He's a great showman. Larry Lynch was on drums — great "metronome" man. Just keeps that beat so solid — unbelievable. Steve Wright on bass. Robbie Dunbar, I think, was on guitar for a while. And this evening, there's Greg Douglass — who I had put several shows on with — Greg Douglass and his band, over the years. He had a band called "Country Weather." They did a lot of Stones covers, and all like that. But just technically an excellent guitarist. Professional all the way. Greg was on lead guitar now…

"Wow! Here we go!"

The show was hot. Very good. PA was… just singing.

The acoustics in the theater – brief rundown, if I haven't done this already – carpeting on the floor, very good. You want to get rid of parallel hard surfaces that create what are called "standing waves." Standing waves are basically white noise. You don't want that at all. So you must soften one of the parallel surfaces. Well, the floor was not parallel with the ceiling, as the ceiling was maybe thirty feet high, and kind-of pitched upward, all made of re-sawn redwood, just a wonderful absorber of stray sound. Now, we did have parallel walls, to the front of the stage and back, from the left of the stage to right. Those were parallel, but – they were also covered in re-sawn redwood. Just a wonderful material; looks gorgeous. Wonderful look for acoustics.

Greg Kihn was on fire that night. At the top of his game. Just… Wow! Steve Wright was singing along with Greg. They had a little *extra* energy. Then they said, "We'd like to introduce a song – duh duh duh – called 'Jeopardy.' Hope you like it."

Jeopardy. I tracked Jeopardy by calling Beserkley Records after the concert, every week, to find out where it was on the Billboard Top One Hundred. I think it broke in at seventy-something. It went to forty-something. It went to twenty-something. This is each week. It went to single digits. It went to four. It might have gotten to two – that's how big that song was. What a song! All my students wanted copies of that song. It went on and on…

We recorded all the shows. We videotaped all the shows. Part of the reason was, the bands knew that these things would not be sold and distributed. So they allowed us to do it. Even my camera people were excited about such a great show. If you've never heard the song Jeopardy, you know, play it. Turn it up a little bit. Greg Douglass did a great job – great addition. You know, not that Robbie Dunbar couldn't have done the same notes. But it just wasn't the same.

When the show was over, the encore request was so loud. By the way, all the bands have it timed out. We helped time it out, to where you're off the stage fifteen minutes before the end of the concert, so that you can come back for encores. So you finish — all the bands timed it so nice.

I think they finished with Jeopardy. That was it. "Thank you very much. Good night." Oh, wow! The fans were not going to let 'em leave. They went backstage where my room was, right across the hall from the theater. They had a water or whatever like that. There was no time for Greg to smoke marijuana — no time! Quick little water, wash your face off. Wipe it off with a towel, there...

Here was what determined if you get an encore. If you could hear the words, "More! More! More!" from my classroom area — which was the backstage area — with the doors open; my doors were open to the theater, but all the theater doors were closed — if you could hear, "More, more, more" through all of that, then you've earned the encore.

And boy, did they earn it. They came back and played another song or two. It was just a wonderful night.

Everyone made money. I started this with Greg. I did it with the Huey Lewis and then Y&T later, but I didn't do it with Journey — it's called a sweetheart deal: Let's say — and this was kind of standard — all the expenses, rent-a-cops, chaperones, everything, PA, all like that, came to around two grand, every time you did the show, so that you're well positioned to take care of everything. You're under control. Two thousand. Okay, if you're charging, let's say, ten dollars for a ticket, I forget what we charged for Greg Kihn — probably seven-fifty, something like that for that big show. So seven-fifty times eight-hundred... whatever that comes to... fifty-eight-hundred, six grand. We'd take two thousand off the top, because that was expenses. Then the band would get eighty percent. The electronics students — my program — would get twenty percent. So on a four-thousand dollar night, they'd walk away with $3,200 and we would make eight-hundred.

Now the concerts were a very good way of making money and bringing prestige, fame – if you would – to the high school. But it wasn't my best money maker – that will come when I decided to give up concerts and work on video yearbooks.

But to finish on this.

We did not meet on Friday. Nope, no more meeting on Friday. We (the Administration and I) met on Mondays. I wanted everyone to feel like they'd gotten all the input from parents, and especially the students at Monte Vista. What'd they think of the show? Was it worth the money? Did you have a good time?

On Monday, we all had a good time.

First time I ever got kudos.

<Administrator voice> "Well, Chester, I think it was well-run. It seemed like the students were just having a good time. They played some good old-fashioned rock and roll."

Hey! Mission accomplished. Done.

Chapter 11

Huey Lewis Concert

In February of 1983, two months before *Huey Lewis and the News* came out with their "Sports" album, Huey Lewis played for me.

He came to Monte Vista! He even called it, "Rock and Roll High."

But why did they come to Monte Vista?

It was a place to play in front of an audience, the same audience that you hoped would buy your albums, listen to your music… and you were making money. Why wouldn't you come? Don't forget: this was in the time when I had started with Greg Kihn, and now also with Huey Lewis — it was a sweetheart deal.

So, if expenses were two-thousand, two-thousand comes right off the top. Pay the bills: chaperones, the police, all of that. Advertising? It costs money. That leaves the net proceeds. Huey Lewis and the News — their band — got eighty percent. The electronics club, called Rainbow Studio, got twenty percent. I forget how much we charged, seven-fifty? In that range. It wasn't quite a sellout. It was seven-hundred and ninety-four.

But the energy surrounding this concert, leading up to it — and the number of people that regretted not going to the show — was huge. You see, there's always a lag at a school. It's not like social media now, where — I mean, *I* don't know how to text — but people text one another, instant messaging, people going, "Oh, all y'all are going to Huey?…" That's it. Boy! The word spread. That's it.

You have to understand, all my shows were open to the

public. No school, no public school in the USA would allow that. Rock and roll? Open to the public? Not closed just to our students? Once again, it was Jerry Grundhoffer who opened the doors. He was the vice-principal and then became the principal. He opened the doors: Let's go for this. Let's do it! He was a tremendous supporter. Once he understood — it's kind-of cute. I'll tell you this little story about Jerry Grundhoffer.

Huey Lewis was playing an encore. It was twenty to ten; they had started at eight thirty. Jerry sees me.

"Uh, Chester, there's twenty minutes left. Are they going to finish on time?"

"Absolutely! Everyone does, Jerry."

"Okay, 'cause it's kind of getting late."

The band played their final number and then walked off the stage. Of course, the cheers — "More! More! More!" were like… like *bone chilling*. It was, like, the best show that had ever performed at Monte Vista. Huey Lewis was such a wonderful entertainer, in an old-fashioned way. He could sing, he could dance, he played saxophone, he played this instrument — I don't know — harmonica. You name it; it don't matter. He was *old school*. He poured his heart and soul out on his shows. Unbelievable.

So, little did we know what was in store that evening. We kind of remember the song on his first album, or his second album, "Do You Believe in Love," and a couple of things — I've kind of heard of on the radio — but I don't know. I don't listen much.

He broke out the entire "Sports" album, the album that was going to be released and send him on his way to stardom. "Back to the Future II" only accelerated him further into the clouds, into the stratosphere. Wonderful show, wonderful show. "I Want a New Drug." All of these things that were on the "Sports" album were like, Wow! The beats, the sound, the mix — once again, the acoustics… Everyone loved playing at the Monte Vista

Theater… period. No one ever complained. They loved it.

So, Huey exits the stage.

<Principal Jerry Grundhoffer> "Is he done?"

"No. He's going to do an encore."

"Oh, no, Chet! We don't have time for that! He's already been playing an hour and twenty minutes. He's going to play another hour and twenty?"

"Jerry, this is not 'do the show again.' When he comes back for an encore, he plays a song or two, but he'll be done by ten."

"Oh! Oh, OK."

Heh, heh, heh… eh, it's a learning process for everyone.

Believe me. It's not easy being the principal of a high school in which you have this renegade, crazy, gonna-do-it-regardless-of-what-you-might-think-anyway — guy… Kind of hard to handle maybe, but we fit it within the rules. It always worked out.

It was a great show. Huey Lewis, after the show was over, came backstage with the band and signed autographs for the fans. I told the audience. There's all these kids stacked up because I — for all my shows, I had a very big long table in my set of rooms where I taught. It was six feet wide, twenty-four feet long, all laminated oak. These were the tabletops that you would use in a wood shop, that were no longer used. The shop wanted new table tops: they were truer. They had been saving these and didn't know what to do with them. I said, "I'd like to make a huge bench out of this." Milo Basker, the metal shop teacher, welded up the giant frame out of pieces bought pre-cut. He assembled it down in the auto shop area. It took twenty kids to carry it all the way up and place it in my room. That's how strong and sturdy it was. The tabletop — what a place to eat on!… 'cause we sanded it and finished it… It was like butcher block, only prettier, longer, more impressive.

So they toweled off, maybe changed a T-shirt because they were sweating because of the lights on stage. We had told the police officers to tell the kids, "ten minutes and we'll let you in twenty-five at a time." We ended up with six twenty-fives. I did have enough posters — I had a hundred and fifty left over. We had felt tip pens. All the band sat at the table.

The kids passed from the front door, right past the table, where they would stop and the band would sign. You would get everyone's signature, then you'd leave. Then twenty-five more.

We did it first cabin. Everything was good. But we never ever had a show as terrific as Huey Lewis and the News, February, 1983.

That's it.

Chapter 12

Y&T

Sometime in September 1985, I got a hold of the manager of Y&T. His name was Scott Booray.

I may have mentioned this already, that Scott had played in the very first mini-concert that I put on at Monte Vista, maybe in 1969, '70… '71 at the latest, for sure.

We chatted.

"It's time for Y&T to come to Monte Vista. You've been putting it off. We're ready for you."

He said, "Let's do it."

One of the things he mentioned was, they had already been booked to headline the Cow Palace in San Francisco in a completely new show, featuring "Glam Rock" – whatever that is… you know, the costumes that they wore and of course the music that they played. It was a very smooth negotiation until we got to the price. Scott Booray wanted to charge ten dollars. I had never before charged ten dollars for a concert. I started at one, then three, then five, you know… and eventually moved up to – I don't know – eight-fifty, maybe, with Huey Lewis. I'm not sure.

But after talking about it, he said, "We'll back off on the percentage." It was a sweetheart deal that they were getting, which was: eighty percent of the profits go to the band, twenty percent of the profits go to Rainbow Studio. This is all after expenses. Expenses for a normal show at Monte Vista High School was around seventeen hundred to two thousand dollars. That's for security, chaperones, equipment, the PA system… all of these things that you have to rent in order to put on a show.

So I played some music at lunchtime like I did before my concerts, maybe a week-long affair: Monday, Tuesday, Wednesday and Thursday itself, the day of the show, so that music could be heard throughout the campus at Monte Vista High School, to draw attention.

The energy level seemed pretty high. The amount of money that we were charging didn't seem to faze. Ticket sales were going good. So I went, "Wow. I think we're going to have a pretty good show here."

I didn't realize that they would bring to *this* show their entire rig, the entire wardrobe of costumes that they were going to use at the Cow Palace.

Here are some of the things that were a little bit *different*.

They had a dual stairway, semi-spiral, that went up maybe ten feet above the drummer. On top of this stair/riser-combination, to get to ten feet, was a six- or eight-foot gong. It was huge — a gong. When you saw it when you walked into the theater, it was like, whoa! We never really had a *set-thing* for rock and roll that went that high above the stage. It was very, very impressive. I think they only used it on one song. Maybe two.

All right, so now we were loading everything in. The stage was coming together. The band was now backstage. They had all these trunks, you know, like wardrobe trunks that you rolled around.

The last time Y&T had come to Monte Vista was maybe ten years earlier. They were known as "Yesterday & Today." Kind of a grunge band, rocked out, had fun. So I kinda didn't understand this new band thing. But I soon became aware.

They wanted security, of course, for all of their trunks and to get ready and such and didn't want to be in the open area of backstage, which was my classroom/lab area. So we went inside the edit suites which were highly secure — but I didn't quite understand.

They started to emerge as the show came closer to the

beginning, you know, maybe a half-hour away, maybe forty-five minutes for them to go on stage. The opening act was already on stage. They started coming out in outfits that I didn't quite understand, you know, they told me it was called "Glam Rock."

Ayee!

They had makeup, and *things*… I went, "Whoa!" I had never seen that in rock and roll before, but I just watched. People helped each other. A couple of gals back there were helping… the hair, the tossed hair, spray nets and all like that… It was *different*.

But, all I really cared about was, did the kids have a good time? Did you like the music? Was it worth it?

You see, most every band that ever played at Monte Vista, I didn't particularly care for the music. They might have had a song or two, each, that I thought was catchy and great. Huey Lewis, he was in a different realm. So when he played in '83, those songs, though I wasn't familiar with them, were *catchy*. It's a little different when you have the hooks and all the necessary things to make a successful song.

Y&T wasn't my style. I remember from 1975, when they were Yesterday & Today, they had a song called "Alcohol." It's a back and forth between the audience and…"Al-cho-HOL!" and then… you know, one of those things. That was catchy.

"Uh, Chet! What did you think about it when they used words like 'alcohol' or cuss maybe?"

It was an act. We were on stage. Let it go.

Very few bands ever took advantage of the situation with a lot of foul language and all like that. Y&T was a little different, but not bad. Not bad at all.

So now comes showtime. I go into the theater from backstage to check attendance. We're up over seven hundred, going to eight hundred.

"Wow. This is fantastic."

The band hit the stage. They did the entire act they were

going to do at the Cow Palace. I circulated around so I didn't really have to be pinned down to listen to the music but the kids were having a good time.

I asked 'em after the show, was it worth it? Absolutely. Do you think we charged too much? No.

Monte Vista once more put on a great little show, courtesy of Rainbow Studio.

What a great night that was.

Chapter 13

Q's House

When I started doing concerts on a fairly large basis — and by that, I mean two-hundred and fifty in attendance, up to over eight-hundred — we had a small problem with some of the musicians, and maybe the roadies. They needed a place to relax — party, if you will — *after* the show, especially. Sometimes, even *before* the show.

We'd go to Q's house.

Q's house was located in Danville, California — I think it was Smith Road he lived on — nice little enclave there, which was literally walking distance from the Monte Vista campus. It was a perfect location.

This way here, the band members, the roadies, and their guests could enjoy their life at the concert without having to worry about administrators saying, "Put that down… empty that beer…" Those kinds of things.

So it was the perfect location. I don't think we did this for Huey Lewis and the News; I don't know if we did it much for Greg Kihn; I know we didn't do it for Y&T. But most all the other bands really appreciated having an off-campus place, where you could go.

This was a little two-bedroom, one-bath place that Bob Quarrick — who was from Pittsburg, California, as I am — had been renting for several years. The husband and wife who owned the house — the husband became ill, and then eventually passed on.

Well, Bob — or "Q" — was, like, the executor for the will, you know, helping out, paying off last-minute bills, all of these things. There were a lot of little details involved. As a gift to Q — to Bob Quarrick — the landlady gifted him the house… at fifty-thousand dollars.

Now, this was approximately a quarter of an acre, in a really nice little enclave in the Danville hills, right near Monte Vista High School. Gorgeous setting. So even though the house may not have been worth much, the land — of course — *was*. I imagine he ended up with, essentially, a three hundred thousand dollar piece of property, for fifty-thousand dollars.

From then on, it was "Katie, bar the door." He was very comfortable. He could easily make his house payments. Then like for a lot of us, he started to refinance and take some money out. He wasn't extravagant, necessarily, but he bought himself a good used vehicle — I think a Toyota pickup truck — it serves him well to this day.

Just a gorgeous setting, especially in the spring or fall months, in which the sun was still shining at 7:30 PM — that type of thing. It was just wonderful; the sun would go down, yet there was plenty of light.

Though the house was small, he had a nice little backyard, nice little side yard, all of these things. It was just a great place to go off-campus for the bands, especially — like I say — the roadies.

Without that, a lot of these concerts couldn't have happened at Monte Vista. It's kind of like, you listen to the bands that play. What's the good thing we did? What didn't we do? We always were evaluating. One of the things we had a tough time with was having the backstage where you had your guests, on a high school campus. It was very restrictive, shall we say.

We made it work. We always made it work. But, having the off-campus facility was just wonderful for concerts at Monte Vista High School.

Thank you.

Chapter 14

Boogie at the Bar-J

When I was teaching at Monte Vista, one of the things that quite often happened was I'd have somebody in class who was the brother of someone that I had taught before — maybe a few years earlier. Or the sister — like that. Family.

One of those families was the Forni family.

A quick aside right here: if you look in the street — those round steel covers that are often on streets, so that you remove the cover and get access to the sewers below — many of them are still engraved "Forni."

<Student(?) Asking> "And Chet, is that how they made their money?"

I think so. I think the owner of the Forni Ranch, Jay Forni, was the son of someone who produced these metal things. Might have been a grandfather. I don't know.

But I think that's where the money started. I don't know the full history of the fabulous little family — the Forni's. Just delightful.

But anyway, Jay Forni, the father, had three sons who came through my program. Let's see: there was Jay Forni, Charlie Forni, and George Forni. There were three brothers — all wonderful kids.

Jay, the oldest: very sharp, very studious. I think he went on to Colorado School of Mines, for higher education.

Charlie, a little more easy going… way friendly… would do a lot of things for you. Great kid.

Then the other one was George. That would be the younger son. I had him in class, too. You know… maybe not as studious as his older brother, Jay, but certainly as much fun as Charlie, or maybe even more fun. He liked to have a good time.

Anyway, I got a phone call one day in which Jay Forni, Sr., calls me, kinda out of the blue.

"Chet, eh, I'm thinkin' about putting a concert on here, at the Bar-J."

"All right, Jay, sounds good."

"And we want *you* to put it on."

Now you have to understand: very rarely have I ever done anything for a profit. This would be my first opportunity. Well, I had put a couple of shows on at the Vets Hall, and tried to make a dollar... you'd kinda break out even. It was a tough sell.

"We wanna put on this show; we want you to do it. You can keep all the proceeds."

Wow! Yikes! How could I pass that up?

"Jay, where are we going to put it on? We don't have a facility on your property."

"Oh, yes we do."

"What is the facility?"

"We built a giant riding arena/horse stall thing, where it'll stall horses — on the sides. The arena will be for riding. We have a judge's stand. The judge's stand is up about three feet in the air, like a small stage. The roof is totally enclosed — all steel roof. The doors are on, so we can close the doors and keep it warm."

This was in the winter time that we did this. The date doesn't really matter that much. Here's what matters.

"We'll provide security. We'll have twelve guys, in charge of security. All cowboys. All *big* cowboys. Each with a gun."

"Ay, ay, yai... guns?"

"Yeah. We're going to keep the peace here."

"I don't want any guns flashing and —"

"No, no... you won't see it. But, they'll all be armed."

At least some of 'em were.

"Uh... All right."

"You've got the big stage. You've got the huge arena, with a nice level-level-level dirt floor. Is there anything else you need?"

"Well, I'd have to bring a generator out there for lights and sound and such, but… we could do that."

"Yeah. Find some good rock and roll band, and let's have some fun." … out on Tassajara Road, Danville, California.

"Jay, I think I can make this happen."

"Well, let me know. That's the deal."

"Let me go over this one more time. You mean, after expenses, I get to keep the proceeds?"

"Yeah! We just want you to do it… Put a few dollars in your pocket. We wanna have a party, Chester. We're going to celebrate this new riding arena. We're going to celebrate Forni Ranch. We're just gonna have fun."

Well, those are my favorite words: "Let's have fun."

So, I picked up the phone, and I called Michael Coats.

"Michael, I'm going to book The Greg Kihn Band to come in at the Bar-J. Publicity is going to be everything in this show. You've got to get the local papers to cover it ahead of time. I don't care about post-concert reviews; if they do that, that's fine. But, we have to get the word around."

"Well, what do I get for this?"

"I'll split it with you."

Now, you don't generally give your publicist fifty per-cent. You know: ten, fifteen, maybe, but… fifty?

Well, wait a minute: I don't want to do this alone. I've got to have that end — the press — the information out to people… that has to be covered.

So Michael and I came to an agreement: fifty-fifty.

Now, the expenses were going to be around a grand, fifteen-hundred for the band… or fifty percent of the take, after expenses — whichever was greater. Book the band for fifteen-hundred. They were supposed to bring a band called "The Plimsouls" — but that band canceled. So they brought another band to warm-up. They brought the lights. They brought the PA.

I wasn't responsible for any of that end. The band took care of it all. I believe we gave 'em fifteen-hundred, or fifty percent of the net proceeds. It turns out the net proceeds were something like… thirty-six hundred?

So, it was eighteen-hundred for them, eighteen-hundred for Michael and me to split: nine-hundred-each… something like that. It was a nice little show.

But, let me tell you how it all began.

Once we booked the show, and I knew I had a date, and I had an address, now was the time to put up your posters. We billed it "Boogie at the Bar-J" — the "J" being Jay Forni, and the Bar-J was his ranch. The "Boogie" was just — we're going to have fun.

It kind-of rhymed… "Boogie" and "Bar-J." That's all.

"Chet! That's a great phrase!" or "Chet! That was stupid." I don't know… it was just a *thing*. It seemed to fit. It rolled off people's tongues. We were going to have a huge off-campus party. Five dollars to get in. Cold beer being sold on the side. We were going to set up a regular situation there, in which beer was being sold.

Then we thought better of it. "Eh, nah, no, no, no no no, no."

The Forni boys sold beer out of the back of their cars/trucks… nothing formal.

Everybody was making money. All the Forni kids were making a few dollars. Everyone was having a great time.

On the poster, we wrote: "Follow the searchlights on Tassajara Road!" We had two of those trucks that have spotlights that go back and forth. We started that fairly early in the evening.

The show hadn't even started… and the night sky was lit up with these beams going across.

We were selling tickets at a music store in Walnut Creek; sold 'em at a music store in Danville. We had tickets everywhere. Ticket sales were kind of slow at first. In other words, I think the show was a Friday night, pretty sure. Might have been a Saturday, but I think Friday night.

The show was all set and ready to go. The only thing we had to do now, of course, was make sure we sold enough tickets so that everyone could at least make ends meet. If there is no profit to be made, well, then, there's no profit.

But awfully hard not to make a profit with The Greg Kihn Band.

We charged five dollars to get in. On Friday while I was teaching, I got nine to ten phone calls in a period of about three hours.

"We need more tickets! We need — bring fifty! Bring a hundred!"

Yikes!

It was five dollars in advance, and five dollars at the door, I think. I don't even think we made a difference. We just took a chance.

We had a great turnout.

Of course there were expenses that go with everything. But, it looked like we were all going to have a great evening. We were all going to make money.

The show started... As you looked up and down this tremendous, grand, horse show *thing*... arena, there were people.

There were not enough bathrooms. But there were all these stalls built for the horses, with no gates yet. No, nothing to fence them in.

So yeah, for the guys — even the girls — take a leak in the corner. There's just... straw on the ground Everyone made do.

Did we have all the facilities covered? No.

Was it a cold evening? Yes.

Did people have a good time? Heh... Wow! Over the top.

Greg Kihn hit the stage. That place was *rockin'*.

We had to monitor the generator outside — the poor

generator was working hard, but it was pumping out enough juice to keep the show going, to keep the lights going, so that we could have a great concert… and we did.

Now, here's the funny part. I didn't really know this was happening. I didn't even pay attention. I'm just collecting money at the door. My wife is collecting money at the door. We're just a mom and pop operation.

Well, these twelve guys — these cowboys working for the Bar-J Ranch… they love to *punch*. And I mean… anybody at any time.

It's funny. What they would do, is they would tell somebody, "Hey, don't sit there. Don't do that…" or whatever. Simple instructions. There weren't many rules.

Maybe someone would go, "Ah… go shove it!" … was their response.

I didn't realize this: *cowboy's don't forget.*

"Oh, yeah, you're getting yours at the end of the show."

I had no idea.

The show was over. I'm on the stage. I'm thanking everyone for coming and telling them to, "Drive home safely."

The only complaint, by the way, that the highway patrol had, was to let *them* know in advance so they could have helped with people getting around. That was it.

How about the neighbors? Did they complain?

They were charging twenty dollars to go park! You're out on Tassajara Road! You're in the middle of nowhere! Can't park on the road. Highway Patrol'll give you a ticket. Sheriff's Department'll give you a ticket. Where are you going to park? Inside someone else's ranch! So they had all kinds of parking. They charged twenty bucks or ten — I forget. You park the cars; you keep the money… and they did.

All the spillover went to the other ranches out on Tassajara Road.

Everybody made a few dollars. Everybody had a good time.

Now. The show is over. I'm saying "Bye, bye" to everyone.

Okay.

Now… it's *"punch"* time.

Nobody's gettin' punched if you came, had a nice time, you acted nicely, and everyone got along — which most everyone did.

But you know… I've said this before, I'll say it again: I'll take dope smokers all day long in attendance of my concerts, as opposed to those people doing alcohol. Alcohol is crazy. You do excessive alcohol, crazy things happen… in your head.

You get mean. You get ornery. You get sarcastic. You get a lot of bravado. At the Forni Ranch, you get punched.

Just beat the *hell* outta each other. What's funny is that when it's all over, then it's all over. But somebody has to declare a winner. I didn't know that. They kind of tapped 'em on the shoulders…

"That's it. He gives up. We're done here. Quit beating on him."

Then, that's that.

There were about fifteen or twenty fights — right at the end. All these cowboys gettin' even for things that were said during the evening. I think some of these people won't be such a wise mouths… in the future.

I'm watching people get beat on — *I* don't wanna get beat on. Yikes!

"Chet! It sounds like it was a rowdy concert."

"No. Perfect concert. Ten minutes of punching. Punch, punch, punch. Everyone tired. Let's go home. End of story."

One of the greatest shows that was ever put on in the valley — I'm positive. No one coulda had a party like that. I don't care what your name is, or where you live.

You'll never beat what we did at "Boogie at the Bar-J."

Chapter 15

Early Flubs

In 1969, '70, '71 — in there — '72 even, I kinda dabbled in trying to get really good bands at Monte Vista. It's hard because, first you have to have a track record. The track record then has to be bands, musicians, and roadies who had a good time, thought the facility was great, had a great auditorium to perform in, a nice PA system — all of those things.

In a way, I was maybe trying to do too much, too soon — an example being the Journey concert.

That was February of 1976. There were a thousand and six people. It was like, "Wow!" — way oversold. But, we got the job done.

But, now we're going to talk about where I *didn't* quite get the job done.

First, is The Steve Miller Band. I wrote a letter to Steve Miller. I addressed it to his booking agency. There was a book out that you'd buy — maybe it was free, I'm not sure — but it had all the correct names and addresses of how to get hold of any of the musicians you'd like to book.

There was another kind of publication, then, they probably do it on the Internet now, but then — they printed the tour schedule. So they're going to be in Waco, Texas, then they're going to be in Austin, Texas. Then they're going to come to Arizona, and they'll be in the Bay Area. You try to book them while they're in the Bay Area — so they could augment their tour schedule, and you could get a date at your nightclub — or in my case, high school.

In the letter I sent to Steve Miller, I told him, "You're

absolutely one of the most popular musicians on the Monte Vista campus."

He had just come out with his album, "Sailor"? He was a very strong candidate to perform here at Monte Vista. So I took a chance with the letter. I don't know — maybe it'd work, maybe it wouldn't.

One day, about ten days after I sent the letter, I got a phone call at my house — I had given both the school phone number and my home phone number.

It was around seven-thirty, eight o'clock in the evening. It was a guy named Gary Miller.

"I'm Steve Miller's brother. Listen, we got your letter and we were very impressed. Some of the bands you've had is kind of impressive."

The school had Boz Scaggs before — I think the Community of Danville put that on in our gymnasium in 1968, maybe, '69. So we had people of some note at Monte Vista, but it was in the early days. I just took a chance.

So, Gary says, "Listen… we're interested."

"Well, we don't have a theater yet. It's yet to be built. But, the gymnasium is in pretty good shape. I've installed acoustic tiles on the wall."

"We want to come in. We want to do an 'Evening with Steve Miller.' Steve'll play acoustic, thirty to forty-five minutes. We'll take a short break — maybe ten, twelve minutes. Move a few microphones around. The band will already be set up. Then the band will play. It'll be essentially about a two-hour, two-hour thirty-minute show… featuring Steve Miller and The Steve Miller Band."

Ah… navïeté. You know, heh, heh… I'm not immune to naïvety. So there we go.

"Gary, listen. There's a local band named 'Country Weather.' I promised Country Weather that the next time I got a good band in here, they could open the show for me. I'm a person of my word. I gotta stick with it. So, how 'bout Country Weather opens up… Steve Miller then comes on and does acoustic… and then his band?"

"No, no! The whole idea of the evening is that we're going to spend that time with Steve Miller and his band."

"Well, let me think it over, Gary. I've got your phone number now," at the hotel he was staying in San Francisco. "I'll give you a call, and we'll go from there."

Terrific show: The Steve Miller Band. You're talking great music, in the gymnasium, which already had Boz Scaggs, who played with Steve Miller on his albums. He's no longer with them. I don't even know if they talk anymore. Maybe they're best of friends. But I think both of them are from Texas[1].

So I thought it over all night long — tossed and turned a little bit. What to do, what to do?

In the end, I called up Gary Miller.

"Hello?"

"This is Chester Farrow —"

"Oh, Chester! Wonderful! So what date do you have for us?"

"Gary, I can't do it."

"What?!"

"Gary, I promised these guys that they could open the show. Here comes the show, and I don't like to go back on my word. So I'll have to pass on this show as it now exists."

"If you want us, it's Steve Miller acoustic and then Steve Miller with the band."

"Gary, I'll pass."

Yikes!

Then, a couple of years later, another opportunity.

I got a phone call from a guy that I knew because he was a guitarist and a good friend of Q's — Bob Quarrick — name was Karl Schwendemann. Technically, a very good guitarist.

---

[1] Now… how I ever pulled that out and said, "they're both from Texas…" I don't know. But I think I read it somewhere.

"Chester! Listen, we go way back..."

"Yeah, Karl. What's up?" I kind of figured he wanted to play. People often called me to play. I would fit him in if I could, no problem.

"I'm working with David Crosby now."

"Whoa! I love David Crosby's voice. His harmonies are stellar. You're going to pick up the guitar parts – Stephen Stills kind of thing... Very good.

"But I've been reading in the magazines, in the local paper: David Crosby has been missing some gigs. Somethin' like heroin or some kind of problem... cocaine. I don't know. He's, uh... you can't count on him. That's not what I'm about here at Monte Vista. I mean, if we put it down that he's going to play, we need to have him play."

"Chester, trust me. I've got David under control. We'll be there. We'll put on a great show."

Now. My favorite band of all times is Crosby, Stills, Nash & Young – Young being the important thing there, because – what a guitarist, what a songwriter: Neil Young.

So, I wanted reassurances from Karl Schwendemann, that David Crosby would be there, that everything would be okay. I had my doubts. Some of the things I had read, I didn't feel comfortable with.

So I passed.

"Karl, I'd love to have David Crosby here, but not at this time."

Now, let's take a look at those two decisions I made. First one: Steve Miller.

<Chester, talking to himself> "Chester! When are you going to learn that just because you promised somebody that they could play on a new concert coming up, and you'll take care of 'em... that you could do the next, or the next one?"

The Steve Miller shows should have gone on. In other words, there's no reason that the Steve Miller Band did not play the

Monte Vista concert... except me, being arrogant.

Like, "I *promised* this, man!"

Get outta my face! This is Steve Miller! This is the Steve Miller Band! Hello?! Songs all over the radio that are popular. How could you possibly turn that down?

I never would again. I'll take 'em any way they come. It doesn't matter to me. I made a little promise? We'll delay the promise. Not *this* show for Country Weather, but the *next* show for Country Weather — sure, no problem.

Now, let's get to David Crosby.

One of the things I've learned over the years: you book a band, keep your fingers crossed, hope they show. That's all.

What do you care what kind of... habits they have? What do I care... what their lifestyle is? The answer is: I *don't* care. It doesn't matter.

I'm... whatever you're into, that's good! Whatever I'm into, that's good! We're all just happy.

You gotta take the moralistic view and throw it away a little bit. In other words, morally...

<Administrator, down on the idea> "What are you doing... bringing someone who's kind-of addicted to heroin, dragging 'em on the stage..."

Ehhhhhh! How many others — over the years — have been on heroin, cocaine or whatever, while performing? Answer: a lot! A lot!

<Chester, questioning himself again> "Well, then, why are you so moralistic when it comes to David Crosby?"

<Chester, answering himself> "Because I was naïve! Stupid — if you will."

Never happened again.

But it did for those two shows: Steve Miller... and David Crosby.

Chapter 16

Bay Area Music Awards: BAMMIES

In 1978, Dennis Erokan, and a gentleman that lives in Lafayette, right here near Walnut Creek, started a free magazine. Evidently, doing free magazines, if people will take them, people will pay you money to advertise. You gotta sell a lot of advertisements. For a magazine like *BAM Magazine,* Bay Area Music, the focus was on Bay Area musicians, their equipment, where they played, when they're going to play again… personal stories, those kinds of things.

He established the magazine in '76. In '78 — January, actually — he held his first Bammie Awards — the Bay Area Music Awards, called the "Bammies."

It started small — it was going to be, like, rock and roll awards. MTV Awards, Academy Awards… Going to be an award show and fun and all like that. Dennis did not expect people to dress up for the event. Come on, hippie era, kind of phasing out of that part in '78. But nonetheless, casual dress, denims, those kind of things, chinos at best. But people chose to dress up. It remained a tradition to the end. That was a pleasant surprise for Dennis. I enjoyed it. My students enjoyed it, too. And I'll tell you how they got involved.

In the first Bay Area music award, it was at the Kabuki Hotel in San Francisco. About a thousand people dressed up, came, and had a great time.

It was successful enough that they felt they needed to expand a bit. So, year two, they went to the Gift Center, The Galleria, in San Francisco. Problem was, the room they had — no tables. No chairs. Certainly, not enough.

So I get a phone call one day from Michael Coats, my former student who was a publicist for the Bammies. It was "Glodow & Coats" at the time, his publicity firm.

He had a problem: he said he needed tables and chairs.

"Michael, you're telling me you want me to get trucks and kids, load up, and schlep all those heavy tables, chairs…"

"As many as you could bring."

Ay.

So we did. It was in a godforsaken part of town. If you don't know where you're going, you get lost… the railroad tracks are high. Your tires want to pop. It's one in the morning as you're taking this stuff back, because — you know, — if you're going to borrow the tables and chairs, let's say like twenty-five tables and two hundred chairs from the cafeteria, gotta be set up in the morning, ready to go for the kids. So somebody's gotta bring 'em back. That was a very, very late night.

But anyway, that's how we got started helping out.

At Monte Vista, I just told the custodian, "See these right here? I'm taking these."

"Eh, do you have authority?"

"Uh… Bob, yeah. *Authority*. I'm gonna put 'em in the truck, I'm gonna take 'em to San Francisco, I'm gonna bring 'em back at one o'clock. I got the key. I'm going to put them back and set them up."

"Don't get me in trouble."

"You won't be in trouble."

And he wasn't.

So that was our start. Five years… another year at the Gift Center on three; four and five were at The Warfield Theater… But we weren't bringing tables and chairs any longer. We just did it for number two. But then in number six, they moved to the Civic Auditorium, now called "The Bill Graham Civic Auditorium."

That's where we got involved in this aspect: backstage at the

Academy Awards or the Oscars or whatever — Bay Area Music Awards — are interview booths. MTV was there, maybe Channel 7 had an interview booth, maybe another station?

The lights are set up and so forth — very nice. People could sit down in the chairs and be interviewed. You could watch this going on. It was just, very festive backstage.

So I asked Michael Coats, "Michael, listen…"

They had moved to the Bill Graham Civic Auditorium. The Warfield was too tight back there, way too tight.

"Michael, you got room now. How about I bring some students, we bring a color camera, couple of camcorders going around, talking, getting footage… for our TV show?"

Our TV show was called, "Just for You."

"To see the Bammies, that'd be wonderful. For our students to be able to interview the musicians, would be a dream come true."

"Chester, we'll start with four. I don't want any more than four. But, I got to clear it with Dennis Erokan…"

A couple days later, Dennis said, "Fine."

<Michael Coats, continuing> "He didn't forget that you brought the tables and the chairs for that number two. That was a wonderful thing to do. You guys were in and out orderly. We expect the same out of the four."

"No problem."

Thus began our involvement, until I retired in 1999, because the Bammies went on till 2005. Roughly, we joined in 1983 or '84. Seventeen years, pretty good, solid involvement, interviewing.

The four people were selected, predicated upon work that they had done all year… coming through… very important. We soon had more students who could come to the Bammies and participate in backstage interviews.

"Are you doing a good job on the television show? Are your recordings coming out? Are you putting in editing time in the recording sessions?" Because there's a lot of hours to put in, in recording — whether it's audio or video, or editing, and so forth.

But my kids were going to get an opportunity to see people like Neil Young, Sammy Hagar, Journey — first gig ever with Steve Perry and Journey. Tom Petty, Greg Kihn, No Doubt, Jefferson Starship, Grateful Dead, John Fogerty, Santana, Y&T.

By the way, The Grateful Dead — it was at a time when they were trying to do two bands, kinda, at once, kinda blend 'em and see... The Grateful Dead: the only band they requested to play with, was Huey Lewis and the News. This comes straight from Dennis Erokan.

Boz Scaggs played; Steve Miller Band; Bonnie Raitt; Linda Ronstadt; Chris Isaak; Tony! Toni! Toné!; Ramblin' Jack Elliott; Linda Perry; Lydia Pence; Gwen Stefani — and many, many others.

Wow, what an opportunity that was open for us. There was no high school, there was no college, backstage being represented at the Bammies. There was a high school: Monte Vista High School. There we were. Here I am with four kids backstage at the Bammies. They're interviewing the likes of all the people that I mentioned. All the people that I mentioned — they all gave interviews, some very tough.

I'm going to digress for a minute.

Some people just don't want to do interviews. They don't like it. They think it's beneath them. Well, whatever. They don't want to — they don't want to acknowledge that the press is involved in... I don't know. They have their reasons.

One of the toughest ones was Santana. Carlos didn't like to do those things. You know, it's funny. My kids came to me.

"Carlos is here! Carlos is here, Chester."

I had learned from the first show: I am of no use. No one wants to look at another adult their age... dressed up, you know, sport jacket or whatever. I used to wear velour sweaters at the time — still do, if I have 'em.

Nobody wants to — "You're an adult. Get out of my face."

What works? Sixteen-year old gal; seventeen-year-old dorky-looking boy. You approach the wife or girlfriend. Don't bother Carlos. You go and you tell 'em, "We're a high school. To do an interview with Carlos would be the Acme, the Apex. Just, if we could do this, if you could ask him for me."

"High school? They let high schoolers in here?," she says, "she" being the wife — or girlfriend — of Carlos Santana.

"Yes. We're a high school. We're called 'Rainbow Studio.' We have a weekly television show called 'Just for You.' We do a musical segment devoted to music and musical happenings in every one of our TV shows. We'd love to have Carlos as the interview for that spot."

"Well, of course he'll do it."

"Would you, could you ask him for us?"

"You go ask him — he'd do it."

"No. No. He kind of said 'no' earlier. He's busy."

"Oh, hell, he's always busy." <calling out> "Carlos! Get over here! Come on, now. These kids are high schoolers. Do you — can you remember back when you were in high school? Come on! To have the opportunity to be interviewing a rock star? Come on! Sit down. You've got five minutes. I'm not going anywhere. I'll stay right here."

Then he'd shuffle over and sit down. All of our questions were generally mundane.

"How'd you get started playing music?"

"What was the name of your first band?"

"Do you get paid for playing?"

"You're pretty good. How'd you get that good?"

Those kind of things. You know what's funny? Even for the most mega-star, when you break down to the background, those are legitimate questions that open up a floodgate of memories.

Carlos goes, "Oh, yeah… I remember this guy… his brother… he had a guitar… and then it —"

Stories that you'd never find on MTV.

But, the kids asked me, "What kind of questions do we ask?"

"Ask what you want to ask. Nothing controversial. Don't ask him questions about: you walked off stage on your last concert, you were angry… that's for other people. It's for rag magazines. Not for us. What do you want to know about Carlos?"

<Student Interviewer Voice> "Carlos, do you like the color red?"

There you go! There you go! That's the heart of it. That's the heart of it – something so simple as that.

He gave a ten, fifteen minute interview, forgetting that he was even being interviewed. He was reminiscing and enjoying himself. He was at peace… for ten to fifteen minutes, in a chaotic, high-energy backstage.

He was with "Rainbow Studio" students. He felt very comfortable.

Now, once we started, then of course there's this part, which is…

<Michael Coats Asking> "Chester, how do you get permission from the parents for their kids to go to a function in which they're going to be backstage? There's free booze, no one checks ID's. There's going to be men on the prowl, women on the prowl. Are you up for it?"

"Well, wow. Let's see, how much can we really tell our parents?"

Here's what I would tell the students: "I like beer." I don't drink it now, but I'm just saying, "I like beer" at the time. I told 'em, "Imma drink a beer an hour, about what I do. The day starts for me at five-thirty, when I meet you guys and we load in and so forth, and uh – you know, so I probably drink six beers during the day, maybe seven. You won't see me stammer, stutter, fumble… anything. I expect the same from you. If you don't drink – don't. If you do drink: keep it cool!"

Imagine, I'm talking to twelve kids. Maybe it's four girls and eight guys. It's kind of about the average, like that. Some of them are so obvious to pick, it's unbelievable. You know, they work hard, they come in after school, they work weekends, helping others. It goes on and on and on. "You're going."

In my class, you're going to the Bammies. Some of the other ones were marginal picks, but the kids kind of voted — oh, I let 'em vote — the kids voted. Same thing as I did for the models for the fashion show. I'd reserve two picks for me. Sometimes they'd pick my pics and that's it. So there were only ten of us going. Sometimes, they wouldn't pick my picks and these two also got to go.

<Administrator Voice> "What did these two do to earn a spot at the Bammies?"

Well, I had a lot of errands that had to be run — all the time or I couldn't complete the project I'm working on.

"... On your way home, could you take your car and then drive to Yardbirds and pick up these screws, and pick up these bolts... I need the ones that look just like this. Here's ten dollars."

<Student runner voice> "Okay, no problem. This weekend. I'll pick it up for you. I'll buy."

Well, that's just as important as anything else going on.

<Administrator Voice> "Chet, that's not so much of a learning thing."

It isn't? Look at the responsibility I'm giving 'em: Getting the right thing. Taking your own car. Spending the money properly. Coming through on time.

Monday morning, "Chet, here's that bag of stuff that you needed from Yardbirds."

"Thank you. Thank you very much." So that kid gets to go.

So what do I tell them now as we prepare to go to the Bammies? By the way, this is a dress-up affair as I mentioned in the beginning. So these kids got to dress up. Ladies looked sharp in their dresses; boys looked sharp in their slacks. I told 'em, "you don't have to wear a tie, but it's a nice thing. You don't have to wear a sport jacket, but that usually goes with the tie. You can take it off. You could roll up your sleeves. You can loosen your tie. Come on. It's backstage, but we're going to dress up."

I told 'em about the drinking, and how they could share that with their mother and father — or not. If you shared, good, and if you didn't, good — I didn't care. If they didn't let you go, sorry.

They'd all go — probably to themselves, "Well, if I tell Mom, eh, they're not gonna let me go because I got in trouble last week. deh, deh, deh…" Okay — and they don't tell Mom.

Others were straight shooters. I had Mormon kids that went to the Bammies. They were, like, pretty strict. Wonderful kids. Just wonderful kids. They'd tell the parent flat out, "There's going to be booze back there. They don't check IDs, Mom."

"Well, I trust you son. I know you're not a drinker…"

Did we ever have a problem with someone drinking too much? It's been a lot of years so I can only remember one gal. She got *smoked*: too much to drink, too much to party. What's nice is that we had a limo bus and the bus driver who stayed there. I told him, "Your responsibility is to listen to the baseball Giants game, do whatever you want to do. Have fun. But I may be giving you a person or two who had too much to drink. Your responsibility is to make sure they don't leave the bus. If they do, you go with them."

"Yeah, no problem."

So, she had to go sleep it off. I had another one. They were both girls. We could talk about girls and women and drinks and getting a little tipsy, getting a little too high, then getting sloppy… but that's for another time. I don't think I'm going to put anything in the book about it — it's just an observation.

But, anyway, so we never really had a problem. Everything was always taken care of. The kids were always safe. They were driven home, back to Monte Vista High School. The parents were awaiting them in the parking lot. They had an experience that you never got, never as a high school student. Could you get to go to the junior prom, maybe? Sure. Senior ball? Yep. Sadie Hawkins dances if they still have 'em? You bet.

But you're *not* going backstage at the Bammies, the biggest musical event each year, in San Francisco, for the Bay Area.

We did.

Chapter 17

My Retirement Concert

In the summer of 1998, it was a regular year — no big year. I had no idea that I was going to retire in 1999.

Usually, when I start something, I go from — till death do us part, as was the case with my wife, Sharon. My barber I've had for 52 years: Bud Lucas. I worked for the A's 51 years. Everything I do is like, kind of forever. This was just a regular year going on. I was only fifty-five at the time. I had no plans to retire.

So this was, like, a Saturday afternoon — maybe Sunday.

Alan Ledford was my boss at the A's. By "boss," I mean, he was in charge of the television crew that was there when later on, in '83, we got a portable DiamondVision. It was a start. He had to oversee that, as well as the scoreboard operator, me, and the PA announcer, Roy Steele.

He came in with his son, Andrew. He brought his son in a couple of times a year. Anyway, I really liked Andrew — nice kid. Alan comes over to where I'm working, comes down. I'm doing balls and strikes and such. The game is going on …

There's about 20 seconds in between every pitch. You watch the umpire: if he *doesn't* move, you put "Ball," and you continue your conversation, face-to-face, if you want. I have an internal clock that knows that it's time for the pitcher to throw the ball. By the way, it's longer if he's in the "stretch" — with a runner on base. Then, it's around twenty-five seconds. You can carry on all kinds of conversations. It's very easy.

So Alan says that his son was taking guitar lessons now, from a gentleman named Bruce Hock. Now, Bruce Hock and I have done many concerts with various bands that he had. He opened for bigger shows, headlined his own shows.

I said, "That's wonderful! Bruce is a great guitar instructor. Bruce is all about music. That's great that your son is seeing Bruce. How long has he been taking lessons?"

"Six months. It's like a shrine in there to you."

"How so?"

"All the concert posters say: 'Chester Farrow Presents'..."

"Oh, oh, oh. Yeah, Bruce and I have done things for a lot of years."

<Chet Inquires> "Andrew's been playing for six months? Has he played a tune for you yet?"

"No! He won't play in front of us. Andrew goes in his room and, uh, plays his music, and uh, that's it. If we open the door, then he stops."

"Well, we'll change that."

"How are you going to change that, Chester?"

"I'll put on a recital, a guitar recital. Yeah! We'll hold it at Monte Vista High School, in the theater. I'll book a date, in May. We'll get a couple hundred in attendance from Bruce's students and their parents. It'll be a nice evening. What do you think about that?"

"Wow! It sounds like a great idea, but I don't understand how you're going to do it..."

"— Eh, don't worry. Leave all the details up to me. Alan, I got this covered."

So, I got a date on the calendar — and by the way, when you're trying to get a date on the calendar, it cost me around five-hundred, maybe seven-hundred and fifty for that date. The reason was, there might have been a play going on and the sets were already up. So now I had to ask, "Er, can you take your sets down, remember where they go, put them back up, and don't use the theater on that Thursday night, for rehearsal?"

There's always a dollar amount that people will come to you, unless it can't be. I said, "Well, if you guys are just rehearsing, is it a dress rehearsal?"

"No."

"Is it your first rehearsal?"

"No."

"Then, if you could cancel it, I could give you … " — and then the agreement was five-hundred, or seven-fifty, something like that.

"Fine."

"Oh! Now we have a date!" That's all I cared about — we got a date.

Now. The year rolls along. The school year starts, my 32nd year, 1998. We're at Christmas vacation.

We have the dates. It's secure now. We get to put it in ink on the calendar.

Christmas vacation went well.

I drove back to school for the first day of classes after the holidays. And … I don't know, something felt weird. They were going to work on my room a little bit, they said, over the holidays. What were they doing? I had a nice little setup there; I had a *kingdom,* for crying out loud: five edit suites, control room, studio, audio; everything solid state; everything computerized now, except the audio was all analog of course, but — I mean we had everything.

The construction people had put in big air conditioning ducts that I didn't need. I had wonderful air conditioning there. The works. These new things were hanging down — it was not in the *motif* I liked. No one consulted me that it was going to happen. Several other changes took place. I took one look and said, "I'm done. I'm all done."

They were in the process of changing over; they were going to rebuild *everything* … I'm gone.

It's the only time I've ever quit anything. If I'm on a softball team with you, I'm playing to the end. Playoffs? All right, I'm there. I don't care. Not gonna quit. May not play next year, for whatever reason, but I have committed to this year and that's it. I commit. You know, I do it forever.

It's just — a thing came over me … I don't want to say it was a *pall*, but I was sick to my stomach. Not consulted. They did things I didn't want … "Could have told you — save a lot of money … put that in later."

But it doesn't matter. I guess the end was near: I'm done.

Now, all of a sudden, the "Rock-and-Roll Recital" became "Chester's Going Away Party."

How'd that happen? Well, one of the people I called to bring in, to "Please, play?" — was Greg Douglass, fabulous guitarist.

<Chester, continuing> "…And could you come and perform maybe with the kids… sit in and play a lead or two? With Bruce and his students?" That was all I was thinking at the time, when I called Greg. He lived in San Diego. I paid him a pittance — three-hundred to come up, maybe four-hundred, two-hundred, I don't know — whatever we could afford. But he was glad to do it.

<Greg Douglass> "Glad to come on your day."

"Wow! That's really nice."

Then I said, "Well, wait a minute, I'm retiring here. Let's pull out all the stops."

So, I picked up the phone and — lo and behold, Greg Kihn was willing to come out with his band. Not the whole band, but with Steve Wright on bass. Greg Douglass, who first played the lead on "Jeopardy" with Greg Kihn — and who was in The Greg Kihn Band for a year or so, maybe two — was going to join him onstage. Wow. We had somethin' special.

Then I decided, "We need a house band, with horns and everything — that will augment the songs that the students would be playing. The songs that the students were playing — because it was a recital — were easily recognizable. Some of them were kinda old — but it didn't matter; old blues stuff, but easy rhythms, easy everything, that they could join in.

When Greg Kihn said that he would come, I went, "Wow! We've got a full party."

So the house band, then — who am I going to get? It turns out that Walter Herbert — heh, what, talk about full circle? — Walter Herbert, the manager of Journey, also had a band. He had a big recording studio at home — a gorgeous recording studio, at home. You know, I guess you make pretty good money. So he's made good money and had nice facilities — but the best was still yet to come.

So he said, "Not only will our band open — I mean, be your house band — if you'll let us do a 30-minute set — "

"Sure, I'll let you do it."

"Well, we'll help out any way we can. I want your kids all to come here and rehearse at my studio."

All these kids of Bruce's that were going to be in the recital, they went on this huge field trip to Herbie's house — Walter Herbert, of Journey — to his private studio. They rehearsed. They spent the day. It was a wonderful experience. Where do you get that? Fabulous!

Kids were elated. Energy was high in the air. Then the tickets, I printed 'em up and they began to sell like hotcakes. We had two tickets: one was twenty-dollars, or thirty-dollars, or twenty-five — I forget — which was your VIP ticket: you'd get preferred seating, which means I'd open the door early for you. You'd get a dinner — Mexican food, from the *New Mecca Cafe*. Guillermo Muniz owned that. We did several things together ... But anyway, it was all set up.

Then there were regular tickets, just to come, sit, and watch the show.

Herbie opened the show. The kids then came and did their thing with the recital. Greg Kihn joined the fray. The house started to rock. Greg Douglass was on guitar. Fabulous set — just a fabulous set — followed by my band that I managed for five years. They closed out the show.

There was seating.

<Administrator Voice> "Chester, you never use seats in the theater ..."

"We are tonight."

"Well, uh, I hear you have probably four-hundred tickets sold, and, uh, we do have five-hundred and something seats… "

"I sold six-twenty-five. We closed it. No more sales."

"Six-twenty-five!? You can't sit six-twenty —"

"Yes, we can."

And, we did.

It was a great night. Everything was just terrific. That was the start of the guitar recitals that I did for seventeen years. After the first one at Monte Vista, I did eight at the Lesher Theatre[1], and then eight at the Village Theater, in Danville.

And that's it.

[1] In downtown Walnut Creek.

Chapter 18

Rock and Roll Recitals: 2 - 17

Rock and Roll Recital I — the same time that I retired in 1999, held at Monte Vista High School — was a huge success. However, it was an unfair way of trying to gauge whether or not the recital could be a money-making opportunity and do it for some more years or whether or not anybody even wanted to continue — my former students all helping me out, of course.

There were a lot of things that were going through my mind. I wasn't quite sure. A lot of teachers were in the audience in that first one, a lot of adults — fathers and moms — of the students, a lot of students — there was a huge mix. I've never had one at a concert like that before, where the ages ran the gamut of 5 to 105.

So, it was a lot of fun. But now I'm retired.

Wow! What to do?

Well, after the recital, we got together at Bruce Hock's — he was the guitar instructor from Danville — over at his place... We watched the tape. Had a little barbecue and all like that. It was wonderful. We just chatted and reminisced a little bit. They all kind of seemed to feel like this was a winning thing.

Recitals are usually piano recitals, violin recitals, vocal recitals — whatever instrument. But this was different: showcasing *rock*... and specifically rock *guitar*.

I don't know if there ever has been a recital before on that; and I don't know if there has been a recital since — in which in another city in this country, a guitar recital was held. I just know we did it for seventeen straight years.

It was a wonderful experience... watching the tears in the

eyes of the mom, who finally got to see her son showcased on stage, performing with five or six other musicians, with a top-notch PA system. It was unbelievable.

That moment: the boy, the girl… 'cause there was a pretty good mix of boys and girls. You never got a chance to really hear how they could be with a full band. A lot of musicians would love to make a song. I mean, they had a song. They'd love to put it together, but you had to pay for studio time. You had to gather in musicians and all like that.

It's funny. I was going to start a business once, called *Chester Records*. We were going to do exactly that. For three-hundred and fifty dollars, you'd bring your song in. We had the house band. We had horns. We had you covered. Let's do the song. C'mon!

But, I never got it off the ground. I even printed cards and stuff. It was funny. We even had a team. I always have a team around me. Why?

What I found: in this world, you can't do it alone. There are some of you reading this now saying, "Oh, *I* did it all alone. Picked myself up by the bootstraps; I'm very successful… Six figures – plus – a year…"

Really? Didn't Mom help? Maybe Dad? Sis? Neighbor? Good friend? Teacher? Counselor? Minister? Didn't someone help you just a little bit down the road? Maybe a cop gave you a break – kind of nice – helped you to do… Boy! Could have had a DUI. You had a few drinks in, and you made it by.

Yourself? Not yourself: add that cop to the list of those people who helped you along the way. It's very simple. No one does it alone.

So, that being said, I decided to go ahead and do a second recital. Bruce was happy and surprised – Bruce Hock. The kids were elated because those that didn't play were in the audience, and they want to play next year. Wow! This was fantastic.

But I didn't want to have it at Monte Vista anymore. When I

retired from Monte Vista, that was it. I went back for one or two Thanksgiving and/or Christmas luncheons by the teachers, and it was already all different. It just — that was not my place anymore.

Do I love it? Forever.

Do I want to go back? I went to a football game once. It's like nobody even knows you after a year. After four years, for sure, no one knows you, right? The freshmen had become seniors and graduated. So it's like, I dunno. Then they started to reconstruct Monte Vista. As I was leaving, in 1999, they were building two- and three-story buildings. Looking like every other university and high school around the United States.

Re-sawn redwood — beautiful — fifty-four acres… C'mon now!… At the foot of Mount Diablo. They changed all the architecture. They changed the whole tenor, the whole atmosphere. So I'm not going back to high school anymore. I want to go to a place where people can have cocktails, if they want to. It's a recital. But it's rock and roll, so it's fun.

Rock and roll and cold beer and a drink or two… C'mon!

What do you do if you ever go to a concert? I don't care if you're going to go see Kenny Loggins or if you're going to go see some quiet Egyptian music. It doesn't matter to me. What are they serving? A little something to drink — lighten you up a little bit.

When you come to a high school, *nothing's* served. Sure, we had refreshments and all like that — but what do you get, a hot dog?

Well, that's not a shot of good bourbon.

I'm not advocating you *do* that. I'm advocating that it would be *available*.

You want to imbibe? Do. You don't want to imbibe? Don't. Very simple. Very straightforward.

So I didn't hesitate much. I chose the Lesher Theater, in Walnut Creek. Beautiful setting. Great building. Nice theaters.

We did most of our shows in the Margaret Lesher Theater. The Hoffman Theater held eight-hundred. We played it once. Oh! It's got the little loge areas, semicircles for the elite, the expensive tickets. It was two levels: five-hundred on the main floor, and three-hundred up in the balcony.

Wow. That's too big for us. But we played it once. The reason we played it was that the Margaret Lesher Theatre which holds three-hundred, was booked. But for some reason, this was not. We did all of our shows on a Thursday night. Same as I've always done: Thursday nights. The mini-concerts were Wednesday.

I have to admit now: I picked the wrong day. What's good about Thursday? Come on, you're at a high school, got teenagers, sun's been out. Warm evenings. Are you kidding me? They want Friday to come, and the weekend, and… party time. Let's be honest. "Party time" could be takin' a long hike, ridin' your horsey. That's party time.

Others maybe, I don't know, have some beers. Go chase girls. They don't cruise the drags anymore, so that's out.

So, Thursday night is a huge anticipatory night.

<Administrator voice> "Chester, a lot of teachers give tests on Friday. Kids have to cram, and whatever, and study for the tests, and wha-"

Then go study. Don't come. I can't dial it around your thing.

"But, Chet! Wednesdays might be better."

It's not a good day. Not a good day. I learned that in the mini-concerts. One of my teachers, Steve Marshall, who I taught with, called it "hump day." I guess they got a commercial, you know, Geico…

<Camel, on commercial speaking> "Mike! Mike! Hey, Mike! What day is it?"

"Eh… Hump day!"

You know, cute.

Thursday is the day to do a show. That's for high schools,

junior highs whatever. Whatever you're gonna do.

"Chet! Plays do better on weekends."

All right, good. Stay with the weekend.

"Choir things are way better on the weekends."

Okay good.

I don't think the attendance is as good on the weekends. I've tried a concert or two on a Friday – even a Saturday, I did one – at Monte Vista. Eh, better draw on Thursday. I call it "anticipatory day."

So anyway, we went to the Lesher Theatre. We stayed there eight years. We did one year at Monte Vista. We eventually did eight years at the Lesher. After, I'll tell you why we got out of there. We moved to the Village Theater in Danville. That's a converted movie house, but it's a nice little setting. It holds around two-hundred and forty-five. That's a nice crowd, two-forty-five. We had two full shows – for one, we had two-forty in attendance – the biggest show at the Village Theater. That was the first time we went there. We called it "Coming Home." And it was.

We drew – let's see: two-forty-five? Well, I think two-forty we drew – that's pretty good. That was the highest of all of them that were held at the Lesher, or at the Village.

The Lesher Theater – now, let's talk about it. It had all the facilities – everything you'd want. They had ushers and usherettes. I know that's not necessarily politically correct these days – you're supposed to call them all "ushers." But I like the idea that I'm implying that it was male and female.

The ushers used to tell me all the time, "I work all your shows. They're the most fun shows that we have. Everything here is so stiff. These concerts are great – listening to the old tunes. Wonderful."

So I had a steady crew. All volunteers. Evidently you'd volunteer your time to usher. In doing so then you're allowed to go into a certain number of concerts or events a year. You'd pick which ones you wanted to go to. A lot of them just liked working the show.

The Lesher had a nice bar. If you had an intermission, then the bar was open... They sold drinks and beers and sodas and waters and so forth. Kind of nice, if you were going to take a break in between, intermission.

Problem with intermission was that fans tended to leave. They'd already seen their son or daughter play. C'mon! Good time to get up.

When they returned, the audience was maybe... half of what it was.

So we only did the bar thing for one year, eh, maybe two. Oh, oh — we did it when we went to the Hoffman Theater, with the eight-hundred-seater, because of conflict of scheduling. We did the bar thing then — because why not? I mean, it's just — it's fantastic. If you ever have a chance to go see something at the Lesher Theater, it's as fine a theater as you're going to find around. Bar none.

However, let's talk about Rainbow Studio, my students, and so forth — and the musicians.

All of my shows, all of my recitals, you could stream 'em. You go to *YouTube.com*, search for "Chester Farrow Videos" and, eh, pick one out. Go to the first one, especially — that was a huge one. Greg Kihn, Greg Douglass, Jeff Campitelli — he was a drummer for Joe Satriani for many, many years. He lived right here in the Bay Area, Pleasant Hill. Just a wonderful young man. He just volunteered like, "I'm coming. I'm helping..."

That's because he had recorded earlier — when he was a high school student — at Rainbow Studio — we recorded his band. I don't know if Joe Satriani was in his band at that time — I don't know. After a while, when you're recording two bands a month... ay, ay, ay! After a while, one band is like another. So you forget — I couldn't give you any details about that.

Now it was the day of the show. This would be Rock and Roll

Recital II, for the next eight shows — okay — at the Lesher.

"Uh... Chet, uh... we didn't have a chance to go over all this on the — uh — on the pre-concert meeting..." The person talking is some representative from the Lesher Theater.

"Uh, yes. What's the problem?"

"Well, eh... you've got camera people, you know?"

"Yeah, I got three cameras, right? I got one in the back and two roving."

"Well, you can't go up on the stage and then come down the stage on the stairs that are permanently affixed to the left and the right of the stage, which leads to the audience areas — 'bout five steps."

"I *have* to. There are shots that we need in front, shots from behind, shots — C'mon! We've got the constant steady shot — the 'cover all,' it's called. From the back — we got that shot. But we need all the interesting shots that we can cut in, when we edit this."

We didn't do the edit live: we shot with three separate cameras, three separate tapes. Ian Williamson, my former student — he graduated in 1993 — was the one who was the genius behind all that.

I had other people doing it for a while, one person — it was a lot of work.

It all boiled down to who stuck with me... Pat Caley helped do it. Ian Williamson did it for many years.

Ian Williamson, should be mentioned. I told him, "Ian, I got a problem. I lose money every year on the recitals. I can't pay you a standard fee of, let's say, two grand — and that's cheap — for all the work you're doing: providing the cameras, providing camera people and then sitting down and editing and syncing three key different camera shots, with the music and such. Would you be willing to take whatever is left that could be considered a profit?"

We started this when we went to the Village Theater, I think.

"Would you be willing to underwrite the show? If the show brings in seven-hundred in profit, it's yours. If the show loses two-hundred, three-hundred: I can't pay you. If the show makes a couple three grand ..."

I kind of rolled up my sleeves when we went to the Village Theater and got people to donate money, a thousand here, a thousand there, five-hundred here — Wow! I was able to spare no expense. When I went to the Village Theater, it was wonderful. The money left over, maybe, would be twenty-five hundred. Oh, good. It's all Ian's, not mine. I'm not there to make a profit; just there to make it happen and not lose money.

So Ian underwrote the show four, five years, in which he made sub-one-thousand. Then he did another five or eight years or — something like that — in which he made nearly three grand... certainly, two. So, they paid off in the end for him, which is good — 'cause you could always use extra money — and it was really great for me.

Not only did they not let us go up and down the stairs with the cameras, but the Lesher Theater would not let us take separate feeds off the mixer. In other words, let's say the mixer has twenty-four channels. Okay, kind of a good sized board — not a great size. But let's say it's twenty-four-channel. Well, then there's twenty-four outlets... line-out, perfect. Let us take those line-outs and then we'll mix it from there. You mix for the house, we mix for tape.

<Lesher Representative> "Uh, Chet. You can't do that. I'm sorry. We don't let anyone touch our boards. We will allow you to take one direct feed, in mono, from the house mix."

<Spit take> "Thanks, but no thanks." I mean — we took it. We've got to have audio.

But my students were disappointed. They were not really involved now. The lighting people didn't get to go up in the lighting standards, and they were better lighting people than the Lesher has... for sure. David West and Pat Caley, former students of mine. C'mon. They've got that covered, in spades.

Can't touch our stuff.

So, we endured. We grew as a recital.

Here's another common complaint: "Chester! Your kids are too loud in the backstage room."

"Too loud?"

"Yeah, the guitars."

"None of 'em have amps. They're not allowed to have amps there. What's too loud?"

"Well, they're *strumming*. We could hear it."

"What?! This is rock and roll! Nobody could hear this. They don't hear us now. They don't hear you. They don't hear me raising my voice to you. Let alone worry about — 'hush-hush, quiet.' That's a drama thing. It's not rock and roll. They can't hear it. It don't matter if they *did*. It's all part of the ambience."

"I'm sorry, Chester. Rules are rules."

We couldn't wait to get out of there.

It was in May of 2008, we went to the Village Theater in Danville. I already told you it's a nice little theater. What'd they let us do? Lights, sound, record... video project — both sides of the stage. Loaned us their projector... anything you'd want to do. Why? Pat Caley used to be the General Manager, the Director of the Village Theater. The new guy, David Lam, kind of took his place — maybe two or three people removed, don't matter. So Pat Caley was as aware of this guy's job at the Village Theater as he was.

Oh, and David West did all the lighting for those people all the time. They knew David. I mean, the manager was like, "these are your people?"

"Yes. This is my team. This is Rainbow Studio."

"You can do whatever you want, but don't put any nails into the side to hold up your snake that goes back from the stage all the way up to where you're mixing from." So we used duct tape.

That was it. *Please don't put nails in the walls.* Now, that's a theater. I don't care if you have benches out there. That's a theater.

Let production people do production. Stay out of the way; give them the few rules that you have, like, no nails in the wall. That makes sense, even though the walls are painted wood. Gee, a nail right there would be perfect and simple... And after you removed it, you will — c'mon, no one's really going to see it.

But rules are rules. Those are fair. The Lesher? Eh! I'll never go back. (I'm not going to live long enough to do one anyway, but...) I won't go back and do a production. Why? My Rainbow Studio people who do all the production for me — I don't do it; they do it, mixing, recording... all of it! editing... you name it, they do it, not me. Can't do it at the Lesher? We're not coming.

So, the Village Theater, we stayed there for eight years. We had a great time. At all the recitals, we had *New Mecca Cafe* as the caterer. New Mecca Cafe is in Pittsburg, California. Guillermo Muniz — who has since passed — and his wife Terry, were the ones who provided the food for us. At first, they charged us — of course. The very first recital at Monte Vista, for twenty-five dollars instead of ten dollars, included dinner, which was a full Mexican dinner — plus fried chicken and so forth... Just on and on. It was wonderful. So we continued that.

Then, pretty soon, I told Guillermo, "I can't afford to pay."

He said, "Don't worry. You no longer pay. We'll do it."

He still does it. Terry, his wife, does it for me at the at the Oakland A's. Once a year, at the end of the year, there's usually a fireworks show on the last Saturday night of the season. During the fireworks show, that means the game is over and it's about thirty-five minutes before the fireworks start. Therefore all the camera people could come in... "Come on in and have a bite to eat." Guillermo pays — Terry — they provide it all: beer, food, salsa, chips... Wow! Fantastic. I would be remiss if I didn't mention that. New Mecca Cafe, Pittsburg, California.

We finished our recitals in 2015. That was the last one. I knew it was time to… let it go. The best attendance we ever had at the Lesher was one-eighty-one. The best attendance we ever had at the Village was the first one, like around two-forty… right in there — I mean, yeah, something like that. Then it dropped down to one-sixty-five. Then one-fifty. Then — *whatever*. "I think it's run its course."

Not that many kids were taking guitar lessons anymore. Things were changing. As the world changed, so did I.

Chapter 19

Rainbow Studio - The Core

To establish a program as big and successful as Rainbow Studio — from, let's say, 1969, 1970, when we really got started, all the way through 1999 — and beyond… when I did the Recitals, these people that I'm going to mention showed up for the Recital — all the Recitals — whether it be at the Lesher Theater, The Village Theater, or Monte Vista, for when I retired.

Some of these people I helped to get placed in the television, radio industry here in the Bay Area. You know, it's funny: when you work for the A's, then you do develop relationships. These relationships are so important to open doors for others.

They knew that I knew what I was doing, that my program was strong — Rainbow Studio at Monte Vista — that the kids coming out of that class could be relied on. Producers — even to this day — ask me, "You got any more kids like this guy, or that one?"

But, I've done all I can do. I retired in '99. I'm really not active in their lives now. I don't have to try to get 'em jobs. They're all on their own.

I'm gonna cover each one. There's nine of them — nine students — who were like, at the beginning. In other words, soon as they came to Monte Vista, they were part of the program. Then were part of it after I retired in '99, all the way up to 2015.

So, we'll go in chronological order. We'll start with the earliest — in terms of graduation from Monte Vista — to the most recent.

=========== Michael Baird ============

The first person that was a huge influence to Rainbow Studio in helping to establish what we were all about — keeping us as professional as we possibly could afford — was Michael Baird. He graduated in 1972. From the very early days that he came into the program, I could tell: this was a star. He was sharp, very smart… wanted to learn… had an open mind. He had a lot of Missouri in 'em… a little "Show Me"…

Oscilloscopes, and the meters — as we designed amplifiers, and such — bore out exactly what we wanted to do.

"… On the scope, it should read this point right here… at 72 Watts peak…" and so forth. The RMS[1] would be 2/3 of that, roughly. And… c'mon. He'd see it on the scope: "There it is." And he would be convinced, of course.

The voltmeter: the voltage should be about 160 at the plate[2]… *Boom*: 161.

I knew I had a winner early on. He was involved in Sesame Street, repairing the TV's. He was involved with all my first mini-concerts and all like that — from the beginning, the very beginning.

Michael had the keys — probably — his second year working with me. What I mean by "give you the keys," it's all the keys to all the rooms. I had the master. There's a lot of trust to be able to turn that over. Without question, it was easy to trust Michael Baird.

Just quickly, I'll mention that I think I helped him get his first steady job, in radio and television production. He was a senior at Monte Vista High School. A gentleman named Mike

---

[1] Root Mean Square value of the AC voltage: https://en.wikipedia.org/wiki/Root_mean_square

[2] The "plate" is one of the key parts of a vacuum tube amplifier circuit.

Marquardt talked to me. He worked at the Coliseum doing the radio broadcast. He was the engineer.

"Chester, I need a kid. I need somebody to do video taping for the Warriors[3]..."

In those days videotaping was reel-to-reel. Certainly all black and white.

"... He's got to be here so much time before the game. Then, after the game, he has to do *this*, and... you got good kids?"

Anyway, to make a long story short, I recommended Michael Baird. Then Michael Baird started to work for Michael Marquardt. Then it started to get real serious, like... steady work.

Michael Marquardt — I remember — called me one time, like, "Hey, he's having girl problems..."

"Listen, Michael. The young man is what, what is he, twenty, now? Twenty-one? I mean... you're going to have those problems."

"Well, he's depressed right now —"

"Well, wouldn't you be? Your girlfriend breaks up with you — or whatever the situation was... C'mon! What're you gonna do, try to throw out the baby for the bathwater? You're little disappointed right now, because he's going through a phase? Michael, back off a little bit."

And he did. Michael Baird continued to work for him. Now, he is the radio engineer for the Oakland A's — and has been for many years.

I 'member a quick story: 1996... when the Olympics were in Atlanta. I told Wendi[4], "Come on. We're getting on a plane. We're going to Atlanta."

"There's no rooms in Atlanta."

"We'll stay with John Moore."

---

[3] The *Golden State Warriors*. NBA. Basketball. They played their games in the arena located adjacent to the Oakland Coliseum.

[4] My long term companion.

John Moore had a room there — we'll talk about him in a minute – and Michael Baird were both working the Olympics. Two of my former students, working television production... which is the class they were in... to be this successful: at the highest, highest level. He's done World Cup games and... fill in the blank. He's getting a little older now... he's still a kid to me, but he's in his sixties! He's done just about everything he's ever wanted to do in the world. Great kid. Nice little family now. He's a grandpa, and all of that... We'll hear from Michael in his own words.

- From Michael Baird:

  "Although I wasn't a student at the beginning of Rainbow Studios, I was part of what Rainbow Studios eventually became – that being an electronics club called 'Zap City' that presented concerts with the equipment we built in our electronics classes at Monte Vista. As a result, I returned for most of the Rainbow Studio productions after graduation bringing with me cameras, switchers and other equipment from the companies I was working for, to help put on their early shows. I also taught a few of Chester's classes in 1973 when he had a conflict working for Oakland's World Series games and the district didn't have substitute teachers that taught electronics. The following year I was working those World Series games as well.

  "During my senior year at Monte Vista, Chester introduced me to Mike Marquardt, Director of Broadcasting for the Golden State Warriors. Based on Chester's reputation, I was hired as a videotape cameraman for the team. (They didn't televise all games in 1971-72).

  "I would come back from an MV soccer game, hop

in my car and head out to the Oakland Arena, change out of my soccer uniform there and set up a B&W 1" reel-to-reel videotape machine and shoot the game. Following that season and graduation, I went to work for Western Electric and was also attending Diablo Valley College when Chester contacted me in 1974 and told me Mike Marquardt was looking for me again. He told me besides wanting me to work for the Warriors full-time, that Franklin Mieuli (owner of the Warriors at the time) also owned a recording studio and a production company hiring engineers for all sports in the Bay Area and many across the country. 'That's College and Pro,' Chet kept saying in our conversation. 'You'll be doing this.... And you'll be doing that.' I said, 'What makes you think I'm gonna take that job?' He said, 'Oh, you're gonna take the job.' I took his sage advice and accepted the gig and actually had to quit college because running a studio in the morning and off to some stadium or arena for a game that night was just too lucrative and busy!

"It all turned out to be the start of an amazing (so far 45 year) career that has seen me working audio for every sport imaginable and working both in the USA and internationally. I now work for the Oakland Athletics, the Golden State Warriors, the San Francisco 49ers, Cal Basketball, NBC Sports Bay Area/California and all Winter and Summer Olympics.

"As my teacher and mentor in my youth and then as a special life-long friend, I can never thank him enough for what his inspiration, advice on life (in my youth) and his continued friendship has meant to me over the 50 years we've known each other.

And I still get to see him at every A's game. Not many people get to say that."

Michael Coats graduated from Monte Vista in 1976. Michael Coats and Michael Baird are very, very good friends — to this day.

However, Michael Coats' interest was not necessarily with the dials and the levers and the faders and the amplifiers and the microphones and the speakers and the cables and so forth. He was more fascinated — when I put on a show — about how we publicize it, how you land the band. I would let him sit in on these — truly private — conversations, so that he could learn the ropes.

Michael learned that... we'd call on a Thursday — the best day to land a contract. Then they'd talk it over on Thursday night. The weekend was approaching... people were excited. You'd get a nice phone call back — usually from band's management — on a Friday sayin', "Hey, we'll do the deal."

Then, of course, you'd gotta take over and do publicity... Because you can't *go* if you don't *know*. That's rule number one. If you're going to put on an event, and you want people to come, they've gotta know about it... somehow. Posters plastered everywhere. Leaflets on windshield wipers. I don't care. Maybe a story in the newspaper. Ah! Michael learned that one fast. Why? It's free. Send them out a press release, tell them basically what it's about, guarantee that you could set up an interview with me, or whoever you're representing, and... C'mon!

Michael gets paid for this. He's a publicist. He's up in Sonoma. I think he's selling his house right about now, and is gonna move, gonna kinda downscale a little bit. He's very successful.

He's had clients in rock and roll, and wine, and now, some

of his clients are doing marijuana and stuff. He's as cutting edge as you can get. He's like a yappy little dog: doesn't get off your cuff. Arrrrrr! Arrrrrr! Arrrrrr!

He won't take "no" for an answer. Then he gives you a good story. A good interview. Maybe a photo op. That's what his expertise is.

He was the publicist for all the Bammies. He could tell you his life story.

Now, I didn't really help him get his first job — I don't think. But I helped him *keep* his first job.

Got a phone call from his boss, Ken Baker — who's no longer with us. He owned "Ken Baker Publicity Services", in San Francisco. He hired Michael on — I don't know if it was my recommendation? Maybe I didn't even know Ken? I'm not sure.

But anyway, one day I got a call from Ken Baker.

"I got a little problem."

"What's that?"

"Michael. I'm not sure if he's really cut out for this..." He kinda had some qualms about the hire, I guess, that he wanted to know. Maybe Michael was being a little moody or something. I don't know. Probably working two, three jobs... and not concentrating fully. It doesn't matter.

I reassured him that everything would be fine, that he had a wonderful hire in Michael Coats.

And now, as they say, "the rest is history."[5]

One of the common themes that you're going to find throughout most of this, is that these people are all freelancers. They fly by the seat of their pants. They live by the quality of their work, and by the positiveness of their personality. Employers have to be able to count on them to come through, do their job, and keep the spirit loose.

Live production is very strenuous. You go home after an A's game — or any production — concert... you name it. You don't

---

[5] Michael now owns his own business, *CoatsPR.com,* up in Sonoma.

go home and go to bed! You can't! Oh! I mean the synapses in your brain have been firing on all cylinders, to make sure that this professional operation operates top-notch. Now, all of a sudden you drive home and you are sleepy now? Heh! Doesn't happen.

Michael Coats was involved in Rainbow Studio from the absolute beginning, when he came in to Monte Vista High School. Smart kid – but his interest was really not in the classroom, *per se*.

There was something special about him that I saw – "this guy's a winner..."

It turned out that he became a successful publicist. I'm very proud. And you'll hear from Michael.

• From Michael Coats:

> *"Chester, it goes without saying that I owe my entire career path to you, my mentor. I was headed to a boring life in forestry or some such until my sophomore year and your electronics class. By age 16, I was working with Greg Douglass thru your association with Appaloosa. Greg and I still roll! You gave me the freedom to explore my muse, and it led right to a career in PR based in SF and clients such as Bill Graham, Doobie Brothers, Night Ranger and from there a myriad of lifestyle clients. You needed someone with a big mouth willing to promote your endeavors and we have never looked back. Butts in seats are what we did and still do. Thank you!"*

=========== Ken Behrens ============

Ken Behrens was another 1976 graduate. Ken was a sharp kid, smart kid. Kinda quiet. Little bit shy.

But he loved rock and roll. He loved PA systems, recording systems. He loved it all.

It's funny. He was involved in everything we did from the very beginning. Helped out along the way from time to time and then many of the Recitals.

I didn't really have anything directly to do with Ken Behrens' profession. I believe that he works for a company that makes bass amps. He lives in Garden Valley, California. He says he's very happy, and doing real well.

He was also the roadie for a little group called "Coinman/Douglass." John Coinman was the lead singer in the band I managed, and Greg Douglass was a lead guitarist in the band that I managed; he was with us for a while. Then the two of them — after the band dissolved — got together... and as a little duo, appeared in nightclubs in Berkeley and San Francisco. Ken Behrens was their roadie: set up, took down, and all these things. I think he might have even been a roadie for us when the band was still together — I'm not sure. Ken can tell you his own story.

But, you could tell early on: when the hook is set... and you're not fishing... it's just — you could see that this kid keeps coming back. He wants to know more. He wants to help out. He wants to help make a "snake," in which we could plug a microphone in two hundred feet away... and then the cable brings it down. Put it together. Changeover quarter-inch phone connectors that are chassis mounted, to XLR. All professional microphones usually have XLR connectors on 'em — not quarter-inch phone. We made the conversion. He was part of it.

Coming back, and helping me... is something I'll never forget. I'll always appreciate — and all these people did it for nothing; I don't have any money. Oh, we did provide dinner for 'em on the night of the show. We did provide — "we?" — *I* provided hamburgers and such for 'em on rehearsal night. But, that's it. He came down — Ken came down — and stayed overnight, two nights, y'know — we're at the Village Theater, overnight. Come in, go to work on a Monday... let's say the show's on a Wednesday. We'd come in on a Monday, do the setup. Tuesday, a lot of times, was a rehearsal. He's right there. It's an arduous process, the rehearsal. But, we got through it. Then, of course, it makes for a better show on Thursday.

You'll hear Ken's story, as you read.

- From Ken Behrens:

  "Aside from my immediate family, no one in my life has done more for me than Chester Farrow. When talking to other former students at the recital shows, I found this to be a common thread with all of us. He introduced me to many worlds that I wouldn't have encountered without his help and guidance. I have worked as a guitar and keyboard tech for many musical acts throughout my life. Everything I know about the music industry and musicians can be traced back to my experiences with Chester and Rainbow Studios. We started with how to properly wrap a microphone cable. How to behave in a professional recording studio was also another lesson learned. And, of course, the knowledge of electronics that has served me in my working life as well as my hobbies of speaker building and guitar repair. But to me, the most important thing I learned from Chester was how to critically listen to music. How to break down a piece of music into its individual components, tracks, instruments, and vocal performances. It is something I use every day, whether just listening for pleasure, or discussing music with someone in the business.

  "That said, working in music isn't what I do as my profession. Chester helped me get a job in an industry that I have worked in for more than 40 years, steel rule die-making. I have started two small businesses during my time in manufacturing and

am currently still working in the field. I started my first business when I was 26 years old. All my success in business I trace back to Chester. He went out of his way to help me when I was a kid. The advice I got from him has been invaluable. Every time I have a crucial decision to make I can hear him say, 'Don't burn your bridges, you may want to cross back over them someday.' Chester has been a teacher, a mentor, and a great friend to me. My entire life would have been different if I had never met him."

=========== John Moore =============

John Moore was an eighth-grader when he first came into my class. He got in because a counselor that used to be at Monte Vista, who was now at his school — Los Cerros — recommended him. Her name was Nora Fisher.

"Chester, I got this student. Very sharp. He loves gadgets and things. You're gonna love this kid."

That was the first time I ever let someone in *early*. John was a 1978 graduate of Monte Vista High School. Up until that point — I'd been teaching since '67, so now it was eleven years later — he was the first student that I ever let in early.

He excelled. Got all A's — c'mon. He'd get everything... and before long, he was — as a sophomore — he was running video tape recorders and things for me. After school, he worked at a job installing speakers in cars, when that was the big rage... your four-track, your eight-track players... He was working here, working there... coming and helping me and so forth. Every concert I put on — if he was around — he would come by. He lives in Los Angeles now. He's an editor.

As I mentioned earlier, he was one of the kids that I went to see at the 1996 Olympics in Atlanta. I forget where he was working. I think Michael Baird was doing tennis… John Moore was doin' — I don't know. I forget. It didn't matter. All I wanted to do was go and bathe in their limelight. I took 'em all out to dinner. It was a wonderful thing: Wendi and I, and Michael Baird, and John Moore. We had a great time. That's the only reason I went to Atlanta.

Stayed there about four or five days. We stayed in John Moore's room. He got a room from NBC. All the rooms were taken, if you wanted to be in downtown Atlanta. So he called room service, had another bed delivered — it was tight quarters, me and Wendi and him — but he generally left by about eight in the morning. Then he generally returned, like, ten or eleven at night. So, it was no big deal. We made it work.

I was so proud.

I never really helped him get a job. But I did help him get into UCLA. He wanted to get into UCLA as a freshman. They turned him down. Then he wanted to get in as a sophomore. He asked me to write a letter of recommendation. The letter of recommendation was a glowing one, of all the things he could do, and the things he had done, and you could trust him to do this and that…

The phrase "my loss is your gain" was used by me four or five times in recommendations for former students — all of them getting a position.

He got into UCLA.

Before long, he was kinda running everything at UCLA's television department. They'd tear down this old truck. They'd rebuild the truck. Patch bays, all these things, you know, like, trying to do one of those nice big TV trucks on the cheap. You'd learn how to do those things at Monte Vista on the cheap. We didn't have a big budget. We didn't even *have* a budget. Gotta raise all of our own funds. Then we gotta earmark what we're gonna do with it.

If you told John Moore we needed to wire *this*, but we can't spend more than this amount of money, he'll stay within budget. He'll make it happen.

That's a lost thing now, in Hollywood. The interns, they don't even understand what's happening. They don't even care. They know they press Button "A" and they get this and Source "B", they get that. Go actually to the patch bay and disconnect, reconnect what you need, and so forth? Forget about it! Forget about it. All they do is they tell whoever the personnel is there, that "I need this for this" and someone else goes back there and patches it together. God forbid, you want to now put an auxiliary piece of equipment on line... And bring it — "Wow! How do you do that?" Heh.

John Moore could do patch bays... blindfolded. He's been to the Olympics. He's been — I don't know — around the world, doing all kinds of things.

He's got a beautiful home in Studio City, California. He and the wife are both editors. How you like that? I guess he met her while editing — I don't know. Then they married, had a child, a lovely daughter, and... Ay! Wonderful.

You'll hear from John now.

- From John Moore:

  "Without a doubt, Rainbow Studios was the most influential experience I've had in my life. The foundation of technical knowledge, problem-solving and teamwork I learned at Rainbow Studios paved the way for my professional career.

  "The chance to be involved in the construction of both a recording and television studio gave me the skills to stand out in Hollywood's post-production community. Producing weekly television shows and multiple rock concerts, with major bands, gave me the confidence to follow my dream and pursue a career in television in Los Angeles.

  "Thanks to Rainbow Studios, I was accepted into the

> *UCLA Motion Picture and Television department, which only accepted 100 students a year at the time. As a student, my Rainbow Studio skill set gained me a student engineering job which allowed me to rewire the entire UCLA television facility including 3 TV studios, several new edit bays and master control. This work led to a position at ABC in maintenance engineering, which then led to editing. I have since edited for all major networks including cable and streaming services. I had the honor to work on the 1984 Olympics, which was a dream I had since Rainbow Studios took a field trip to ABC Hollywood Prospect Lot my senior year. I also edited on all the Olympics in the '90s and I was not the only Rainbow Studio alumnus working the games. None of this would have happened were it not for Rainbow Studios.*
>
> *"I am forever indebted to Rainbow Studios and Chester Farrow, who has been a lifelong teacher, mentor, and friend. I am blessed to have been a part of Rainbow Studios at Monte Vista High School Class of '78."*

Pat Caley graduated from Monte Vista High School in 1982. Now, Pat Caley was a little different, in that he was more… He just wanted to learn the practical knowledge… to keep understanding… to grow… He wanted to be involved with whatever we could do. He kinda got hooked on lights. So he's my source for lights. He became an expert at that.

Now, he's an expert engineer who installs big video board projects. The Dodgers. The Giants. He did the A's board a couple years ago.

It all kinda started at Monte Vista High School. He went on to San Francisco State and discovered that their program was not very strong, that in fact, Monte Vista's was stronger.

He always kept us appraised as to equipment that we might be able to purchase... things that had come online that maybe might work, and such. We were always trying to do more with less, when we purchased equipment.

I got as much input that I could get. I'd get a lot from all my former students. Very important. What are they using now? How's it holding up? How's the final product? Those kind of things.

Pat not only did lights, but he did directing for my television show, "Just for You." *Our* television show, I should say. We did that for over twenty years. Pat was one of the directors. When you become a director for me, you're at the about the highest level — there's nothing much more, other than letting you take the keys. You take over and produce. I tried that a few times, and it was like the kids kinda weren't ready for all of that, necessarily.

So, the director just wants to direct, and the technical director just wants to press the buttons, and the graphics director just wants to make sure the cameras look good, for when we show graphics.

Pat went on to San Francisco State. Then we reconnected again. He was there for all of my concerts, if he wasn't working. All shows. Any project I'm working on, you can count on Pat. That's very important to keeping a program strong. We needed these alumni to come back, to let us know what's going on in the world today. I don't mean ten-thousand dollar software packages like an "Avid," and so forth. No, no. no. What could *I* use? What's available for a few hundred? Maybe a thousand, at most? Pat was a tremendous resource — still is, to this day.

I get a big kick out of this, which is, this all started with Pat — the big scoreboards, and all like that — when he and I were partners in my consulting business from 1999 — after I retired — to about 2006… whenever the recession hit.

Consultants. I've said this before: last hired, first fired. That's the way it should be. When things are going rosy, then you could bring in the consultants to help you think through a project… help you develop it. But, in the recession, then there's just not the money. The teachers need the money for raises, just to stay up with the cost of living.

Pat — I remember — also was an Eagle Scout. I went to his ceremony. So that helps you understand, kinda, a little bit about Pat Caley. He's got a couple brothers. I taught one of his brothers, and the other brother was always around rock and roll and lights and stuff. So my mini-concerts and those kind of early concerts were a natural for him. This was, once again, an example of a family thing. Not uncommon.

You know, it's funny: when you teach and you teach long enough, pretty soon like, "My *mother* had your class."

"Oh, yeah. Wow. That's nice."

And then, pretty soon… "My *grandmother* had your class."

Yikes!

But, that's the way it goes (heh). You'll hear Pat's story, from his own words, as you read. Thank you.

• From Pat Caley:

> *"What did Chester teach me that helped with my career? Well, as Mr. Rodgers in the counseling office told me once, yes you can get life science credit for electronics class, because Chester will teach you about electronics… and life. I still remember a student in 'Electronics I' who was thinking that moving out of her parents' home, finding a job and sharing an apartment would be easy. Chester spent half a class listing out on the chalkboard what it could cost to live on your own away from one's parents. That was a lesson in life.*

"Chester has always been good at reaching students. Besides the basics, like Ohm's law, soldering and cables, cords and connectors, I learned that the key to a successful production, whether it is television, recording, or concerts, is everyone needs to work as a team. All members of the team must not only do their job proficiently, but work in unison as a team, encouraging each other on, backing each other up, just like a sports team. This holds true in my work, how building productions systems takes a team."

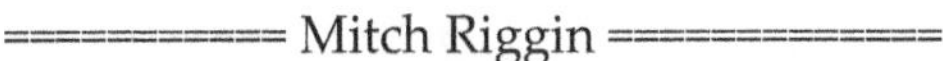

Mitch Riggin was a 1985 graduate of Monte Vista High School. He was a cute kid, kinda skinny, kinda an afro haircut-thing. Big tall hair. He was a drummer.

He liked his band. He was all proud. We recorded his band. We let the band play at Monte Vista High School.

You could tell right away, this kid was awful sharp.

"Chester! How do you identify 'awful sharp'?"

I'll give you the opposite example. I had a student who wanted to get into TV productions. I told him, get a perfect score on an exam on power supplies in "Electronics I"… and help me in the back where we were sheetrocking walls to build more control rooms — "edit suites," if you will. He aced the test. He did a good job.

Now, we were doing the sheetrock. There's a rhythm. It's like, "Hand me about three screws…" or three nails, whatever I was using… then I'd go and I'd put 'em in. I'd reach around, you're going to hand me three more. That's kind of how it'd go.

He'd hand me *one*. He'd hand me *nine*. He wouldn't be there when I needed him. He'd come back, "Oh, yeah, Chet. How many are we doing again?" That kind of thing.

So that's the opposite. I let him in TV productions, too, and he did a good job. He was a good boy. He went on to be a roadie. Successful, you know, in what he was doing. But a lot of times, you go, "Who knows?"

But Mitch, I could tell right away: sharp kid. He was a director for me. As I said earlier, if you end up directing for me, you're about the highest I go. Unless you take my job… as producer. By the way, Mitch could have done that, too. He didn't care. Some are just natural leaders. Some are not. Most of us are not natural leaders. But anyway, he did a fine job in school. Acted in *front* of the camera, if I needed it. Got behind the camera. Directed. Ran camera. Whatever. It doesn't matter. TD[6]. Didn't matter the chore. He was right there. Gotta make sets? Gotta make backdrops? He'd help. He put in the time.

One day, then, he goes off to college. Not sure where… maybe Chico? Somewhere up north. I had told the kids that, always, if you go to a college and you graduate, and your major is television production or a related subject close to it, then I will get you a job in the Bay Area… probably in sports, because of my connection with the A's.

So, here comes a phone call from Mitch Riggin.

"Chet! I graduated, duh, dah, dun… Everything was really good…"

Oh! He had come back to Monte Vista a few times to show us the work that he was doing at the college. I always encouraged that: show 'em what you know. What were you doing? How'd you do that? And so forth. The kids were always fascinated and learned from people that were quote-unquote "supposedly" ahead of them.

"Chester! I can't find a job in the Bay Area. I've graduated from college. I've heard no responses from my resumé."

"Well, wait a minute. Did you send one to *Sports Channel*?" That was a new channel that was being developed at that time and they had jobs. "Did you put my name down as the number

---

[6] Technical Director

one person with a recommendation, the first one on the list?"

"Chester. You're first on the list. Bold letters, even."

"I can't believe it. Who'd you send it to?"

"The producer, Michael Ireland."

"Michael Ireland? He eats in the Press Lounge. I'll talk to him tonight. See what's going on."

I sat down with him that night.

"Michael…"

"Chet! What's up?"

"I got a former student who said he has submitted his resumé to you — wanting a job — three times. He hasn't heard back from you."

"Chet. You know, we just throw them away in the trash can. It's who you know, y'know."

"Well, I'm representing this kid."

"What's his name?"

"Mitch Riggin."

He laughed. "Yeah, I just threw his latest one out…" — whatever.

"Michael, open it up and take a look and you'll see that I'm recommending him. I don't just recommend *anybody*. I got a great kid here. He'll be good for your program. You need this guy."

"Chet! Bring me the resumé again tomorrow. I'll act on it right away."

Make a long story short, within the week, he was hired — I think, as an intern, at first. You'd go from intern, to running camera, to graphics, to TD. But his road to being a director was blocked. He was blocked by a guy named Tommy Adza, who had been and would be the director of A's television broadcasts for quite a while. He was not going anywhere.

Jim Lynch, over at the Giants, he's not going anywhere either. He *has been* their director for a long time, and he intends to *be* their director for a long time.

Don't forget, director is "above the line." Yeah, there's no union contract. You negotiate your own. Some of these guys were getting a thousand, fifteen-hundred, two-thousand a game. You multiply that times eighty-two games, or eighty-one games… Wow. That's big money.

So anyway, Mitch gets the job. He works his way up. Wants to be a director. He knew he couldn't do it here, because the road was blocked to directing. So he leaves, and he goes to Milwaukee.

"I'm going to Milwaukee. I got a job with the Brewers."

"God-forsaken… Milwaukee!?" I mean, he *was* living in Half Moon Bay. Gorgeous. Foggy… but, c'mon. "And now, you're going to go to Milwaukee, where there's snow, and that kind of stuff?"

"Chet, I have to do it for my career."

And that's it. It's an opportunity. He ended up working for — not just the Brewers, but the Bucks, for basketball, and other things. Finally, he moved to Arizona, as the director for television broadcasts for the Arizona Diamondbacks. He introduced that one, where if you ever watch Diamondbacks broadcasts… somebody hits a home run and it goes into the pool — and then he has a stock shot that he had pre-done, which shows the ball coming into the water from a camera deep in the pool… very nice. Very dramatic.

Now, he's with the Los Angeles Angels. I got a chance to see him this year, already. We played the Angels in the first home-stand at the Coliseum. Big hugs all around… it's like a love fest with these guys. Just unbelievable. And… well, Mitch'll tell you his story.

• From Mitch Riggin:

> *"I've said it many times, but no one outside of my immediate family has had more of an influence on my life and career than Chester. He caught my attention by becoming the first teacher I ever heard*

say 'fuck' in class, but other qualities made him the coolest teacher I'd ever seen.

"I gravitated to his classes, to him as a person. I soaked it all in. Before I knew it, I was spending anywhere from three to 14 hours a day in his classroom, editing, mixing, recording, running camera. It was so stimulating, and I wanted it all.

"He gave me independent instruction in Scuba diving even though he doesn't swim. He gave me a passing grade in math class, so I could get into college. He set up my first internship in sports TV, a field I've worked in for 28 years. He even had my rock band open for the MTV basement tapes winners at our high school. It was the first and last time I ever signed an autograph. He gave me the keys to the high school recording studios and left us alone all by ourselves. We finally locked the studio at 2:00 am.

"The trust he had in me enabled me to trust myself. Chester showed me not only a career path in television production but showed me that adults can be cool, funny, swear, care and make a difference.

"Chester's advanced TV production class was hand-picked by him. It was a mixture of smoking-section stoners, musicians, nerds, geniuses and social rejects. It was perfect. His classroom was a magical place. It was our space. We built the desks and collected carpet squares to cover the walls. It even had its own walk of fame painted on the floor. I was entrusted to fill and stock the Coke machine— it was quite the honor! But more important than anything, was Rainbow Studios. It was where we produced our own half-hour show. We worked our asses off for that half-hour on cable access each week. More work, care, and preparation went into that program than many

shows I would go on to work over the next 28 years. "It's really difficult to describe just how important a person Chester is in my life. Had it not been for Chester, I would not have gone to college, nor would I have had this wonderful journey of a career, traveling the country and world covering live sports for television. He taught us to care, to fight for what we believed in, to K.I.S.S. Keep It Simple Stupid! He also taught me what comes around goes around. I really do believe in that. Treat others like you want to be treated. Chester has touched so many people's lives. I'm so thankful that I am one of them. He's one of a kind and I love him."

=========== Seth Worden ============

Seth Worden graduated in 1986, just after Mitch Riggin. I could tell right away the first time he ever came into class — this tall, skinny kid — he's got a brilliant mind. Solve any problem.

I thought I might go into engineering when I was going to San Francisco State. C'mon! I get confused when the gears turn this way and that, and… oh, my!

For Seth, problem-solving is a natural way of life. Seth would repair just about anything that I had. I remember teaching soldering. He caught on real well. Then he learned the little techniques of putting together these connectors, and such. You gotta be patient. You can't have one little wire accidentally touching one other little thing — no, no. Now you've got a short or something like that… there's no danger of electrocution, but there's danger that it's going to fail while you're using it.

Seth was just very expert. He would go, like, "Well, I could make this…" And he'd make things. Our studio got better because of Seth.

After he graduated, he'd come and he'd help out whenever

he could. All you had to do was call. It didn't matter that I was having a concert or something, and it was advertised in the local paper… Seth, maybe wouldn't hear about it. But if I made a call and told him I could use his help –

"Right away."

So when I started the Recitals, Seth Worden called me and said, "I wanna be a part of it."

"Wow! Of course! Sure!"

As the years went on, we went from analog mixers to digital mixers. I would be lost with digital because I'm an analog man in a digital world. I've said that before.

Seth learned all that stuff on the fly, as we put on the concerts, the recitals.

It was wonderful.

I wanted to do video projection. He found video projectors. I didn't have screens. He'd make screens.

Every year, we'd get better. For sure, the recital we had at the Village Theater had one screen. The following year, we had two. And then, two better ones, and then two with better units and better screens… and so forth and so on.

He was our go-to engineer. I don't care whether you're talking an electronic engineer or mechanical engineer. He's an engineer.

Obviously, he was very important to the backbone of Rainbow Studio.

- From Seth Worden:

  "I'm not sure what I expected that first day when, as a freshman, I walked into Electronics at Monte Vista High. Chester was certainly a distinct character. He greeted the new class with his characteristically animated 'Oh… Oh, Hi!' The times were quite different in the early 1980s. Kids were teased, and not only by each other. Chet elicited quite a few laughs at various students' expense. During one

particular roasting, I remember thinking to myself that maybe he was having second thoughts about picking on me, when he interjected 'But seriously, I'd let Seth go out with my own daughter.' I thought, 'Okay, maybe,' and then he said, 'Because I know she'd be safe.' The class erupted in fits of laughter. Those kinds of things definitely would not fly these days. Despite the introduction, I went on to take classes from Chet at every opportunity: two years of Electronics and two years of TV Production, as well as independent study. In retrospect, I believe these experiences helped break down a lot of barriers between students, and certainly helped steel us from being paralyzed by embarrassment (which is important if you want to be in front of a crowd, camera, or on-air). We learned many practical skills for life and work in his classes; such as how to work with others as a productive team, how to work with deadlines, how to organize and produce shows and concerts. We learned to read schematic diagrams, to follow signal flows, how components and circuits work, and most importantly how to fix them when they don't—a valuable skill which has saved me lots of money over the years. We learned the importance of prioritization, and the value of persistence. Chester also allowed students the freedom to fail and learn from their mistakes. For me, the greatest gifts were: learning how to find some humor in even the most trying situations, the value of not taking things too seriously, and the importance and rewards of getting out of your comfort zone, because that's where the real learning and experience is found. It was a great adventure and I'm forever grateful for the knowledge and guidance I've received from

Chester over all these years."

Ian Williamson graduated in 1994.

It's funny. There was, like, controversy when he first came in class. The computer teacher expected him to come from his middle school and be a star-shining example of an up-and-coming, smart kid. 'Cause Ian is very smart. All my kids are very smart.

She was complaining on Day One.

"Chester! You stole my student."

"What student?"

"Ian Williamson."

"I don't know Ian Williamson."

"He's in your electronics class."

"He is? I dunno. Do I have a Williamson?" I did. "Oh, yeah. He's in second period or third period. Good."

"Well... you know, he was supposed to be in taking to computers and..."

"Well, that's not my fault that he took my class. Wadda ya want me to do?"

"Well, maybe you could encourage him to —"

"I'm not going to encourage anyone to leave my program. I'm not silly. You say he's a good student? Thanks!"

And the rest, as they say, is history.

Ian was sharp from Day One. He might've even have come in as an eighth grader. I don't even know. He had spiked, purple hair going one way. He was a skinny thing. He's not skinny anymore. I'm skinny. He's not skinny anymore. He kind of filled-out, like we hope everyone gets in adulthood.

Ian was central to everything we did at Rainbow Studio while he was there. Always available to help out in any way possible... setting up video, directing the video, for a concert. It doesn't matter. Ian Williamson was always part of the formula, once he started at Monte Vista High School. We started the video Yearbook 'cause of Ian Williamson.

Ian had the skills to be able to use a three-quarter-inch editor. This was not "non-linear" editing. This was as "linear" as you get. You'd lay down a little scene... five scenes later, you'd like to change that? Hah! Good luck! Oh, yeah. Now we had to go back, and try — Oh, boy!

With the computers these days, very easy. You move this to here, and this to there. There you go.

So, because of his capabilities then, I felt, "Why don't we start our own video Yearbook?"

The way this really started, was a couple of years earlier, these people came...

"Hey, we represent a video yearbook company..."

"Oh, good. What's in it for us?"

"You, your kids take this camera. You go shoot a bunch of shots. Then we edit it. In the end, when we're all done, you'll have a nice half-hour video Yearbook..."

"What do *we* get?"

"You earn that *camera* after two years of doing it."

"So, we shoot for free... shoot for *free*... and you keep the money? I mean, I don't understand —"

"Yeah, but you get a camera at the end."

Get a camera at the end...

"Get outta my face! I'll do a better Yearbook than whatever you got." I looked at his sample, and I went, "Phaaa. Nothing! Get outta here! We're going to do better than that, just from the get-go."

And so, in 1993, Ian was able to single-handedly — after my students logged the footage for him... in the senior section, the junior section, the baseball section, the choir section, the PE section, the *whatever*... launch the video Yearbook.

That allowed us to earn from ten-thousand to twelve-thousand dollars a year. Now, in the days in which we did just concerts, we might make four-thousand a year. My budget was around a hundred dollars; we fundraise four thousand. So, to jump from four-thousand to ten to twelve-thousand, was a huge leap, allowing us to buy much better equipment, to replace some of the older stuff, and such.

I kinda got Ian his first job, at *Sports Channel*. In this case, it was Seth Magdalener. He had been my boss at DiamondVision[7] for a couple years, and had moved on to being a producer at Sports Channel. Sports Channel, I think, later became the Comcast Channel that you watch the A's and the Giants on. You know, they were purchased, and so forth.

The reason I got Ian a job was, I got a phone call from another former student, Chris Gunnerson.

"Chet! I just graduated from…(some school. Doesn't matter.) You said you could help us get a job in the Bay Area."

So I called Seth.

"Funny that you called! Because not only do I need an editor, I might need two."

"Whoa!"

So I set up the interview for Chris Gunderson. He got the job.

Then, I called Ian Williamson to see what he was doing. He was in-between jobs.

"Would you like to work at Sports Channel if I can get you a job there? You'd be editing the A's-lite broadcasts." The "A's-lite" and "Giants-lite" were a little half-hour encapsulation of each game.

"Oh, yeah! Regular work!"

So, I called Seth.

"Uh, listen. I know I just talked to you on the phone, and that we arranged for Chris Gunderson who's coming down. You got a job for him. I got another kid. He's way sharp. I'm not saying sharper than anybody else. I'm just saying he's way sharp. You

---

[7] At the Coliseum.

need this kid on your team. If push came to shove, I think he could probably do both: A's-lite and Giants-lite, if that ever were to come to pass."

And as it turns out, Chris Gunnerson stayed there a few months, then went on to an audio-visual position with a big hotel in San Francisco.

Ian kinda took over both of them, doing the Giants and the A's. It just turned out that way.

But, Ian has helped me out from the beginning. Always there for me. Started the video Yearbook with me. Did a wonderful job.

You know, it's a lonely existence inside an editing suite, all by yourself. The only thing I'd tell him at the end of the day, "Progress."

Progress. When you're doing linear editing, that's all you can hope for, is progress. Because it seems like you're never done. And then you finally are.

Ian is a freelancer, now. His first regular job was the one I got him at Sports Channel. He's had a few other things that he's done. He worked for the Monterey Bay Aquarium, seven or eight years, doing all their video stuff. He made over — almost — two-hundred thousand a year for a while. You can make big money in this industry. It's just getting in and getting your — you know — foot in the door, and... who you know.

For all my recitals, Ian Williamson helped me out. In fact, I was losing money on one, two, three — I dunno — the first five or six. I asked him to underwrite the show. He did. Which means, I would pay him — instead of the standard two-thousand, or twenty-five hundred for video production — you'd get whatever's left. Some years, it was six-hundred... maybe four-hundred... maybe eleven-hundred. Then, when I moved to the Village Theater, I started to get donations — a thousand here, five-hundred there, and so forth — Ah! now the budget was bigger and Ian was rewarded. For a lot of those times, I'd pay him twenty-two to twenty-five hundred. He made some pretty good money. Actually, it was the money he was supposed to make. But at least, I was paying him what he was supposed to get.

Here's Ian's story.

• From Ian Williamson:

> *"I owe the course of my life and career to Chester Farrow. Without his influence as a teacher and mentor in high school and as a friend beyond, I have no idea where I'd be now, but I know I wouldn't be anywhere near as happy and fulfilled with my life.*
>
> *"The idea of the teacher that influences their students for life is common. Then there is Chester. He didn't just teach the subject matter of his classes — he would also teach us about life and being our best individually. To take a class with Chester in high school was to deal with a teacher treating you like an adult with all the expectations that would go along with it.*
>
> *"Much like many of his former students, Chester helped me start my career by recommending me to his former students. That's what he does; he is a mentor at heart who doesn't just inspire you to work hard, but he also puts his reputation out on the line to help you get started. The network of Chester Farrow's students is large and deep, spanning across many generations.*
>
> *"Additionally, and personally, Chester has been a second father figure for me. His support over the years has been incredible. Since I first met him as a teenager, he's been nothing but extremely supportive and always interested in what's going on with me. Chester Farrow remains an inspiration for me, and I forever feel lucky to have him in my life."*

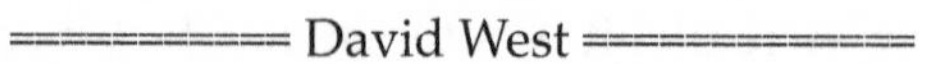

David West

David West graduated in 1998. That's the year before I retired.

So, the students I'm highlighting here… spread between 1972 and 1998.

David West was, like, — right away — caught on with doing lights at Monte Vista. He was in charge of doing the lights — especially for the dance show, which was a big production in May.

So, Pat Caley had an apprentice, so to speak. Well, when you learn from Pat Caley, you learn the correct way. You learn all about lighting. You learn all about power. You learn all about shading. You learn all of those things. In some cases, you both learned together. So, David West had a wonderful opportunity, in which, a resource like Pat Caley was available, because he lived in Pleasanton. If David needed Pat to help out on a drama play or something, Pat would come and help out. David got very good at that.

Then, he kind of spread his wings into TV productions. We even had him in front of the camera, once or twice, which was not his preferred thing to do. But, y'know, at Rainbow Studio, if we're going to have a concert review — somebody went and saw Elton John, and was going to review the concert, maybe they were sick that day. Well, we'd need someone to step in and do a review of some concert. Maybe you read about the Elton John concert and you could summarize it, and whatever we needed, for a one minute segment on the television show. Everyone would roll their up sleeves and help. Did they want to be in front of the camera? Most of 'em, no. But they would do it, because: The Show Must Go On. It wasn't very complicated.

So David ended up being Director for me. He ended up going to the Bammies a couple times.

He couldn't go one time. He was selected to go. He was a director for us. He did a wonderful job… and certainly *deserved* to go.

He came to me.

"I can't go to the Bammies."

"What, are you kidding me!? It's the highlight of the year! What do you mean, you're not going to the Bammies!?"

"Um… I just can't go."

Something — he did something wrong, maybe, at home. I don't know what he could possibly have done wrong. But, he couldn't go.

I tried to persuade him.

"Let me talk to your mother. I'll straighten it out. Y'know, whatever you did… we could forgive and forget. Or… whatever. Or… work on it. Or… c'mon!"

"No, Chet. I just can't go."

And, y'know, he was very honorable in that respect. He loved his mama. He loved… Y'know… he was just a great kid. He took that punishment better than I would take it. I mean, he didn't even fight it. Just… that's it! Can't go!

That was his junior year — I think in the senior year, of course, he went… y'know, the Bay Area Music Awards… headed up our crew. Helped set everything up: lights, camera… all that… even though his expertise — you could say — was in lights. He knew all that. He helped out and did a great job.

I think he works for a lighting company, now. I believe the lighting company makes lights for big time — y'know — Broadway… wherever you need beautiful lights and things. The biggest theaters, the best, expensive equipment, the best that they make.. That's what he does.

He lives in Brentwood, California. But he was not only always there for the shows that I did, but now in retirement, doing the recitals — there was David West, along with Pat Caley… doing our lights.

No one really enjoyed, much, being at the Lesher Theater, because they didn't want our hands on the lights. They didn't... ah!

But the Village Theater, no problem.

I mentioned before, Pat Caley used to be the Executive in Charge of the theater, in Danville — whatever they call that position. He'd book the shows. Made sure everything was working. That was his responsibility. He was paid by the town of Danville.

Pat did a lot of things before he got into the engineering, with the scoreboard displays and all like that.

But anyway, David West — he was what I would call, "The Little Big Man." While only a sophomore in high school — freshman, I dunno — he was already adult. Just good manners. Smart kid. Not argumentative. Eyes wide open. Willing to learn. Wanting to learn.

What more could you possibly ask? He was good! So he ended up directing my TV shows. He did all of those things. In charge of the Bammies? C'mon! Some student has to take over because I can't be backstage at all times with the kids. It's just a fact of life. I got my own seats. I come to watch the show. I'll come back and check on you every half-hour or so. And by "checking on you," just make sure you're alive. Hopefully not bothering anyone... and so forth.

And you know what's funny? We never had a problem at the Bammies. My kids were accepted from the git-go. I told you, we used to get placed right next to MTV. They'd come on down the line — they gotta come by our spot.

We got all the interviews. David West was a very key part of that.

- From David West:

  "Professionalism. That's the number one word that comes to mind when thinking about Chester and TV productions. Sure, for many of us our Chester time

started with Electronics class. For some, as early as Freshman year. However, even then, we were taught about professionalism. It was shown in the way he carried himself in the class and the stories that were passed down. If one was to stick around long enough, they would start to see the TV production students come in and out, feverishly getting equipment for a shoot or stressfully editing a clip for the video Yearbook... all the time though, showing respect for not only Chester but their fellow students and the projects at hand. Over time, various alumni would come in... some to work on live recordings in the studio, others to help repair equipment. All with absolute willingness to teach the next generation. It was in Chester's classes that so many of us learned to work well with others, put out literal fires, and all make sure we did it on time. Now decades later, as both a Lighting Designer and a Sales Representative in the lighting industry, not a project goes by that I don't think about things I learned in Rainbow Studio. It may be as simple as soldering but usually, it's about making sure my actions would make Chester and fellow alumni proud.

"It doesn't hurt that I use the Rainbow Studio backpack I received as a thank you for doing Rock and Roll Recitals for so many years. That backpack travels with me to nearly all my meetings. I wear it proudly, knowing that there are so many out there that may recognize the logo, but also because the logo is such a symbol of high-quality productions. Thank you again for all of this, Chester!"

The "CORE"
L-R:: Michael Coats (1976); Ian Williamson (1994); Mitch Riggin (1985); Seth Worden (1986); John Moore (1978); Michael Baird (1972); Chester Farrow (1967-1999); David West (1998); Pat Caley (1982); Ken Behrens (1976). Photo by Dan Cummins

Chapter 20

CHILDREN'S DAY AROUND THE BAY

Sometime early in 1990, maybe February, January/February, I get a phone call from Michael Coats. Michael is a former student of mine. Think he graduated in '76 from Monte Vista High School.

"KRON, The Mercury News, K-FOG, BAM Magazine, and 7-Eleven are all gonna sponsor 'Children's Day Around The Bay.'"

"That's nice. What is 'Children's Day Around the Bay'?"

"It's a big fundraiser for the Bay Area[1], and the proceeds go to Children's Hospital at Stanford, and the Ronald McDonald House."

"It sounds wonderful. What are you? Why are you calling me?"

"Well, every year they like to have three or four different sites, kinda like hosts at each site. When they're done talking, they might throw it to another host or go to commercial first or so — but it's an all-day… *telethon-thing*, with entertainment."

I think they were at — what was then known as — Sears Point… the Raceway. Steve Page used to work for the A's — and now he's the President. Then it became Infineon Raceway. I think it's *Raceway of Sonoma* now. I guess they race some cars there, for entertainment. Maybe some people get to try out cars. I don't know.

There was going to be a concert. The concert was going to be held at Cal State Hayward. I had successfully put on a concert at Cal State Hayward featuring Greg Kihn, for the student body.

---

[1] San Francisco Bay Area.

It ran just flawlessly, in their gym. Raised a lot of money for the school. They had all the confidence in the world that I could do this.

However, they had a gorgeous football field at Cal State Hayward with an all authentic, synthetic track going all the way around. All eight lanes painted. The relay spots, where you must hand-off — all the lines were in. It hadn't been there but a couple years, if that long. We were going to put a concert stage ninety feet by forty feet in the corner of one of the turns, so that it would face the audience with the biggest grandstand. They had stands on one side and maybe not the other, or big stands on one side and small stands on the other side. But nonetheless, we wanted to reach the big stands where all the people were and also all the way through the lawn, because we had lawn seating. It was a great little show.

<Chester> "Well, it sounds like fun. What do you want me to do?"

"You know Y&T. You know Greg Kihn and those people. Line them up. We want to hire you. You're actually going to get money for doing this."

"Wow!" — 'cause it's very rarely I've ever gotten any money. "All right."

I was the promoter for the show. I worked with a television producer — nice guy — Richard *somethin'*. I forget his name. But anyway, he was in charge of the TV end. I was in charge of arranging entertainment.

I called Scott Booray who was managing Y&T at the time. Scott Booray played in my very first mini-concert that I ever had at Monte Vista High School, with his band called "Copperhead Creek." We've always gotten along real well. I asked him if his band would like to headline... we couldn't pay as much as we normally did, but we could pay. He said yes.

Then I called Victor Rocke to see if The Greg Kihn Band could play. Victor said the band would play. It was on Sunday, June 3rd.

Usually, it's kind of foggy and kinda cold at Cal State Hayward. It was on Friday night, when I brought the overhang that covers the top and sides of the stage. I riveted together yards and yards of shade cloth to make a big giant shade cloth, to put on the overhang.

It was kinda cold that night. We stayed over in Hayward in some hotel — motel. Then Saturday, we erected everything. The stage was already built on Friday. We had to actually place the stage on some of their track.

But it's funny, you put little half-inch plywood squares, three inches by three and four by four inches… put it underneath and the pressure is relieved in many many points because you're doing this at each piece of the construction for the stage.

It's all scaffolding. That's what staging is, is scaffolding. That's what I had to do, arrange all this. I called the scaffolding company. It was in San Jose. I didn't know they had so much scaffolding. I compared prices. The San Jose people were the best. I went with them and learned all kinds of new things.

Putting on a concert outdoors is very different. I did some during the early years at Monte Vista, on our football field.

You understand how outside sucks up all power. Yeah, you got a nice amplifier system. Sounds good inside a gymnasium. Now you bring it outdoors. Oy! Where did it go? The wind blew it away. Y'know. That's why it comes in waves. Sometimes it's windy. Oh, it's crazy.

But believe it or not, the Saturday and the Sunday were drop… dead… gorgeous. Maybe seventy-eight to eighty degrees? No wind. Sun all day. Setting sun was gorgeous, as we were finishing up the concert. Y&T was on stage — backlit by the sun. Just gorgeous.

My co-hosts were Grace Slick and Gary Radnich. And it's funny. I called Gary one time on the radio and asked him how he felt about working with Grace Slick. He remembered me, and remembered — I think — that I was scoreboard operator for the A's.

"We got along great! And you know what? She's a nice gal." She was celebrating her fiftieth birthday. 1990.

They were the co-hosts. The lineup was basically The Greg Kihn Band, Y&T, Big Bang Beat, Rattle Shake, Tramaine Hawkins, Taiko Drums, Chaz Ross. I don't even know these people. I just lined up the two: Y&T and Greg Kihn. I guess maybe somebody brought them along so they could also play or they were their friends. I don't know. We had comedians, too, in between each set, in between bands. Some of you may know these names, I don't know — Dr. Gonzo, Steve Kerry, John Boyle, Sean Murphy, and Marga Gomez.

We decorated with balloons, all filled with helium. Big arcing set of balloons, red, white and blue — over the stage and such. It was a wonderful event.

Then they'd come back and forth.

"Okay. Now we're going to take you out to Cal State Hayward, where… *somebody* is now performing."

They'd cut in live. The band would get some air time, because that's what we promised. We got the okay from the producer? Yeah. Each band will get some time. Kihn and Y&T will get more. Okay.

We had about three thousand, thirty-five hundred there. We charged ten dollars to get in, twelve-fifty at the door. So that was a big house. We raised a lot of money for charity.

Later on, I was presented with a very nice… piece of graphic art. It was presented to me out in Palo Alto. You know, they do everything kinda first-cabin… Stanford. Everything in appreciation, you know, so it was like an expensive framing, an expensive… *whatever*. The artist, Laurel Burch, was there in person. She signed it… Just wonderful.

But nonetheless, everyone had a nice time. The school was happy the way it was run. We did not ruin or do any damage to their track. I understand. Y'know, I used to coach at Monte Vista

High School: football and baseball. It's like, your facilities are everything. When you get a brand new artificial track — Please! What are you doing putting this event on here?

But it's funny. The owner of the scaffolding company assured me that nothing would be — he said, "You'll see nothing when you're done. We've done this before. More than once." Therefore I passed the assurance on to Cal State people. But — I don't know — I'm taking the word of a man. But the man seemed, you know — I never met him; it was on the phone. But he seemed quite knowledgeable, very confident. Everything worked out perfectly.

Everyone made some money, including the bands and the comedians… all of our help. A lot of donated help. Students at Cal State Hayward helped out. Very nice. They got in free and I think they got a T-shirt. That was nice. But I'm just saying they didn't get really paid. The concession stands were going and flowing and just hoppin', because it was a gorgeous, gorgeous weekend. Sunday was the event day. It was… spectacular.

It was a lot of fun being involved with Children's Day Around The Bay.

Chapter 21

Vice-Principal for a Weekend

In the year 1976-77, somewhere right in there — maybe even a little earlier… maybe '75, '4 — a job opening came up at Monte Vista High School for a vice-principal. I decided — kinda on a whim — that I would try out for this job, the reason being, the vice-principal makes more money than a teacher. To start making some extra money, and more money than teaching, I thought I'd try administration. I've got ideas. I've got… y'know, I could do this.

If you wanted to interview for it, you had to go down to the District Office. You'd fill out your papers, and all like that. They'd set up an interview for you. So I went and interviewed. I thought I nailed it pretty good, y'know, for what they wanted.

Very conservative; you gotta be careful with your ideas. But, I had some ideas about keeping roll, keeping track of kids, and such.

I did pretty good. There were about four or five people who tried out. One of them was a guy named Jack Mansfield. Jack Mansfield was a teacher at San Ramon High School for quite a while, then came up to Monte Vista High School. He was a teacher and he applied for the job. Jack Mansfield was ex-marine — maybe twenty years older than me, something like that — really together. Great sense of humor. Would make a great administrator.

So anyway, to make a long story short, we *both* got the job. Now, how do you both have the job? Well, they couldn't — they added up the points at the end of the interviews, and they couldn't distinguish between myself and Jack Mansfield. Felt that both could do a good job, I guess. So, for the first time in — I think ever, in our district — two people get the job. What's that all about?

Here's how they were going to do it: you would teach half-time — like, in the morning — and you'd be the administrator in the afternoon. The other one would be the administrator in the morning, and teach in the afternoon.

You're going to do half-time teaching, which means two — or three — periods. I don't know — exactly know — how many, 'cause usually you teach five at Monte Vista. And so, how you do that in half, I don't know. But… anyway, that was the situation.

So we go in to interview, on a Friday, with the principal — now that we have been selected to be vice-principals. Jack and I were both outside the principal's office, sitting down at Monte Vista. They called my name first.

The principal says, "C'mon in, and we'll get started… get to know everybody —"

You know everybody already, but I'm just saying, you know, they're going to talk about — I dunno what? I guess, responsibilities, and such and…

The principal at that time was a guy named Sam Zackheim. He was from the Los Angeles area, and was… It's funny. He thought of himself as a liberal, but he was a very conservative guy, especially as he got older. Didn't want to take risks. Was always scared (chuckle) of my concerts… "Yikes! Another concert? Eh! What are we going to do now?…" And so forth.

I go in and we sit down. The first thing that Sam Zackheim says to me… is, "Chester! You're on *our* side, now."

Yikes!

I'm on… *your* side? Ay! I don't even understand… "sides." Isn't this a *team* thing? Isn't this… "us trying to help our teachers who are trying to help our students?" I mean, isn't that — ?

These things were going through my mind. My head was a

swirl. It was, like, "What are you talking!?" ... I'm on *this* side now. Aren't we all on the same team?" It was like, kinda weird.

So anyway, I finished the little interview session. He says (to me), "You guys are going to start on Monday, both of you. We'll figure out who does the morning. We're not worried about getting started..." And so forth. "So, enjoy your weekend. We'll get together again, on Monday."

So I left.

"Jack, I think they're going to call you next."

"How'd it go in there?"

"Well... I dunno, Jack. It was all right. Good luck in the interview..." And that's it.

I went home. Over the weekend, I thought about it. I said, "I don't wanna work for this guy. I don't wanna work for any situation — any person, any situation — in which, I'm limited in any way. In which, I'm part of *your* team, but not *their* team." I mean, I don't even understand that.

My mother had arranged for a nice dinner for us to go out. We did, my wife and I, and my mom and dad. They were both still alive. We went out to eat somewhere. Maybe it was the River View Lodge, y'know — I'm not sure — in Antioch. My mother used to work there, for many, many years... as a waitress.

"I dunno if I want to take this job."

"Oh, no! You're crazy! You're an administrator now! You're going to make good money! You'll do a good job! What are you talking about!?"

"Ma! Take it easy! It's just a simple decision. I don't think I want to do it."

"You better go think about it! You know, I dunno. Who raised you!?"

That's always a — heh, *who raised you?* I love that. It's a great phrase. Y'know. But, they're trying to say, "Wow, how strange you are. We don't know you. Where's this thinking process coming from?" But it's just — that's how I am.

I thought about it and thought about it. "I'm not doing this."

So, in our very first meeting, on Monday now, in which we're going to get our assignments and decide and so forth… they did it the same way again… which is, they called me in first, and Jack would be second.

So, I go in… sit down.

Sam Zackheim, the principal, said, "Well, Chet, eh… have you thought about it?… Eh… Are you going to be a member of our team?"

"Sam, I can't do this. This is crazy. I can't work for a situation: 'we'… 'they'… I don't even understand 'we,' 'they.' I thought education was 'us'. We're all in this together… trying to educate our children. But first, we gotta make our teachers happy. If they're happy, they'll do a better job in the classroom… and the kids will get a better education… just because the teachers are happier.

"And you have this divisive, 'you're on our team now…'?

"Sam, I pass. I think the job needs to go to Jack Mansfield. When I leave this office right now, I'm going to tell him it's his, because… I'm out."

I left. I came right to Jack Mansfield.

"Jack! I turned the job down."

And you know what's funny? Jack had mentioned — 'cause he had thought about the same thing that I was thinking about in a way, but he was thinking at a different level: just splitting the job responsibilities to half-time/half-time, each… is crazy. So he didn't want to really be part of that. But now that I had left the scene, it was wide open for a full-time job, for Jack Mansfield.

"Chester! You handed a job — an administrative job — to another teacher at Monte Vista, just like that…?"

Just like that.

He was thrilled. He was shocked. It cleared the way for him. They hired him that day, full time. Which was wonderful.

Now, I saw Jack Mansfield. He showed up at my retirement,

just to say, "Thanks."

I couldn't believe it, after all these years. This was 1999, I retired. 1975, maybe, is when these interviews took place. But he never forgot. He always appreciated. He lived a good life... financially. That's good. He did a good job as administrator — that's even better.

Then, he got afflicted with some kind of muscle... *thing*... I don't know... in a wheelchair after a while, and so forth. So I don't know how long he stayed as an administrator or whatever, but... he was there for my retirement. We hugged, and so forth. He really appreciated what I did. It was no big deal for me. It was an easy turn-down.

You know, it's funny. People wonder, "Why do charter schools get started?"

Because of administrators like that! Because of roadblocks that administrators put up! No wonder people want to start their own charter school! I wanted to start one before there *were* charter schools! "I'll pick the best twenty teachers that I know — fifteen of 'em right off the bat from Monte Vista — and start my own school."

It crossed my mind. I thought about it.

But it's hard. It's not easy getting off the ground in 1975, or whatever — whenever you want to start these things. There were no such thing as charter schools.

And, so... that had to be let go...

But... that was my experience about being vice-principal for a weekend, and I'm sticking to it.

Chapter 22

DISTRICT CONSULTANT

In 1998, a year before I retired, I had no idea I was going to retire.

One of the things that I promised a principal at one of our elementary schools, Tom Ladaceur — he asked me, "Chester, when you have time — I'll pay you for your time, to help us here..."

I never charge for my time, ever, when I worked for — somebody gave me a six-pack once, when I fixed their stereo that was humming, because the turntable wasn't grounded to the amplifier. I connected a wire. The hum went away; he was thrilled. I said, "I don't want anything..."

"I gotta give you something, right?"

"Give me a six-pack, maybe a twelve-pack... something like that."

I don't — I basically just do these things, because.

So he asked, "Could you install a studio for me... to where we have a nice set, couple of microphones, and the kids could do 'The Daily Bulletin' at our school?"

"Tommy, as soon as I get some time, I'll take care of it. Trust me."

"No, no, Chet. I trust you."

My word is my word; so if I tell you I'm going to do something, I do it. It's just that simple. It might not be today. But, in the near future, I'll get to it.

Well, as it turns out, in January of '99, I had made up my mind — as soon as I walked in the classroom, and saw all the changes that were taking place — I'm outta here. Thirty-one and a half years: fantastic. And then you make all these changes, and you don't consult me? You don't let me know? We don't discuss these things? Get outta my face! I'm done. Done!

It was over; anger lasted… a day.

So, my financial advisor — it's someone that the school district brings in, and you pick from one of these people to help you put money away for retirement — I called him up immediately.

"Let's get together."

"Uh, why, Chet?"

"'Cause I'm thinking about retirement."

"When you thinking, Chet?"

"I dunno. June of '99, I'll be done."

I was, and it worked out. I was making — I make enough money every month to make ends meet — plus some. Having the A's job is a godsend: just, fills in all the blanks, and more.

So, turns out I retire in '99, in June. I'm all done. 'Bout ready to go home for… the next *whatever* years. Hope I make five, maybe ten years, in retirement. '99… I dunno…

I'm at twenty years. I'm way — everything I've ever done is way longer than I deserve to have, you know.

So, I was working at the elementary school installing the studio for Tom. Really all I'm doing is interrupting the Comcast feed, putting that into an A/B switch: "A" — flip it on "A" — that will be your regular Comcast TV that goes into the teacher's classroom. Flip it on "B" — ahh! Now, you've flipped on our studio.

The feed that comes from our camera — or cameras — now goes to that output — you know, out of the mixer, whatever you want to call it — that's basically how you set up a separate station.

Whenever they wanted to do a 'Daily Bulletin,' then you just flip that one switch, and on the teachers' TVs will be your channel — if the TV is on, and it's on channel three or four, then whatever channel we're using — you're live, and everything's good.

While I was installing this for Tom Ladaceur, a fellow named John Threshie came by. John Threshie was a former student of Monte Vista… from way back. I think he was in the — I was still coaching… no, I had just left coaching. So maybe '73, '74… I forget what year his was.

But he remembered me, he liked me, and he saw the work that I was doing for Tom.

"Listen, we want to hire you as a consultant for the district, to do exactly what you're doing at all the elementary, intermediate, and high schools."

"John, you want to hire me as a consultant? I haven't even retired yet." In fact, I really didn't retire until July 1, and this was in June of '99. "I'm not really retired yet."

"What would it cost me to hire you?"

I thought for a minute. Without even — that's it. There was no question about it.

"I'll give you a deal: a hundred and twenty-five an hour."

Now, have I ever been paid a hundred and twenty-five an hour? But I mean, that's a lot of money: a hundred and twenty-five an hour. So… no, I've never been paid a hundred and twenty-five an hour.

"Chester, I can't afford one twenty-five. I could afford a hundred."

"John, I'll make you a deal. I'll start at a hundred. Then, when you think that I'm worth one twenty-five, let the future checks reflect that: pay me at a hundred and twenty-five. If I never reach one twenty-five, I didn't do my job."

"You got a deal."

Well, now… I can't do this work alone. I was able to do it, but it's hot and it's sweaty, and you have to be on a ladder, and all these things… It's like — I forget — I think I was fifty-six at the time.

But, me and heat — we don't do too well. When I play softball, I melt at 80º. The other day was 90º, I think. I think later in the day, it got to 90º, but I — you know. I'm not saying it almost killed me, but it took away all my energy.

But nonetheless, I got a hold of a former student of mine, Pat Caley. He was an integral part of the Rainbow Studio. So, I hired him.

"Pat, listen. We could work on weekends. We'll work around your schedule... after school, whenever you want. We'll start knocking out these schools. We'll make each studio that we do — each control room that we have — even better than the first, 'cause we'll learn as we go along."

And we did. We did a wonderful job. Pat Caley would do most of all the connecting of the cables. These are — most of the stuff is now digital. I don't know from digital — from a USB port — from anything. I've said this before, I'll say it again: I'm an analog man in a digital world. And it's just fine. The geese look just as pretty in this digital world as they did twenty-five years ago in the analog world. The sun is just as bright. The sky is just as blue. No change. Not for the things that matter to me.

By the way, every contract, every deal I ever made — or flubbed — over all these years... this book that I'm working on... all done by phone. Never met the guy who's going to — I forget, what do they call it? Ghost-write — yeah, yeah yeah: never met him. A Bay Area guy, great guy. Steve Wagner. Ever meet him? I did, finally. He flew out here. We chatted for the day; had a good time. He went back after seeing his girlfriend for a few days up on the coast. Nice little trip. He went back to — I think — Missouri or somewhere there... I dunno.

But, my transcriber... he's in Oregon. Haven't seen him in five years. Been a long time. Larry Goldman.

How are we doing all this? Phone!

He takes over my computer and we do it on the Internet. He just tells me, "Plug the back of your little recorder into the computer, and I'll do the rest." And he does. Then he says, "I'm done." Then he starts transcribing.

So all this latest: Twitter... Zitter... doesn't matter to me. Same phone number I've always had. Not going anywhere. You want to get ahold of me, you know where I am: in the phone book, even. I don't even think they *make* a phone book anymore.

But I digress.

So, Pat Caley essentially was all the backbone of our little business. I paid him by the hour. We worked for about five, six years... mostly, like, during the summer... especially when the teachers weren't there. You got to run cable and such — wonderful time to do it. There's a custodian, maybe, and a librarian there, in the summer.

Unless they have summer school. It's easy to work around; summer school's over by noon. So you start the day at one, you work till seven — you know, whatever you need to do. Just easy to work around.

After so many years, then, John Threshie kinda had to tell me — he said, "Chester, consultants are last-hired, first-fired."

I was making around a hundred hours. I'd do contracts at a hundred hours. So there may be one contract — could be two contracts — a year, I dunno. Normally one. So it's about $12,500, for the year... working during the summer times.

Then you'd go over there, like if somebody's having a problem. Pat and I would go, we'd meet, and we'd resolve their problem — usually it was a connector somewhere that had gone bad. Hmm... occasionally a solder connection, and so forth. But, normal wear and tear — especially with kids.

But, see, not only did we install, we taught them how to do a production. We showed 'em who directs, who the TD[1] was, who the audio person was — all of that stuff — floor manager... your talent. What're you gonna do for a set?

<Student> "Well... we're just going to —"

---

[1] Technical Director

"That looks kind of hokey. Why don't you dress it up a little bit?"

And they would. It was a great little thing for those schools that wanted Daily Bulletins.

Now the thing is, we didn't even have that ability at Monte Vista High School. There was no way for me to really tap-in, other than to go into the closet and do it. The school didn't want it — it was weird. So at my own school, I didn't have a thing to where I could broadcast to every classroom. And I taught television production. Go figure.

It's all right. You know, sometimes you don't get a lot of cooperation. Sometimes your dreams are shot down by those... who like the status-quo. Takes a lot of guts to be an administrator and forward-think. Forward-thinking might get you fired. There's always that. Forward-thinking might get you fired.

I understand: a lot of pressure, especially when they say, "No, we don't want that. No, we don't think it's a good idea at any of the schools."

Then you say, as the administrator, "Well, *I* think it *is* a good thing."

How long you think you last? You might last the year.

But they'll be looking for someone more *cooperative*... immediately.

That's one of the things that's very sad about education. When I first started at Monte Vista, it was an experimental school. Anything went.

You want to bring in the Black Panthers? Bring 'em. They came to our library. They talked... power salutes and all.

Simultaneously, I'm with Justin Herman, Executive Director of the Redevelopment Agency in San Francisco. We're in the small Science Theater. Another hundred and eighty people — packed — to see what this man has to say.

That's taking chances.

They named a plaza after Justin Herman. Now, they took it away for his work done in the Western Addition. He had a different style; I couldn't work for the man. But I was — he offered me work. He didn't believe in getting input from the community. Nothing. Bulldoze! Get out! Get out! Bulldoze! Rebuild! Bring back!

It's probably one of the worst examples of urban renewal thinking... in my lifetime.

They took the name of this plaza away. There's no more "Justin Herman Plaza." I don't know all the politics, but — I dunno — some people in San Francisco didn't like what he did. I didn't like what he did; but I'm just "Chester"... it don't matter.

They took away his name and all of that.

But anyway, John Threshie came to me, after about five, six years.

"Chester, last-hired, first-fired: We gotta let you go."

By that time, we had done just about every elementary and junior high school, but we hadn't yet touched the high schools. Somehow, the high schools got grants and kind of put in their own expensive hundred and fifty thousand dollar program... two-hundred thousand... floor cameras, three-chip — or three-tube in those days. But anyway, just... Wow! After I leave, they upscale at the high school. Pretty good.

Why is that? I dunno. I quit wondering about it... uh, in 1999.

So, what happened then? Okay. Well, we don't do that anymore. We're all done. You're a consultant: you work for a while, then you don't.

Pat Caley then went on to install the big video boards at the Giants' stadium — I think it was called "AT&T Park"[2] at the time. He installed the big boards — two of them — at the Oakland Coliseum, about four years ago, three years ago. He was the Project Manager — on-site. The *Man.*

... Former student of Monte Vista High School, with training

---

[2] "Pac Bell Park," maybe.

in the consultant business, installing studios for elementary, middle — but not the high school.

What's the difference? Let's go like this: ten-million dollar installation. The finest cameras and lenses; maybe two hundred-thousand dollars, each set-up. Maybe you got five. That's a mill, already. Whoo! More than that! Wow! A million, two-five! Very good. We do the same thing at the schools, for… a thousand, fifteen-hundred. Couple of small cameras, whatever, they got the cables. They go into an inexpensive mixer. What does a mixer cost, for example?

At the Coliseum, where this beautiful installation is: ten million dollar board… and another million dollars on the PA system and… Wow! Really upgrading.

Pat Caley parlayed the work we did as a consultant to becoming Project Manager of many big installations on the West Coast. He's kind of calmed it down a little bit — just back to engineering and so forth. Doesn't necessarily need the responsibilities anymore… He saves his money, which is a very good thing. He's an Eagle Scout.

But, I had a lot of fun, got a chance to watch a former student of mine climb the ladder… to the top. There's nothing bigger than the installations at the Coliseum, or the new Oracle park, or the old AT&T. It doesn't matter.

Don't get any bigger than that.

More of the same. But it's still top of the food chain. These aren't five-hundred dollar cameras including lenses, that we're talking about. All expensive. All top-of-the-line. You're expected to have the outcome to be flawless. Ten million dollars worth of gear, and it's up to you.

You look at Pat Caley's work right now at the Coliseum: it's got the consultant job that he had with me, all over it.

We started out, I said, "Pat, you got to label these things really good at the ends. Where does this go… right here?"

"Well, I put a mark *thing* on —"

"Well…"

So he buys labelers and things… now, everything is marked. A village idiot could wring it out, find out where it goes… find that it's patched-in in the wrong place. Um-humm.

All came from that program. And you know what? We had fun, too.

Chapter 23

Break-in at Rainbow Studio

In the late '70s, maybe 1977-78, our wonderful little control room that was next to the classroom which was used as a studio, so that we could record bands... was broken into.

How'd they get in? Well, they went in through the wall. There was an outside wall that was in the drafting class...

I kinda knew who the two were that were involved, but I could never pin it on 'em. But I know who they were. One of 'em was a fat slob. The other one was some skinny guy. I never liked 'em from the git-go. I could never prove that they did it. But in my heart of hearts, I knew who did it.

They took all my good stuff. Monitor speakers. These were studio monitor speakers, like in a professional recording studio. No different than that at Wally Heiders'... *His Master's Wheels... The Record Plant*. Doesn't matter. Your finest recording studios', is what we had. The same thing.

Our amplifier was a *McIntosh 2100*. All tube. Fifty watts a side. Very powerful. Very quiet. *Gone.*

They took my mixing console. Outta here! — Yikes!

They took my tape decks. Ay, ay, yai!

Thousands of dollars of equipment were stolen.

It was done over a weekend. We came to find it on a Monday morning. Big hole in the wall, and so forth.

Well, we reinforced everything. We put rebar everywhere. We reinforced the doors. Bought alarms. We were the first facility in the San Ramon Valley Unified School District to have alarms. They said, like, "We budgeted for it. Then in a couple years..."

"I can't wait one year. I can't wait one day. I'm gettin' an alarm company... *now*. I'll do it on my own. It will serve this school."

I didn't care.

The district went ahead and paid for it, as well as expanding it to all the other schools that had equipment worth stealing. Eventually, the entire District was alarmed. That's a wonderful thing.

But it didn't help us out.

Well, it turns out that the equipment... some of it was found. They suspected these guys. They went to their house. It turned out... that a lot of the stolen equipment was found. Not just mine, but from other places.

I had to go to court in Redwood City, because that's where they discovered it.

So, I go to Redwood City. I go to court. The district attorney says, "Mr. Farrow, can you identify this?"

"Yes, that's my — that's our thing. Take a look underneath: it's engraved..."

He'd flip it over. "Oh, here it is: 'Monte Vista High School... Rainbow Studio.' Rainbow Studio."

So I got half of my equipment back.

Then I looked at the two perpetrators, or whatever you call 'em. I said right to their faces, "Where's my Mc 2100? That's a vintage amplifier. It's not here!? What'd you do, sell it for a hundred bucks!? C'mon on, now!"

I guess they were found guilty, and all like that. That was nice.

I was going to go home now. I got some of my equipment back. I had my little Toyota pickup truck. It fit in easily, with plenty of room to spare. Got my speakers back. Very nice. Very nice.

As I'm leaving, this detective — I didn't know he was a detective at the time, but — he comes up to me.

"Can we talk outside for a moment?"

<Chester, to himself> "Oh, wow! Maybe I'm in trouble or somethin'. Maybe I shouldn't have talked directly to the defendants about my Mc 2100. I dunno."

"Chester, listen, we have a problem, maybe you could help us with."

"The police? Uh… What could I do?"

We were outside for a reason.

"Chester, we think the interview rooms are bugged. In fact, Chester, we *know* they're bugged. It goes straight to the chief of police of Redwood City."

Now, I would name that chief of police, if I knew what his name was. All I could barely remember was, it was around 1977… '78. So whoever was chief of police, they didn't trust him. "They're bugging their rooms," is what the detective said.

"What do you want me to do?"

"I want you to go inside this, right —"

He was very — we were sure not to be within microphone range. We were outside. He was pointing…

"… in through that door, we're gonna go. It's in there."

I think it was Interview Room "B". There were about three or four of 'em in a row, in Redwood City. They're all the same, just like you see on TV. There's a table, there's a — *whatever*. There could be a recorder going as someone was talking… and so forth.

"Well, I'm going to need a few tools."

"Anything."

"I could start with a couple of screwdrivers, one, a regular screwdriver, one, a Phillips. I dunno. We'll start with that…"

'Cause I'm not going to delve too deep into his situation.

So, I go in the room with my little screwdrivers in my pocket. I entered the room and closed the door. I thought it real weird — which was, "I'm being listened to, maybe, as we speak."

So, I made sure to make very little-to-no noise. I did not speak while in the room.

The detective was waiting outside. He was kinda smoking. Kinda pacing.

I even told him, "This may take a while. I dunno."

"Whatever you could do. We won't forget that you helped us."

Now, those words, ... *we won't forget that you helped us...* was a nice incentive. They're not going to pay me cash — they're just cops... same as teachers — we don't make money. Where're you gonna get money?

But, I don't know, you might — maybe he owes me a favor, after, or somethin'. Then sometime I'm in Redwood City, maybe I get a "*get out of jail free*" card. I dunno.

It was an adventure... just like life itself. I don't know what's going to happen. Let's go find out.

So I walked into the room. I scoped it out. What was I looking for? I'm looking for... electrical outlets. Are they located approximately like in your home, like in most businesses? About a foot, or a hammer's-length, off the floor? *There* was one. *There* was one. *There* was one. *There* was one — just like it should be.

But what a minute, against this wall, to my left... was a table. On the table was... *nothing*. Just, a table against the wall. Just above the table, was an electrical outlet. That means the outlet is about three-and-a-half to four feet off the floor. What's *that* doing there?

At first, I thought, "Well, wait a minute — that makes sense. They might put a recorder on the table, there. Then they — we gotta plug the recorder into something." It's not like today, the little recorder I'm using to write this book — seventy-nine dollar, Sony. It does everything. It's fabulous.

But it made sense, that maybe it was there for that reason. But, I wanted to take a look. Ah! I take a look. It's just: non-Phillips, regular slot screw.

So I used that screwdriver. I took the cover plate off.

Something looked way weird.

The electrical outlets themselves — the actual device that you buy at *Ace* or *Home Depot* or *whatever* — was... it didn't have the *depth* that it's supposed to have. They're generally about three-quarters of an inch thick. This was like... I don't know. It looked *suspicious*.

I removed further. These weren't electrical outlets at all! It was a built-in microphone, that went somewhere.

Yikes! Eureka! I have found it!

I was completely surprised. But yet, I wasn't. They said it was bugged.

It was a neat little device, too. The microphone kind of fit right — it's like something you could buy — maybe a few years later — at *Radio Shack*... in your little "New Releases" ads that are in *Sportsman's Magazine*, or, I don't know — *whatever... Spy Magazine... something...*

You could buy one of these. You'd just install it. Put your microphone in and... send the signal somewhere. And you're bugging it. You'd record it. Kinda ingenious.

I put everything back together, the way it was. Went outside... By then, the detective had smoked five, eight, cigarettes. I don't know. I went outside to meet him.

"Chet! Did you find anything at all?"

"Yeah, I did. I found your microphone."

I told him what happened. I told him where it was located.

"That signal must be going up to the chief of police. You say the chief knows everything that you're doing, even before you do it? That's what made you suspicious? Well, there you go. Follow this wire. You'll find that it goes somewhere, maybe in a closet, with the chief of police. I dunno."

His face beamed. *Beamed*. Holy criminy! They knew that they were being bugged. They couldn't find the bug. Here, this high school teacher of electronics and TV productions... finds the bug. With a screwdriver. It wasn't that complicated. They hadn't thought to do that. They just assumed that that was a good outlet. It wasn't; it was just camouflage.

He says, "Come with me."

Then the detective was like — he lit up another cigarette, smoked it like... he was like... on cloud nine. Oh, man! He couldn't wait to tell his fellow police officers what we found.

"Come in this room with me."

We go in the room.

"I know you want that Mc 2100. The Mc 2100, as you know, is not here. But is there anything else in here, that you might like? Anything at all."

Wow! I'll take these speakers. I'll take these two amplifiers. I'll take *this* mixer, and *this* mixer.

Oh, yeah! I'll take these microphones. Oh, yeah.

So, not only did we refresh all of our stolen equipment which was gone. We were now better for it.

All thanks to that bug... in the Redwood City Police Department.

My, my.

Chapter 24

Longs Drugs Ripoff

One day at Monte Vista High School, I got a call in the afternoon. It was a secretary of — Steve Long. He was the owner of Longs Drugs here in Walnut Creek. They also have one in... Maui — a Longs Drugs — still goin'. But the current one in Walnut Creek is now a *CVS*.

This was circa 1980. I know it wasn't the '70s. I don't think it was as late as the '90s.

But anyway, I got a phone call from Steve Long.

"Chester, listen. We have a problem here at Longs Drugs."

"What kind of problem?"

"We bought a lot of Christmas tree lights."

This was like, in October, maybe. It's funny, we had just had a back-to-school night, a couple of weeks earlier. Steve Long was there. Why? He had a couple — maybe three — sons, they all had my class. One of 'em was currently in the class. So he came to see what I intended to do that year. That's what back-to-school night was all about. He felt I had my stuff together. I don't know why he called me.

"Chester, we bought a bunch of Christmas tree lights... It says you could string ten of them together. Ten strings together."

"Wow! Very nice. So what's the problem?"

"After we hook up two or three, they blow out. They have fuses in 'em, and they go out. We'd like you to come to the store — to the office, actually, on Civic Drive in Walnut Creek..." I've only been there a couple of times, just to see Steve. But, anyway.

"Well, I'll come to the store — I mean, to the office — and check it out."

And so, I did. What I found was lots of lights strewn all over the floor. There were three or four people in there, kinda plugging 'em in, kinda — they were all in disarray. What's going on?

He tells me that the investment in the lights was over $50,000. Now he's got a problem. How to get his money back. Some of his money — I guess — was already paid. Then some — I don't know. It was very expensive and they were not working.

"Chester, anything that you could do to help us correct this situation and find out where the problem is... I'd really appreciate it."

"All right. Give me a set of lights with — "

"Nooo! Take... twenty sets. Play with them. Put them together. Find out what's wrong."

"All right. I will."

It turns out they were — they were *under-fused*. When you linked these together, then, every time you plugged in another string of lights, because they were in parallel with each other, you were drawing more current. What happened was, they had about a two-and-a-half amp fuse — maybe it was just a two amp fuse. You hooked two or three strings together, it had no chance. It was just too much current. I don't know why they even said you could do ten strings. I didn't understand.

The wire was heavy enough. It was just... if the fuses were the correct sizes, then several strings could be hooked together. Ten? I don't know about ten, 'cause you'd have to have a big fuse on each string.

That was just the first thing I found. All right. But, we already knew that, didn't we. We knew that the lights didn't work once you plug in two, three, four strings — sometimes, two — it'd blow out the fuse. Sometimes it took five, to blow out the fuse.

I was digging for something more.

I don't know if you've ever noticed, but on electrical items, there's a li'l tag that says, "UL". It stands for "Underwriter

Laboratories." What they do is they test all of this lighting, and such, to make sure that it's up to snuff. According to the UL, Underwriter Laboratories, it gave their seal of approval.

"Wow! How could Underwriter Laboratories give their seal of approval to lights that can not be strung together with ten sets of lights, even though it says it can?"

I jotted down the number on Underwriter Laboratories' tag, and I called Underwriter Laboratories. A lady answered.

"How could I help you?"

"I have a string of Christmas tree lights here. I'm just wondering if it's really been UL approved. It has your seal on it. There's your tag, 'Underwriter Laboratories,' with the circle around it — standard procedure — but I can't believe that you guys authorized this, that you have said that it was fine."

"Do you have the number, for the Underwriter Laboratories?"

"I do." So I gave her the number.

She looked it up. "That company is defunct. Out of business. This tag is no longer legal, or binding."

"Oh! Thank you very much."

"Who is this? What product are we talking about?"

I hung up.

I didn't want to go into the investigation, and all like that. All I wanted to do was to verify that they had no UL number. They did not.

So I called Steve. I told him what I found out. He said come to the office. That was the second time I was at the office. I've only been there a couple times.

I told him what I had found out. I showed him what I was talking about. We went over the UL number. It was not certified. This was phony. It was a defunct number that they were using. You were being scammed.

"Wow!" Steve smiled. "Thank you, Chester. Thank you for doing this research."

He was very effusive in his praise. I hadn't done that much. But I just did what I could.

"Chester, we want to pay you for your research. Anything. Whatever it takes."

I was thinking twenty-five hundred, maybe... Then I said to myself, "Self? C'mon. You did about an hour's worth of research — maybe two — finding out the current drain for the several strings of lights. That took a while. But the UL information was — that was gleaned in a fifteen-minute phone conversation. Done."

So I said, "How about a $500 dollar gift certificate from Longs Drugs for my wife?"

"Done!"

It was a great little Christmas for us, because $500? Longs Drugs had some nice things that you could give as gifts and such — besides food, and all like that.

But, that's how we solved the Longs Drugs ripoff.

Chapter 25

My A's Years

When I first got hired by the Oakland A's in 1969, I got hired along with Ray Crawford. Ray Crawford was a coach – like I was – and a teacher. He eventually went on to become an administrator, and a superintendent, I think, up in the Oregon schools; I'm not exactly sure where. We had a great time for about five years, working as a pair.

But lemme just kinda tell you where I sit, how it goes, what I do, and those kind of things.

In that very first year, and then for the next ten years – eleven years – there was just four of us in the room. Our room was located, basically, just above Section 217… just a little bit to the third base side of home plate. Wonderful view. We were right next to visiting radio, which was right next to visiting TV, which was right next to home radio, which was right next to home TV.

That's kinda how it breaks down.

"Chester, are you saying that all the announcers and such are basically right behind home plate?"

Yep. Just above Section 216, right in there. Right behind home plate.

Some are to the first base side and a couple are to the third base side of home plate. All the announcers have great views.

The press have wonderful views. They're not right behind home plate. They're kinda more down to the first base line. Auxiliary press, down the third base line, but still wonderful views.

There were just four of us in the room.

The sound guy, whoever that might be — or gal... but in those days, there was no gal; there still isn't, I don't think, doing the audio for the Coliseum. But somebody has to oversee the power and make sure that the amplifiers are working, the speakers are working. This was the responsibility of the Coliseum. Bill Gentry was one, Fordi Ramirez was another, Red O'Dell was another. They're all great guys. We used to chat and talk all the time, because there's — y'know — about twenty seconds in between pitches. So it's very easy to converse... everybody kind of shuts up when the pitch is happening, so that I could focus. But, that's about it. After a while, you learn to talk and keep score and all of that, all at once.

There was also the organ player, who for many years was Lloyd Fox.

Our announcer was Roy Steele. He came in '68. I first met him in 1969. For those of you who never have seen Roy Steele, he used to be like five-ten, five-nine, two-thirty?... powerfully-built man. He used to work out in college with the weights. I think he played football in JC[1]. Roy was a minister, and later... kinda gave that up, and broadened things... He was the announcer for the water ski show[2] in Redwood City. And, oh, for the Oakland A's. Also, the announcer for the Warriors, in the early days. I think also he did hockey. Mr. Finley brought a hockey team here. So, Roy had a lot of experience, and some income.

Then there was me and Ray Crawford. So what is that?... Five in the booth.

We're located today — we're, like, right above 221. Further away, making it a little more difficult for me to see the right arm of the umpire, because basically, I do balls and strikes now.

---

[1] Junior College.

[2] Marine World in Redwood City:
http://www.redwoodcityhistory.org/blog/2017/3/10/zm6utap2wmxcyjo4b15w4yorx8utsn

But anyway, let's go back to the early years.

We don't have an organ player anymore… Well, we have Jack. He comes in on Sundays, and — you know — performs in between innings, and maybe during a rally. Evidently, according to the union, you have to have an organ player on-site and/or pay for an organ player. In those days, I wasn't really too involved.

That was it for about eleven years.

I brought candy. In the early days, we'd bring beer! We'd have beer on ice, in an ice chest. How could you do that? Well, wait a minute — one of the things that we had with Mr. Finley, in the early years — from '69 to about '75 — not only was our dinner catered — and a delicious dinner and nutritious and delicious, from *Maraglia Catering*; I believe, maybe they were out of San Leandro — but, we had an open bar! The bartender's name was Joe Beckius. Y'know, the old phrase, "…set 'em up, Joe!" It was open two hours before the game. That's when they opened the Press Lounge so that we could go eat, before the game.

By the way, let me just stop for a moment. When do you ever get fed when you go to work? Think about that. A full, sumptuous meal… sit down… relax… cocktails… wine… beer. It was, like, assumed that you're going to have some libation before the game. Now, wait a minute. After the game, it was open for another couple hours. Well, who gathers around the bartender there? I don't know… Mel Allen, from the Yankees… Harry Caray — he worked for us for a while, for a year. All the big names in broadcasting and play-by-play people. The national press. They'd stand around and just tell stories. All night long.

I kept looking at my watch… time to go. Why? I'm a high school teacher! I gotta get outta there! Our games — in the early days — started at eight o'clock, not seven, like today. Eight! You didn't get through till eleven… eleven-fifteen. Now, you're gonna go down, have a few drinks, and get on the road? Yikes!

But that's kinda how it was. Then it faded away… and that's a good thing. Now, there's no drinking in the booth. No, none of that. Very nice.

I think once a year, we have beers… we kinda celebrate. During the last homestand, there's a fireworks night. So we get some food from the *New Mecca Cafe* — they donate it. They bring a case of beer, too.

There are twenty-five of us — at least, now — that work… more! Camera people, camera cable haulers, all the… y'know. There's a lot of people now. But, that's the only time we have beer. It's a fireworks game and… there's a half-hour — or a little more, even — between the end of the game and the start of the fireworks. This allows the camera people, and such, to all come up and have a bite to eat. All we have is burritos and beer. That's our lone, "have a beer" day. So, it's pretty civil, pretty straightforward up there.

But in the early days, it was just the four of us. There were no rules. We had no bosses — I mean, our boss was… Mr. Finley. He was always in Chicago. So, it was pretty easy and straightforward…

But, here are some things — maybe — that you'd like to read, or hear about.

I never even thought about it. I mean, I've thought about it, but we've never calculated lately… Let's say there's 300 pitches a game — that's about average. Might be 297, but it's around 300. And, let's say you did 84 games a year.

"Chet! It's only 81 on the schedule."

Yeah, but with the Giants[3], and then any playoffs over the years and World Series… So, you throw all those extra games in… Let's just call it 84.

I've completed 50 years.

---

[3] The annual pre-season finale "Bay Bridge Series," Oakland A's versus San Francisco Giants.

I didn't start out at the beginning of the year last year, 2018. I had surgery, and the recovery time was like... took me a long time to recover. So, I didn't come back till June 7th, last year.

It's roughly 50 years. So, you multiply 300, times 84, times 50... comes to 1,260,000 pitches. That's how many pitches I've recorded. Not just watched, but recorded. In other words, by "recording", you've gotta call it a ball... you've gotta call it a strike... fly out... ground out... fielder's choice... double play... line out — whatever it is — pop foul, y'know.

The total games — this surprised me — was a much smaller number than I thought, 50 years, 84 games a year... 4,200. That's how many games that I've observed.

"Chet! Have you missed any games?"

Well, when my father passed, and then my mother passed... those two, I took some time off. I might have missed a game or two. But, other than my surgery — basically, no. I've done almost all of them.

Also, we found this out about a couple of years ago, that I'm the senior computerized scoreboard operator in the major leagues, by about four to five years. The way we know this is that some emails went around with the organization that is all the scoreboard supervisors. They all go to this meeting — maybe in Las Vegas, or something — and they exchange ideas, talk about new things they want to do, and such.

They're all connected on email. I think the Baltimore Orioles sent an email out which was, "We have a guy that'll be celebrating his thirtieth year..." At that time, I had forty-five, or forty-six. "He's celebrating his thirtieth year. Is he the longest-tenured scoreboard operator in the majors?"

Someone else responded, "We have someone at thirty-six." The highest was — I think, at that time — forty, or forty-one... and I was forty-five, or forty-six. So, that's a little tidbit, y'know.

I could actually say, "Hey! I've been running computerized scoreboards for the major leagues longer than anybody in history."

It's funny. I've done a lot of things over the years. You never think about what you do or what you've done... until you write a book. Then, you see it in black and white. I'm not writing it; I'm just talking... but I mean, you think about it... then you get the pencil out... and you start *multiplying*... and... wha—? You find these numbers out. You go, "Wow! That's fantastic!"

"Chet! After all these 1,260,000 pitches you've watched... you have a good time up there?"

Wonderful.

First of all, I love baseball. Love watching it. Love playin' it. So that helps... a lot.

Some of the people that work — and they're supposed to get the crowd kinda fired up and stuff — they don't feel that maybe a rally is coming. There's really no way to — well, we'll talk about that.

First of all... I loved it... loved playing it... love watching it.

You kibbitz all the time... We've talked about everything from, y'know, rainbows... to laundry detergent — doesn't matter, you name it. We'll talk about anything, at any time. It doesn't matter.

By the way, one of the things I do from time to time: break out in song. Just... you know... Why? Because it's fun.

Do some people laugh? Yeah.

Do some people find it annoying? Ah... I dunno; I never thought about it.

We're all just having a good time.

It's just like fans in the stands — break out in song when you want to. Isn't that wonderful? You could do all that at a baseball game? Fantastic.

So. My view is fabulous. The pay is good. In the early days — like I say — there were just the four of us...

By the way, it *could* get a little boring, especially — like — on a Sunday... day game. Oh, how about a doubleheader on

Sunday? Ay! So you're tired. Everything's dragging. Nobody feels like conversing. We're just enduring.

"Chet! You mean, in the old days, you didn't consider a doubleheader, like, wow, something extra?"

No. Never have.

I played some tournament softball — you gotta go play three, four games a day! After one game. I'm shot!

"Wha- We got more?"

"Yeah, you gotta rest for an hour. And then we're going to play again."

Ay, ay, yai! Y'know.

So doubleheaders are just a drag. They're no fun for anybody. Now, don't get me wrong. The players, they take off the old uniform… they put on fresh clothes again. They look sparkling, ready to go. But, c'mon. They're tired. I'm tired. We're all tired. Yet, we have another game to do. Uch!

Thank God there aren't very many doubleheaders anymore. At least, not really *scheduled*. Now, if there's a rainout, then… you have to make up that game. They want everyone to play 162 at the end of the year.

"Chet! Uh… my… my favorite Padres… uh… they only finished 161 last year!"

Yeah, because they're in last place. Their (makeup) game was insignificant to the team that they had to play. So it didn't matter to either team. You're not going anywhere. One's a fifth-place team, one's a fourth-place team. Then they don't play it. But that's the only reason they wouldn't play it… is that, it was clearly, both teams were out of it. It's insignificant to either.

So, let's move on now to… my software that I use. When I first started, it was a company called Information Concepts, Incorporated… ICI. They wrote a wonderful program. They wrote two programs — there were two guys: one did baseball, and one did messages. I don't think I mentioned: I did both things for the scoreboard for about fifteen years. All the rally messages that you saw in 1969, '70, '71… all those things… when I would start a rally in the first inning… That was me.

Only thing I didn't put on the board was, who the scoreboard operator was. Speaking of putting it on the board, I think I was in a program[4]… once. Mr. Finley put me in, in 1973. So, if you go to the program to find out who the scoreboard operator is… not there.

"Chet! Did you ever say anything to them?"

Nope. It doesn't matter! I'm doing it. I'm enjoying it. I don't need the notoriety. I'm not doing it for notoriety.

The two fellows from Information Concepts, Incorporated – while they were developing the software, right in front of our faces, as we were being trained, in very early April of 1969 – they would ask us… 'cause Ray and I both played ball, Ray Crawford and I – They would say, like, "When a guy is on first, and the next guy gets a single, don't you think that most of the time the guy from first goes to second?"

"Oh, absolutely."

You know, you gotta have like a big heavyweight guy at bat, maybe left-handed, with a man on first… and he pulls it down the right-field line. Okay, when you pull it down the right-field line and it's fair, the guy from first usually goes to third. If the runner's not fast, he can't get a double out of it – only a single. So, for most all situations, a single will put the guy on second.

I said, "If there's an exception, let's put '+' right next to it: which is… "H", space – "H" for "hit" – "H" space "1"… "+". The "+" is a baserunning code. So, instead of the guy going to – just second, we put, "1+".

Therefore, "H 1+" means: the runner not only goes to second, he also goes to third.

"Chet! For some reason, would there be a thing called, 'H 1++'?"

Yeah. Guy gets a single. That's a single, "H 1", and the

---

[4] The printed baseball program sold to fans at games.

baserunner — assuming, that he would go to second — the first "+" says, "Oh, no, he went to third," and the second "+" says, "No, he came on home." I don't mean to be very complicated here, but it's pretty straightforward.

That was the software that we started with. That's the software that we used... into the '80s.

Then a gentleman named Larry Goldman came on board. He upgraded everything that we did, computer-wise.

First thing we did was we abandoned the IBM 1131. By that time the hard drive maybe — maybe — had two-million bytes — you know, two megabytes. That's it. When we first started, the IBM 1131 had five-hundred-thousand, "500K", for memory. If you tried to do any kind of animation, n' stuff, it just chewed up all of your memory. But it worked good enough for static messages, like, "Today's Lineup" — home team, visitors. Those are on separate files, so to speak.

Then, Larry came on board. He used an Apple ///. What we did is, he wrote the software — the best software I've ever used — from just talking to me. Larry didn't know baseball, *per se*. He's a baseball fan now. But he didn't know baseball.

"So, what do you wanna use for a base hit?"

I said, "The one from ICI, I already know: 'H' is good. Makes sense."

"And when a guy gets a base hit or a walk, I'll just put the guy on first?" Yes.

"So, 'H 1', or ball four — either one — or an error by a player, puts the runner on first base?" Yep.

End of story.

Today, with my fancy software — by a company called "Daktronics"... I think it's the leader in the nation — it goes like this:

"In-play" — you gotta hit a button called "In-play." All right, so you hit "I". Then you go, "H" for the hits. It wants to know who'd it hit it to? I mean, where'd it go? I just... *where'd it go?...*

who cares where it went? Got a base hit. All right. So it says, "Okay. The guy's on first." But... it's lit up. It's asking you, "Does he stay at first?"

What do you mean, *"Does he stay at first"*!? Got a hit! Got a walk! He's on first! We're done! This is 2019!

These people, when they come and they try to upgrade the software... like, currently, the things that I have...

"What's highlighted right now?"

"Well, it's waiting for a Ball. We're going to default, first pitch will be a Ball. Each pitch will be a Ball."

Oh good. It was a Ball. Good. Hit "Enter". Okay. Good. That's highlighted in yellow. If it's a strike, it's highlighted —

"Now — my highlights went away! All gone!"

The software's like, squirrely right now, like, doesn't want to take the information... but finally does. C'mon.

Larry Goldman wrote software, in the early '80s, for an Apple ///, that took care of every circumstance that could possibly happen. How about now?

Here's Larry Goldman's software:

The bases are loaded. We're up. We hit the ball out of the park. "H"... a number... "4". "H 4" Oh! Four-base hit. Oh! The guy from third scores, the second scores, the guy from first scores, and the guy who hit it, scores. Yes?

What is it now? 2019. How is it now?

Okay! Hits a grand slam! Here — on this one, here, the key — hit the key "F12". So, in-play! "F12" for the home run. The guy on third base lights up. "What do you want to do with him?" He advances! C'mon! Wait a minute! It wants to know: "where'd he advance... *to*?"

Base number four!

Okay, good. Now there's a guy on second. It's aglow. Wants to know, "where does he go?" *Where does he go?* He advances home! Well, you better not just hit "a" for "advance". Why? Because it'll default to third. And it won't score the run. All right, so you make sure you...

Aehhh! Wears me out just talking about it.

We had better software — I believe we made a proposal to this company, and they passed on it. We were willing to sell Larry Goldman's software, for a crisp hundred thousand dollars. If they want it today, we'll make a deal. Larry needs the money. I could use the money, too. Contact me. Contact the publisher of this book. They'll get a hold of me. We'll make a deal. All of your software and all of your major league parks... that are lousy... will be wonderful. I make you a simple offer. You want it? Get a hold of me. We'll make it happen. Larry's building a house up in Oregon. I could always use a few dollars. I'm working on my deck outside. Very nice. Let's make a deal.

But... it's funny. Things... the years go on. Sometimes, you go backwards. I don't understand. But — I digress.

Around 1983, '85... Uh-oh! We were invaded. It was no longer Chester Farrow and Roy Steele and Red O'Dell on audio, and Ray Crawford, and Lloyd Fox on organ.

Ray had left — He left around 1975, '76... something in there. So, I was doing both jobs. Of course, I got a raise, 'cause I'm doing both jobs. So that was nice.

But... in comes... a thing called DiamondVision® — and a crew. The crew was, like, — yikes! — maybe fifteen people. I don't know. We *were* a quiet little thing. It was very nice, nice and private... and we get invaded. Who do we get invaded by? Well, it's the new DiamondVision crew for the Oakland Coliseum.

I think what we did, we rented, portable display boards... they stacked on each other, these things. They looked like... storage containers. But on one side, then, were all these lights and stuff, y'know, so you could have video. I guess that was the precursor to us installing our own.

I'm not exactly sure what the names were in those days, or who the company — I think, Mitsubishi, DiamondVision — but

I'm not sure if that's the one we rented for a while… I'm not sure.

But anyway, the crew expanded large… way large. It was Jim Lynch. Jim Lynch is now the director for Giants'[5] television. There was John Ward. John Ward is now — he produces replays, I think, for Giants' television. They got great jobs. They get to pick when they wanna work. I think Jim only works baseball. I dunno. Maybe he works other sports.

The people who came in to our scoreboard room were all bright. All sharp. Y'know, all fresh out of college. All… that kinda thing. Got a little experience under your belt. This was a wonderful opportunity that opened for them. In fact, all the television we do now, which is — all the networks we have, local ones — was wonderful for the industry. The industry is driven by seniority. Not at the director level — that's called "above the line" — but all the other jobs: camera, sound… and so forth.

It's all regulated… But, it all pays good. When you're working as a freelancer… independent… the goal is to fill up your calendar to your liking. How many days a week you wanna work? Maybe you start out, you say, "I need six, seven." Well, that's a whole calendar thing. I see eleven open spaces. You keep working on those eleven, reminding the guy who's doing the crewing for whatever sport that's going to be televised, that you're willing… if they need you. I guess you do that for a while. Then, pretty soon, you get established… and your calendar is full.

Of course, that's when freelancers are the happiest, which is, they're on their own. They have no guarantees. They have no guarantee of a job. I mean, I'm a freelancer. Same thing. Could be fired tomorrow. Do something silly… say something silly… you're gone. No recourse. I don't have any contract. You're flying by the seat of your pants, which is wonderful. But it's a little risky.

---

[5] San Francisco Giants Major League Baseball team.

If you're not stupid, you just act nice, do your job well, you just keep working. Why wouldn't you keep working? Maybe you don't shower and people don't want to be next to you? All right, that's an issue. Maybe you use sexist phrases and can't calm it down enough. That's an issue. But I mean, if you just… watch your p's and q's…

So now, we have all these extra people that are in the room. There's people to one side, the other, just all kinda crammed in. But before, it was very roomy… now it's very crowded. But hey, it worked. We all got along. Had a good time.

One little aside I want to mention is that Jim Lynch, when he came in — he was about the second or third director who came in… someone named "Phil" came in first, and then someone else, maybe, I think, and then Jim came — he was awful loud. I told him to quiet down — a couple of times. I guess that was surprising, because you don't really tell the director what to do. But I'm a scoreboard operator. What do I know? I don't know. You're gettin' loud. I can't hear. C'mon. I can't even concentrate.

"Use your headsets! You're trying to yell to 'em like he's all the way out on the field. That's what the microphone and the amplifiers are for."

Anyway, anyway… we all got along great… we did things together… I had a couple golf tournaments. They were a part of it, and that was fun. All of that. A great crew.

It's now changed, over the years. It keeps changing. But, when I say "keeps changing", there're some people that stay for a lot of years. So there's continuity. There's thirty-year people, and twenty-year people that are working for the A's… and also… working the television for "in-house", they call it. It's called a "board" show. But it is just the same as if — instead of going to the board, it went to your TV. C'mon. There's no let-up. There's no like, "oh, it's just a board show." No.

That's how you learn. You do board shows… you get paid pretty good money to direct… then pretty soon, you work in the truck — and such — if that is your goal.

You wouldn't want to make a move from director of the board show, to... a graphics guy inside the truck. You don't want to do that. It's hard to move over, when the directors don't quit. They just keep on going. Stay young and... y'know. So, Tommy Adza for the A's, and Jim Lynch for the Giants: they're not going anywhere. Why would they? They're doing what they love, although Jim Lynch really does like hockey — better. Yeah, that's his sport. He's a hockey nut. But, I digress.

So, now we have this huge crew. They're working with this temporary board. Alan Ledford used to be my boss at the A's. He just returned a call to me, in which I wanted to know, "What was the year?" 1983 is when the portable DiamondVision came in. Then in '85, it was permanent, the two big boards, and such like that.

There was another set of software. Instead of Larry Goldman's software — which was smooth as silk — I had to — and I balked at this — my bosses remember. I balked at this, which is, "Why are we changing software? Why are — we have a wonderful thing going here? It's so, like, you couldn't ask for software any better. No major league scoreboard operator would rather use anything but Larry Goldman's software, if they had it. We've got it. Why do we wanna change?"

"Well, it, uh, corresponds to..."

I dunno... What?

"... And then it, uh... Major League Baseball wants..."

I don't know what it's all about. It doesn't matter.

What I'm saying is, we had some horrifying software, 1985-1995. You gotta struggle through. That lasts about two years. Finally, you change.

Now, to give Daktronics some credit, when we got their software — I forget when we did; it doesn't matter — it was an improvement over the other couple of software programs we tried. Not an improvement over Larry Goldman's, but an improvement.

Now, I really understand their design. They designed it so a secretary could do it. So, you go, "H", you know, in-play, got a hit, "Enter". Okay. Now, he went to first. "Does he stay at first?" "Enter", again.

"That's all. Just follow the program. It's not that hard, Chet."

Well, wait a minute. When you're doing millions of keyboard strokes over your career, why do I want to do *more* keyboard strokes? I want to do *fewer*. I want it to be quicker. There's no easy way out. You put up a *ball*... and it's a *strike*? — to change it is like, Ay, ay, yai. Delete this... now put that... All right. Y'know.

There's a lot of little things that could be done to make it easier. But... that's the way it is.

Not only did we used to have like fifteen people, now we've got like, twenty-five. We got all brand-new scoreboards a couple of years ago. The budget was ten million. Whether they spent most of it, or all of it, I don't know. But they're gorgeous.

A former student of mine was the Engineer-in-Charge of that installation. He was also in charge of the big one that was put in by the Giants, maybe eight years ago, ten years ago — I forget — six years ago. They've got a new one now. He's done 'em all around the United States; mostly on the West Coast, though. That's a big thrill for a teacher, to watch a former student do the installation.

Now the crew is about twenty-five. We're no longer behind home plate. As I said, we're right above Section 221.

In the old days, you used to be able to come and knock on my door, for example, where I work and...

"Uh, is Chet workin' today?"

You know, that kind of thing.

"Chet! You got a visitor..."

You know, like that.

There's fewer visitors. Hard to get up to where I work.

They've got passes for everything. They check your passes to make sure you're supposed to be on the floor. They're trying to keep a vigil... They're trying to keep a close eye on who comes in, because you never know. They do check with the metal detectors, and so forth, before you come into games now. Everyone has to do it. So it's pretty safe.

But now, with a crew of twenty-five, it's like my view isn't so good. I'm looking over the left shoulder, really, of the umpire. I wanna see his right hand, right arm, right shoulder... movement... in case he calls a strike. The people at the A's installed a monitor for me, which is the same view as the centerfield camera — as you get on TV at home. Every once in a while, I have to use it — for a given umpire — in which he barely makes a movement with his right arm... but he made a movement. He might have lifted it from being, you know, perpendicular to the ground, to parallel to the ground. But he didn't move it forward and he didn't — Ay! So...

"Chet! They called it a strike!"

Ay! My, my... called it a strike? So, I have to make the change.

That helps me. I know it's going to be a long night... because I gotta watch the TV. Then I gotta record it.

"Chet! Do you mean there are some nights you really don't... watch?"

Yeah, but they are few and far between, where you can't see the movement. I've had cataract surgery, so I can see better at night. That helps. I can see pretty good from long distance; not so good reading. I wear like, bifocals — or whatever — at work... something... "cheaters", they call 'em. Yeah, you know... you go to CVS and you buy 'em and... or the Dollar Store. They're all good. Works for me.

With the crew that we have now, it's like... there's computers everywhere. Here I am, an analog guy in a digital world. I'm in the middle of a digital world, where I work. It's all these computers and all these things and… Ay, ay, yai! Way over my head. But I know what they're supposed to do, and why they're doing it, because there was an analog equivalent of what they had, years ago. Then it was changed over. It's all digital now. I retired from teaching — in '99 — while digital was getting big.

It doesn't really bother me in what I do. They're great… they're great tools — computers — fast. They could be fast. With the right software, then… everything instant. You're done. Done. Everything's taken care of. Don't worry about it.

When everything is running smoothly… and there's no squirrely-ness… and everything is lit up like it should be… and everybody's being advanced the way they're supposed to be… then it's a very simple job.

My only responsibility now… I used to have a responsibility of firing up the audience, getting rallies started, and so forth. That was fun. I work right next to the people that do the rally messages now. I don't even know if they realize that I used to do what they did, for fifteen years — as well as balls and strikes.

My job is a lot easier now than it used to be. I'm not responsible for any of the messages.

It's a great group of people. Some of them have been there twenty, thirty years. David… Angie… y'know.

Dick Callahan has been there like, fourteen years already. Where'd the time go? It was Roy Steele for all these years… and then… gone. Now Dick arrives. Wonderful. It's like we didn't skip a beat, except we tried all kinds of people in between, when Roy Steele was ill. It was fine. After an operation, he was having a hard time recovering. He had to be covered for. Then he started to lose his voice a little bit. And… wow… then he was no longer the stadium announcer.

But, in all these years, I have to say I've never had a bad day at the A's. Oh, I've had an argument or two. Y'know… you get a little puffy-chested. "Wow! I'm gonna draw the line in the sand", and wha-… I'm not a "draw the line in the sand" guy. We could always work it out.

Y'know, sometimes you argue for nothing. Then when it's all over, you go, like, "What were we arguing about?" So, if you have to think about what we're arguing about, and it only happened a few times in fifty years... pretty sweet... awful sweet job.

Chapter 26

Mr. Finley and Me

A lot of people ask me when I met Charlie Finley, who I always referred to — and I think he appreciated it from day one — as "*Mister* Finley."

We weren't close or anything. It's hard, you know... He was my senior by thirty years, forty years. So, he was always "Mister Finley," to me.

When I first got the job — at the A's — nineteen people tried out for the job, as the scoreboard operator for the Oakland A's. This was 1969.

I negotiated with Mr. Finley over the phone. He wasn't going to pay for training for the two people who were left that won the job — because you had to do a lot of homework and stuff — a lot of the people might be an insurance salesman. Another one might be a bartender... another one might be something else. It doesn't matter. But they all had families. They couldn't put the time in to learn about computers.

Ray Crawford was a teacher with me and a coach with me at Monte Vista High School. He was athletic director. He and I worked together for about five years.

When we trained, they said, "You'll get the job, but there's no pay for the training." We had to train all during Easter vacation. Those days off for a teacher with a family — those are precious, precious days.

We heard about the job through guy named Don Warner, who was Assistant General Manager of the Coliseum. But more importantly, I guess — his son was a defensive back on the football Varsity that I coached. His name was Eric Warner. He had asked all our coaches if we wanted to try out for this job. Ray and I were the only ones who really tried. We got the job.

I asked Carol — I told Carolyn Kaufman[1], "We need two-hundred fifty dollars, each, for our training before we start the year." We started on the road, I think. My first game ever was April 8th, 1969.

"I can't authorize that. You'll have to talk that over with Mr. Finley, himself."

That was now going to be my first encounter with him.

"Uh, fine! I don't have his phone number."

"Here's the phone number."

So Carolyn Kaufman gave me the phone number for Charlie Finley: Area Code 312, WE9-2475. I could call his apartment, if necessary: 312, Area Code, 467-0442. I believe Mr. Finley did insurance work for malpractice — one of the first in the nation. He made millions doing that.

He made a lot of money, enough to get into Major League Baseball early on, with the Kansas City A's. He was ten, eleven years there, I think — something like that — and then came here. When he came here, he was really nobody's fool. I read a lot of things that he had said in the paper — but never really met him. The first time I met him was when I called him.

He said, "Hello."

"Uh, Mr. Finley, my name is Chester Farrow. I'm your new scoreboard operator for the IBM 1131, along with Ray Crawford..."

As an aside, you need to understand one small thing. When Ray and I went for the job — went the first time for the job — it was on a Monday. All we did in the morning was talk about what we were going to be doing, the hours we were going to spend, those kinds of things. "I hope you know something about computers..." Nobody did. I taught Electronics. I taught *binary* and I taught — it was at the early stages of computers, but who

---

[1] Secretary for Mr. Finley at that time.

knew computers? Card sorters, maybe, but computers — what was that all about?

Mr. Finley said, "What can I do for you? Chest..." No. "What could I do for you?" he said — it's all he said. He didn't call me "Ace" at that time.

"What could I do for you?"

"Mr. Finley, we trained awfully hard during all five days of the Easter vacation for teachers in our school district — Ray and I are both high school teachers. We feel that all the training we put in here and all the homework that we put in...that we didn't get to see our children, only for Easter — we want $250, each."

"Or what?"

"Or we can't work."

"$250 each?"

"Yes."

He paused for what seemed... *forever*. He finally said, "All right."

I was going to ask him, "Could we have it in *cash*?" It really crossed my mind. I don't know this man.

I didn't. I bit my tongue.

"Great."

We went there on the very first day — the first night — on the 8th. There were two envelopes, one for Ray Crawford and one for myself. "$250, Oakland Athletics," blah blah blah... Their checks were good? We didn't know. We went right away and cashed — we went to the bank — fast — how fast can we do this?

I'm not making a joke. It's really the truth.

The money was good.

That was my first encounter with Charlie Finley. I really didn't meet him until — oh, by the way, every year I called and I got a raise, for the first five years.

Oh, I was going to tell you earlier: one of the things that we did — that Ray and I did — is we agreed. We went to the first meeting on a Monday, then he said, "Go to lunch. Come back in an hour."

So we went to lunch — a little drive-in-thing, a hamburger… just somethin'. We were sitting in the car.

"Ray, now this is very important. If we're gonna do this, we gotta do it *together*. We can't separate. He fires me, you quit. If he fires you, I quit. I'll do all the negotiating."

Ray felt a little uncomfortable, like, "I —"

Not me.

We started at twenty-five dollars a game. After you start working on the computer, and how complex it is, things you gotta learn, what you got to know… pretty soon, you're an expert. There's only thirty of us around the country. We were the first one with a computerized scoreboard, fully computerized.

So, there's a lot of leverage there, in a way. When I had to call him for a raise, I'd call around March 15th. Why? I hadn't heard from him. Am I hired? Fired?

By the way, with all the owners that I've ever had, I've never had a contract. I've never had a handshake. It's always just an agreed-upon price, and we go from there.

I've had no guarantees. I've flown on my own, by the seat of my pants, all these years.

Been nothing but fun.

But anyway, I digress —

So every year, I'd ask for a raise right around March 15th. Every year he'd go, uh — that's when he started calling me, "Ace."

"Ace?" Then he'd laugh. "That other guy… I call him 'Parson'…" (He was referring to Roy Steele, who used to be a minister.)

"Very good Mr. Finley, but I need more money. Here's why, here's how much work we did… we had no idea."

He even tried to do a double header in which you don't get paid the full amount for the second game because you're already there — eh! — Didn't fly with me.

Every year, it'd be the same thing: March 15th. I call. He'd say the same thing.

"Why are you calling so late?"

"Why haven't *you* contacted *me*? I didn't know if I had a job. I didn't know if you had hired someone else. No one let me know, Mr. Finley. But I need more money, and here's why. Here's what we do, that no one else does..."

He liked — you see, when I ran the scoreboard, I had a personality.

<Big Scoreboard Messages> "I can't hear you!" ... "That's all you've got? C'mon!" ... "LOUDER!" ... "There you go!" ... "Better!" ... "Whoa!" ... "Now we're cookin'!" ... like that.

Let's have some fun. Let's put some personality into it. No scoreboard operator today does that. If I were in charge of messages that went up, I'd instantly put my personality into it. *"I can't hear you!"* — and they'd wonder, "Who's that guy? Or gal? Who is that person ... with the personality?"

You'd intersperse with little jokes here and there, you know, the ones that work. They're easy. They're simple. *Mundane*. All religions could get a chuckle. No controversy for me, but we're going to have fun. Not done these days.

Mr. Finley liked it. He let me go.

It's funny. When you do something in the Finley organization, it gets reported to him immediately.

<Staffer in the Finley organization> "Mr. Finley, you know what was on the board today?"

They would call, thinking that he was going to take some action... and he'd laugh.

"That Ace! heh, heh..." Then he'd go, "Well, what was wrong with that anyway? Why'd you call me?"

"Why, I just thought you should know —"

"Eh! We got a game going on!"

Mr. Finley used to listen to all the games, in Chicago. One of the guys that helped him listen to the game — because the A's weren't broadcasting in Chicago in the 70's — would be "Hammer" — MC Hammer, Stanley Burrell.

He was just a little kid — twelve, thirteen — when he came and helped out... bat boy, ball boy, whatever.

Then, they called him "Finley's confidant." Because if Hammer saw you do something or something that was reported to Finley, you know... well he gave him what the score was and who was at bat. Nice kid though, nice kid. His brother was nice — his brother loved him. I don't know what the brother's name was. But I remember when Hammer was just coming on the scene, and the pantaloons and the *things*... Even before that, the brother was, like, pedaling the music. He'd find me in the parking lot.

"Chester, can you get them to play this?"

I'd do my best, to get them to play it — you know — the music in between an inning, and so forth.

Ground floor: Hammer. MC Hammer. Very cute.

So anyway, that was the situation with Mr. Finley.

We actually met in person at the 1971 playoffs. Finley hosted a very nice, catered dinner — affair. Everything was first class, from Mr. Finley, in the early days. Everything was A-number-one, and, uh — "show man" — and they spent the money. Just had a good time. You know.

So, that was our backdrop. That was our thing. I met him at the playoffs, talked on the phone each year. That's about as far as I knew Mr. Finley.

Then comes 1972. We're having a great year. We're going to win the pennant. We're going to the playoffs. Looks like Detroit is our opposition. We clinched the pennant about eight days before the 1972 season was over. It was an evening game, night game — might have been like on a Thursday night, maybe Friday night. Let's just say it was a Friday night. Pretty nice crowd, all like that. They're all excited — we're going to the playoffs again. We had gone in '71. Lost in the playoffs, but we were going again.

We had Rollie. We were ready to go. We had everyone, everybody from '72. What a great team. Not a ton of hitting, but enough; great defense, great pitching… great combination.

So I decided I wanted to go to Detroit. It was around the sixth inning of the game on — let's say — Friday night. I asked everyone, I told everyone in the booth, "I'm going to go ask Mr. Finley to take me to the playoffs in Detroit. Anyone else want to go?"

Roy Steele raised his hand; Lloyd Fox, the organist, raised his hand.

"Red, what about you? Red Odell?"

"Nah, I don't wanna go."

"All right; Ray, you wanna go?"

"No, I can't go. My wife is eight months pregnant — eight and a half, something like that. The baby is due in two weeks. That's about when the season — you know, the timing is just bad. I can't go."

"Okay. I'm going to go ask — and if he says, 'okay,' I'm going to ask for you guys."

<Guys> "Uh, Chet, eh, be cool, man, because you're gonna lose your job. You're going to —"

"Eh! C'mon, c'mon, c'mon. We're so far beyond that…"

By the way, you need to understand one more thing. Day in and day out working for the A's, you can get fired at any time. I have no contract. There's no such thing as seniority — you've been there 51 years? Yeah, it's just a number. I've done everything I've done fearlessly, knowing that the end could come anytime, anytime, anytime. In fact, when I first started with Mr. Finley, I didn't care whether it was money, something I didn't have; now I don't have to teach night school, summer school, all like that. Wonderful thing. What a great second job.

"I'm going down, talk to him."

"Good luck, deh, deh, deh..."

Opened the door. Went down the hallway. Walked to the owner's suite. That's how it was in those days. It's reconfigured now — you can't walk in *anywhere*. In those days you could. It was open.

So I walked in. There were all kinds of press standing around him, interviewing him. He was like, holding court, in his suite. The suites weren't plush, like they are now. They just had regular seats, but it was under an overhang. Good views. Nice place to watch the game. Not fancy like it is today.

So I walked in.

"Ace! What are you doing here? You should be working!"

"Mr. Finley. Ray's got it right now. I've come to talk to you."

He looked at me. "Whatever you have to say, you can say it in front of all of these people. We have nothing to hide."

"Uh, fine! Mr. Finley, the reason I'm here is... I want to go to Detroit with you. I think I could be a lucky charm. I think I have the pulse and the feel of this team. I need to be with 'em."

"Ace, let me tell you something. Nobody goes to the playoffs. Now! If we go to the World Series, that's different, Ace. Then we could, eh, work something out, if we go to the World Series."

"Mr. Finley, last year, 1971, we could have gone to the World Series. Did we go? No. Is there any guarantee that we're going now? No.

"I've never been anywhere north of Crescent City... east of Reno, south of Tijuana, west of San Francisco. Essentially, I've never been anywhere, Mr. Finley. I'd love to go on this trip."

He got quiet. Very quiet. We were talking — several press, and Mr. Finley — as he thought. Then he looked up at me.

"Ace, you're going. You're going to Detroit."

Then, like the stupid village idiot that I am, I said, "Mr. Finley! Ah, Roy Steele and Lloyd Fox, they want to go, too!"

He stared at me. Well, he *glared* at me. He pointed, and he said, "Ace, you don't speak for anyone but yourself. If those people want to go to Detroit, have 'em come ask me."

<Chester, reiterating to himself> "Wow! Have 'em... come ask me."

"Mr. Finley. Thank you. Thank you." I shook his hand. "Thank you." The press was like — kind of — jaw dropped.

There'll be press, in Detroit. But no guests.

I'm one.

I told Roy and Lloyd what they needed to do. They went down one at a time. Each one — I don't know how the conversation went — he said, "you're going, you're going."

Roy and Lloyd were roommates. I had my own room. Got meal money every day. Tickets every day... Unbelievable.

So we go to the playoffs. Who's my seatmate?

See, they hand you these tickets when they give you your meal money.

"Here's your ticket for today."

We go to Detroit. Where are the few people that are Finley's guests going? Second level. So we just walked up to the second level.

"Oh no, sir. You're right behind the Detroit dugout, in the box seats."

I went, "Whoa."

So me and Roy went to the box seats. Lloyd never made it to any games, I don't think, I don't know. He was in Detroit cruisin', having a good time.

My seat mate was the mayor of Detroit's wife. Lovely lady, she was there for all three games.

We had beaten them the first two games — in Oakland. Now, we were coming to Detroit. We just had to win one more game.

I had — what would I bring to the game all the time, in my coat? In my left pocket was licorice — black licorice drops — in my right, were sunflower seeds. I told her what I had. She said, "I love both."

"Well, just put your hands in the pocket anytime you want.

Help yourself."

We went to a party at her house. Very gracious, it was just wonderful. Couldn't believe it.

Best seats in the house... everything. Additionally, when we left the hotel to come — for the first time — to the Detroit ballpark, there were two buses and two limos. The limos were behind the buses. Mr. Finley's limo was right behind the bus. So, we got in the bus with all the press and whatever and sat down — I don't know where we were... in a bus.

Finley's eldest son comes to the door.

"Uh, Chester! Roy! Lloyd! Come with me!"

"What's wrong? Were we on the wrong bus?"

"Yeah, somethin' like that."

We got out of the bus. He points to and opens the door to the limo in the back.

"This is for you guys. That's all courtesy of Mr. Finley."

Pretty sweet.

I got meal money, tickets... How about this: Finley wouldn't let — *Mr.* Finley would not let me buy a drink — none of us. He'd be at the bar. You have to understand we weren't pals. He'd be at his — imagine the bar is in the round, only a rectangle. Bartenders working both sides, both ends, you know, like that big, you know, hotel bar. Hoppin'. World Series time.

Mr. Finley would be on the other end. He'd wave over for another drink for us... Like, another one's coming. I'd wave like, in appreciation, "Thank you very much."

But, never spent a nickel.

On the way from Detroit to Cincinnati... I had a great time in Detroit, great time, but it was like, I wanted to get back to school, I think. This was enough. I had done baseball all year. Now I had seen the playoffs. I didn't know if I wanted to go to Cincinnati.

<Guys> "Chet, you said you wanted to go to the World Series. Now you're on your way to the World Series. You're

flying in a charter. It's wonderful. Enjoy!"

Yeah, I don't know. I was kind of maudlin, kind of, "nyeh," kinda, "I don't know." I was ambivalent.

Mr. Finley comes over and he says, <gently> "How is — How are you fellas doing?" He was working the plane saying, "Hi," and whatever, on the way to Cincinnati. "How you fellas doing?"

Lloyd Fox says, "Chester wants to go home. If you could bring his wife here, he'd be happy."

He looked at me.

"Ace! Is that true?"

"It is. I miss my wife. I miss school…"

"No, you don't want school! You want to go to the World Series! Soon as we arrive in Cincinnati, you get on the pay phone —" (That's what they had in those days or the hotel phone, in your room) — "and you call your wife and tell her to fly out…"

She did and we had a wonderful time.

"How am I going to pay for that?"

"Oh, no, no, no. Your wife will pay for it, keep the receipt. You turn it into Carolyn Kaufman. She will reimburse you."

And I did. And she did.

We went on to Cincinnati.

So here we go.

My wife arrived and came to the hotel. We just had a great time.

We won the first two games in Cincinnati — first two out of seven. We were flying high when we left for the charter to go back to Oakland, up 2-0, over the mighty Cincinnati Reds, 1972.

From that world playoff and World Series experience that Mr. Finley treated me to — also Lloyd Fox and Roy Steele — I'll forever be so grateful to have had that opportunity. A kid from nowhere-land, getting a chance to go to the World Series, playoffs. Especially, when nobody goes really to the playoffs, from the front — maybe some front office people, but that's about it — normally in MLB, Major League Baseball.

However, it's funny this led to something else. Which is, out of the blue — kind of nowhere — in, I think, January or February of '73, comes a phone call to my house. Now in those days, there was no call waiting — just a regular phone. Nothing high-tech about it at all. You answer the phone.

It was late at night, about ten-thirty. For the school night — for me — it was kind of late. It was Mr. Finley.

"Ace! What are you up to?"

"Mr. Finley? What are you doing? It's ten-thirty at night here, must be twelve-thirty in Chicago where you are — " at his offices. "Wha - what's going on?

"I dunno. What's going on with you?"

"I don't know, just kind of relaxing here.

"Well, hey... Listen, I got an idea."

"What's up?"

"What do you think about — you ever golf?"

"I do." — and I did at the time. "I do. Little bit."

"You know, they got *colored balls* now."

"I know — I use an orange one myself."

"That's what I wanted to talk about... Orange baseballs!"

He'd call about designated runners. He'd call about — always about Bowie Kuhn and complain about him.

<Guys> "How often did he call?"

"I don't know. Every couple, three weeks."

One night, he called. My wife, Sharon, and I were entertaining Janice Worthington and Chuck Herndon when the phone rings about 11 PM our time.We're sitting around my small little kitchen table.

"Hello?"

"Ace! What're you doin'?"

"I'm partying. Got guests."

"Me, too!"

You could hear the tinkle of glasses and the giggles, and the laughter…

"Sounds like a good party!"

"Yeah. Yeah —"

But he didn't call about the party. He was bored to death with the party, I think. He would get a few drinks in him, he'd wanna talk. His mind would go, like, fast. Fast… ideas.

"What do you think about that?"

Sometimes I'd go, "I dunno. I've got no thought."

"Well, then, *have* a thought." Heh, heh, heh…

"All right, let me think about it. I don't know. It sounds kind of weird."

"It is, huh? It is, Ace!"

But he was one of those guys that believed any publicity is great publicity. No such thing as bad publicity. I mean, unless you do indecent exposure, that kind of thing. But I mean — talking about how you're crazy and your ideas are stupid. So what?

That was Finley — I mean, *Mr.* Finley. That's the way that was. We did this for about three years: '72, '3 — then he had a heart attack. I don't know when the heart attack came, but that's kind of when it ended.

Then Mr. Finley was, like, more bitter, kinda. Not fun, poking fun, happy-type thing. More…

Also, free agency — after a while — it killed him. Broke his spirit. When they didn't have free agency, you'd offer the contract: take it or leave it. If you didn't do it, stay home — I don't care. Play — for this pay that I say — or don't play. It's your call. Anything you'd like to do… unless you feel desperate. Mr. Finley never acted in a desperate manner. Was not his style.

We got along real good. All right, excuse me. Say it again. We got along real *well*. We were not friends. We didn't hang together. He was a regular part of my life for five years, with the late night phone calls.

They were entertaining. They were a pain in the rear. They

were everything. Sometimes I was in the mood, "All right!" — when it was him on the phone. I didn't know if it was him. I'm just saying... But if it was — all right. I always worried late-night, something's wrong — family member, *something*. Phone calls at eleven aren't good.

From '72 - '76, they were a regular part of my life.

That's it.

Chapter 27

It Was a Dark, Moonless Night

When I went to the playoffs in 1972 with the team at Finley's invitation — I asked him if I could come; he didn't invite me. I asked if I could go. He said I could and he treated me like a king. But anyway.

We were in Detroit. We were staying at the hotel — I forget the name of the hotel. In one of the chapters I mentioned how I didn't pay for anything. I'm in Detroit with Roy Steele, the stadium announcer, and Lloyd Fox, the stadium organist at the time — as guests of Charlie Finley.

Roy Steele and I had finished dinner long ago. We were having cognac in the evening. In those days we smoked cigars occasionally. I bought some nice cigars and there, at the hotel, I told him, "Roy, let's step outside and have a cigar."

"Yeah, sounds good."

So, we go outside. It was like the side alley, where we wanted to go. You open the door from inside the hotel, and there was a covered area that's maybe twelve feet wide and twelve feet deep — very nice. You know, one of those old ornate hotels — like an alcove, if you will. Roy and I went outside to smoke cigars.

The door — not the doorman…it was… not the concierge, but it might have been — he said, "Where are you gentlemen going?"

"We're just gonna step outside here in this alcove and smoke cigars."

"All right, but don't go any further."

"What do you mean, don't go any further? There's a rib joint right down the street."

You could see the neon sign.

"I think we're going to have a cigar and then we're going to walk down and get ribs."

"You can't be going out there. You can't be going out there. Gentlemen, this is *Detroit*. It's one a.m. in the morning. If you want ribs, we'll have someone get them for you. We'll have a cab. You pay for it. We'll get it and bring it to your room. But, these streets are dangerous."

"Well, is it okay if we just have our cigars out here in the alcove… like, right here?"

"Yes, sir. I'll keep an eye on you. Don't step off those steps."

Whoa! Kinda scary.

All right! One o'clock in the morning, we fire up our cigars. We're talking, having a good time, chatting away… anticipating the following day, which will be the first day of the playoffs. We had won the first two in Oakland. We needed one more victory — in those days, it was three out of five. There weren't all the divisions they have now. There were just two in each league. That's it. So if Detroit wins, *they* go to the World Series. If we win, *we* go to the World Series, representing the American League. And we're in pretty good shape.

So, we're out there smoking our cigars chatting away. These three limos drive up.

Now, you have to remember, there's no moon out. It's dark. Not even maybe a one streetlight — I don't know why. We're a hundred eighty degrees away from the main entrance to the hotel, and *it's* well lit. But I didn't understand why the side door leads to… kind of a darkened street. I don't know. But that's the way it was.

These three limos drive up. Now right away, you're smoking cigars, you're enjoying yourself, we'd finished a cognac or two. In a while, we were going to eat something because we were hungry. Then we'll go to our rooms. But, it was a nice evening and these limos drive up.

"Well, who's this? VIP *something*?"

In the front car three guys get out. You could see they were wearing holsters with guns. From the back car, three more guys got out... holsters and guns.

Wow!

Little beknownst to me — I didn't even think about it. They were lit up enough that I could see them. We were not lit up, could not be seen. I didn't realize it. Doesn't matter.

These guys get out. They surround the car's front, back — they're looking everywhere, everywhere. Not looking at us. We're standing right there. We're not hiding our cigars — we're smokin'. You could certainly see the embers in the cigars. We're not trying to hide. We're just... hangin'.

The guy inside the hotel said, "You could be right there; don't step off the curb." Wha — here we are. We're not steppin' off the curb. Just smokin' our cigar.

Out of the car comes George McGovern, who at that time was the presidential candidate — who I voted for. He lost. Uh... that's the way that goes.

But, it's George McGovern. I recognized him from TV.

He was with another guy — not his wife, I don't think; no. Another guy. The guy was kind of standing behind him, leading him in... to the alcove. They were going to go in the side entrance. That guy inside had been waiting for them.

But unbeknownst to me, I didn't know that. It was pre-arranged for him to park there. We kinda, had inadvertently messed up the plan, like, "Why can't I go out there and smoke? Can't stop me. It's America!" One of those things. I didn't have to say that, but I'm just saying, that was in my favor, to stay there. Purely accidental.

Anyway, George McGovern comes walking. I step off the curb, shake his hand.

"Senator McGovern? Chester Farrow. I'm the scoreboard operator for the Oakland A's. I'd like to introduce you to Roy

Steele. He's the announcer for the Oakland A's. Both of us are voting for you."

He shook our hands and turned around and looked at the — you know — special services, whatever they are; I forget what they're called, you know those personal security.

Absolutely unaware. We could have killed him in an instant. He had no chance.

But, we weren't there to kill anybody. We're just there to say, "Hi"

By the way, we were there *first*... smoking cigars. We weren't bothering you.

Anyway, that's my encounter with George McGovern. He was shocked. He's good... He appreciated the idea that we said that we would vote for him. But the plan did not go as planned.

We encountered him faster than the Secret Service could have defended him. That was a no-no. It's a good thing that we were good guys and not the bad guys.

Chapter 28

The Band

In the early 70's, while putting on little-mini concerts at Monte Vista High School, one of the bands that came through and played four or five times — never exactly the same band, but the people were ... a couple of the personnel might change; you could tell a band was forming. But the constant was a fellow named Josh Harris. Josh, he's like Greg Douglass. He's like Bruce Hock. They just want to play music.

They don't want to write checks. They don't want to go to the store. They don't want to do garden chores. They don't want to do any of that. They just want to play music. What's funny, is that he struck me — a great little personality. Lo and behold, within the next year or two, Josh Harris approaches me.

"We have a band. We'd like you to manage 'em."

The band contained John Coinman: vocals and guitar. Chuck Phelan: vocals, bass. Lloyd Ferris on drums. They weren't such great musicians, as they were harmonizers. They had a great harmony: three and four piece harmony. A lot of the arrangements of the songs were done by Josh. A lot of the songs were written by John Coinman and Chuck Phelan, I think.

"Well, if I can get my friend Bob Quarrick — or "Q" — to co-manage, I'd do it."

I won't do the booking, though, it's too hard. Josh says, "I'll do that. I'll contact the night clubs and so forth."

So, they made it fairly easy. I did it for five years — maybe, only four. But, it was a time in my life where... "Bring on another challenge!" I was into music; "Let's try this." They sounded a little bit like The Eagles? — their tune structure and harmonies? But we lacked the song that had the hooks, the things to make a hit.

We entered the Country Music Awards, very first time. Lost, lost, lost, rejected, rejected, rejected, because basically our music was country *rock*. We played in high schools. They played for me at Monte Vista — several times. Why wouldn't you book your own band to open a show? You'd be silly not to.

<Administrator voice> "Yeah, Chet, but you usually only do two bands."

"Well, each of the first two will play a little shorter, 'fore the headliner."

"Gee, Chet, why're you making that change?"

"Duh. My band! I'm the promoter, the producer. I could do that!" — and I did.

We played Santa Cruz. We drove everywhere to go play. It was fun. For a while, Greg Douglass joined us. Name of our band was originally "Black Jack," then it turned to "Appaloosa," then it turned to "Deluxe." While it was "Appaloosa," was when Greg Douglass was part of it.

It was a great experience, but let me just tell you: I have to relay this. This is a common thing.

The nightclub, let's say in Berkeley, San Francisco — name it — would say, "You guys are going to open the show on a Thursday, at this time. We'll give you one dollar for each paid admission."

I didn't do much other than just go watch on occasion. I'd go and say, "Okay. I'm going to watch this set." Then, I'd have to collect the money for the band.

By the way, we never made a profit. Our roadies, who were former students in Monte Vista, or current students, they were the roadies. They'd drive the truck, they'd do everything. Usually, we'd make around sixty dollars, forty dollars a night, and it just went towards the truck and the roadies.

So we essentially played a lot of times for free, over all the years. That's the way it goes.

But — getting back to a nightclub. This is, without naming names, this is a nightclub in Berkeley.

One dollar for each person paid.

<Chester Inquires> "Can I see the guest list? Take a look? Is the guest list is complete?"

"Yes, it is."

I take a look. There's twelve names.

"Very good."

So the people come in. It's kind of easy to count. There's four, there's six ... four more ... night goes on — oh, hey! More! Eight... twelve... So I get — let's say — I saw the twelve — they came in in fours — who were on the guest list — got that. All the rest were paying members ... I get a hundred eighty-four.

So I need a hundred eighty-four dollars from the manager of the nightclub when our set is over.

Our set finishes. I go to the guy.

"Uh, I hope you enjoyed it, deh, deh..."

"Oh, yeah, everyone seemed to appreciate it, deh, deh, deh... um, I'd like to book you guys again for a couple weeks from now, on Thursday again. Are you guys up for it?"

"Oh, yeah, well, it sounds good."

"Good. Okay. Here's your money."

Now I'm expecting a hundred eighty-four. ... He hands me $67.

"*Sixty-seven*? Uh, I get one eighty-four, and, uh..."

"You'll take sixty-seven and come play in two weeks, as though this conversation never happened. Or you'll never play here again."

<Tsk> "Okay. Thank you," — then you leave.

Common practice? You bet. You wonder why musicians distrust promoters, producers, managers of nightclubs. It's hard to find someone you trust. Hard, why? I don't know why that is in rock and roll, why there isn't more honesty. Money-grubbing, one way or another, why?

You took a loss on the night. You took a loss? — then tell me.

<Apologetic Club Manager> "... I didn't have enough, uh, expense, way —"

I never got that. All you gotta do is say, like, "Gee, we were hoping for a hundred fifty, and only forty showed up. I can't even afford really to give you the forty dollars."

I would take whatever you had.

But to lie? Be deceitful? Rob? Fill in the blank! It's disgusting. Someone needs to step to the fore. By the way, when you read articles about someone being really good in this field, promoting shows, nightclub manager and so forth, you think they're just talking about, "Very nice, and she says, 'Hello'"?

She follows through — he follows through — with their commitment. If I say it's a dollar? It's a dollar. If we can't make it, I'll come on bended knee telling you, "This was a bad night. It rained. People just weren't coming out." All bands would take whatever you had, and say, "I hope we could do better." They'd be feeling guilty — like it's our fault: we didn't have enough draw. You know, just one of those things.

Anyway, the band got an opportunity to play at the Oakland Coliseum — twice. First time, they were "Black Jack." The second time they were "Appaloosa." How'd that happen?

Well, I called Mr. Finley, owner of the Oakland A's.

"Mr. Finley? Listen, I manage a band. We have eleven, twelve doubleheaders every year."

Doubleheaders were very common in the 70's and before, to try to give you as much value as possible. But today, people just want to give you a couple hours and go home. I understand... you know. Everything is so fast paced these days... You know. I get it. I'm not part of it, but I understand it.

"Mr. Finley, listen, uh, double-header... there's thirty minutes in between each game. How 'bout I have my band on a flatbed truck ... in which we've already tested the equipment.

So they drive in on a flatbed truck, amps and everything all set up. We just plug into the PA system at the Coliseum."

The gentleman's name was Red Odell, and his son, Gray — very important in our life.

"Fine. Remember now, uh, only thirty minutes... and we don't want to get in trouble —"

I laughed at him.

"Mr. Finley, when have you ever cared about being in trouble?"

We both laughed.

"Well try — try to finish in thirty... Ace." He called me, "Ace."

"Try to finish in thirty."

We played, and we did. We did a great job. The people enjoyed it and everything.

The second time we played, we were "Appaloosa." This time, remember, "Appaloosa" had been joined by Greg Douglass. Well, Greg Douglass for one reason or another couldn't make the gig. Twenty-two thousand on a Sunday, and you can't ... make the gig.

Ayuuuu!

Anyway, so the band says, "What're we gonna do, Chet? Greg's not here."

"All right, we could do the songs that he doesn't play, or can you cover his lead?"

"No, I can't cover the lead."

"Josh, can you fill or something on keyboards?"

"Eh, I don't — "

We were going over the set list. I said, "Well, how come 'Sadie' is not on the set list?"

"Chet, uh, I don't — "

"Eh, what? It's a good tune!"

<Chet, singing, snapping fingers> "Sadie, said that she loved me, doot doot doot do do ... doot."

I don't know; it had a good beat, a good fun thing. Come on!

You need to understand something though. I'm not a lyrics guy. What do I mean by that? I make up my own words as I go along, and that's it. I never really —

"Chet, you mean you missed the whole meaning of every song that you've ever heard?"

Absolutely.

Now if you go back to rhythm and blues and all like that, I get that. Then those songs make a lot of sense for me.

<Chet, singing again> "I sit in my room… looking out at the rain. My tears are like crystals, that cover my window pane. I'm thinking of our lost romance, and how it should have been. Whoo, if we only could start over again. I — "

And so forth. I get that. Anything else? I — I don't hear.

"Chet, why'd you spend so much time explaining why you don't —"

Well, we're getting to that.

So anyway, they're saying, "Well, Chet, Chet! We shouldn't really do S—"

"We're doin' 'Sadie.' C'mon!"

They performed about six songs, each one about three minutes long — fits right into a double-header. Why they don't do it now, on a double-header, is simple: there's no more double-headers.

But it was great entertainment.

"Chet, did you start something new?"

I don't know, and I don't care.

"Chet, had you ever seen rock and roll on a flatbed truck? You were there since 1969. Did you — have you ever heard or seen that?"

No.

"Could it have been the first?"

I dunno.

I don't think about things like that. I only think about things like that when I'm — like now, writin' this book. Then you look back and you go, "Who did that?"

"Nobody did that."

"You did it!"

Maybe so, I don't know. But it was fun.

So anyway, getting back to the "Appaloosa" show.

All done. Everything's good. They played 'Sadie' — very good. Thought the crowd really enjoyed. They laughed, and all that — beautiful. That's the same reaction we get in nightclubs: laughin'. Twenty-two thousand people all laughing in unison — it's wonderful.

I wasn't down on the field. I'm up where, like, behind home plate in those days for — at the computer — to do balls and strikes ... outs... fielder's choice, double plays, whatever.

Show is over. Three guys — I didn't even know we had that many front office people. The front office was Carolyn Coffin, secretary, and about 3 people. Four, three — I don't know, we didn't have many people. They bust in...

"Chester! Mr. Finley's on the phone."

I said, "Wha—?"

"Mr. Fin — and he's *angry*."

"Uh... He's angry? What's he angry about?"

"Chester, Jesus Christ! You can't, uh — you can't use that kind of, uh... *filth* at a baseball game. This is America."

Filth... baseball game... America...

Ay! My head is spinning. Yikes!

"I'll go downstairs and talk to him, in your office."

"No — we'll go with you."

It was like, they delighted — like, "Got you now, you son of a gun. Finley's always liked you... Too bad for you! Job open! You're outta here."

The people in the booth were kind of stunned, Roy Steele, Lloyd Fox, Red O'Dell. They were like, "Ayyyyeee."

Red O'Dell said, "I didn't hear anything wrong, Chet."

I went, "I dunno. I don't think my band did anything wrong."

So I go down there, get on the phone. The guys were all hanging around. All three of them. They want — they want to see me go down in flames, like ... I don't know.

I said, "Hello!"

"Ace! Mr. Finley here."

"Ah, Mr. Finley, hi! How are you?" I said, "The music was really good and people had a good time. Uh, people were laughin' and clappin' and... I don't know."

"Chet!" — I mean — "Ace! Is it true that, eh, you talked about, uh, one person in the song, on top, and the other on — wha, wha?"

I went — I said, "What do you — that song, 'Sadie!"

Sadie! ...*Person on top...*

I started to go through the lyrics as best as I can recall, from all the times I've seen it played in nightclubs and high schools. I should have it memorized.

<Chet, singing to himself> "Sadie said that she loved me, don don deh, ehhhhh, and we get along best when she's on the bottom and I'm on the top..."

"Whoa. Mr. Finley, I just thought about it."

"You just thought about it now!?"

"Yeah. I never even really listened to the lyrics. Everyone in the nightclubs —"

"This is not a nightclub, Ace!"

"Mr. Finley, everyone had a good time. There was no foul language. There was no malice intended."

He laughed, and said, "Go back to work, Ace."

Those guys there were stunned, when I hung up the phone. They said, "Where you goin', Chet?"

"Back to work. Mr. Finley said, get back to work."

<clap/clap> That's my story, and I'm sticking with it.

Bye. Bye.

Chapter 29

Reggie and Me

In October of 1972, Mr. Finley took me to the playoffs and the World Series. This included Detroit, and the all-powerful Cincinnati Reds with Johnny Bench, *et al.* Just an amazing team, Cincinnati. They were called "The Big Red Machine."

One evening, it was the night before our first game in Cincinnati. It was 0-0. Cincinnati had the better record and therefore opened the World Series *in* Cincinnati.

It was the night before the game. Mr. Finley took myself and Roy Steele, and one of the ball girls, and his son — a couple of his sons — to dinner, along with him and his wife and his older son and some other people.

Essentially, Mr. Finley needed a chaperone for his kids. You know, it's funny. I don't care. Got free food at a very nice restaurant. Tablecloths. Great service. Are you kidding me? Private room. Talk all you want, as loud as you want. And it's free? C'mon, now? What do I got to do, babysit? I dunno. The kid is like fifteen years old. No big deal.

So we sit down. After dinner, Charlie Finley — Mr. Finley's — son threw out a question that I got entrapped with. It's funny. When you're young, you do silly things, sometimes, like pontificate on marriage. I had only been married — what — nine years at the time? Like I know all about marriage. But he asked the question, I believe because, Mary Berry — the ball girl — was at the table. I think her and Reggie[1] were friends.

"Chet! What do you think about… *mixed marriage*?"

I'll tell you almost word-for-word what I told him.

---

[1] Reggie Jackson, powerhouse player for the Oakland A's at the time.

"You know, marriage is hard… period. It's not an easy, easy road. Compromise. Sacrifice. These are not fun words. But they're all part of the necessary ingredients that goes into a pretty good marriage. Open communication… never lie to one another… all of those things.

"I married my childhood sweetheart. Her name is Sharon Farrow. She's flying in tonight. I'll be seeing her tonight. Mr. Finley flew her out so she could be with me — you know — so that's a wonderful thing…"

"Who's paying for it, Mr. Finley? Oh, wow, good for you."

"Yeah. So anyway, I've known her all my life. I've known her and her brother Rodney. My wife was named Sharon Clawson. Her brother was Rodney Clawson — is: he's still alive. My wife is — she passed in 1992.

"I've known her all my life. Her mother and father and my mother and father were best of friends, before they had children. Then they had children. Remained good friends. When I say 'best of' — I don't know — you'd see 'em certainly every couple weeks, one month at the latest, you know, since you saw 'em. Everyone was working in the mills — steel mill, pulp mill, wherever — in Pittsburg.

"We started to date in high school. I dunno, maybe I was a senior, she was a junior. I dunno. I forget.

"We dated for the longest time. I sang love songs to her from a Johnny Mathis album… '… chances are… 'cause I wear a silly grin, the moment you come into view…' — that kind of thing… she'd be laying on my lap. I'd be combing her hair or whatever… all very sensual, all very leading to… marriage.

"We discovered we were pregnant… time to get married! That was 1963, my junior year in college.

"But, that was neither here nor there. It was just, where I came from, yeah, you impregnate your girlfriend? You got responsibilities. They're lifelong. I made up my mind right there and then: I'm married to this gal till I die.

"There was no — who else? I mean, she was the love of my life. Even with all of these things...my parents and their parents bowled together; my parents and them and we'd go to the bowling alley, as kids. We'd watch 'em bowl. Sharon would be there. It doesn't matter. Everyone knew everyone in this relationship. Everyone was happy with one another in this relationship. So you don't have to worry about bringing the girl home, or bringing the guy home, to meet the parents. Everybody knew each other. It was, like, seamless.

"And yet, we still got problems. I'm more daring. She's more conservative. There's a lot of things that go on. Holding two, three jobs at a time. Gone a lot. It's like, not easy being married.

"It doesn't matter the color. It doesn't matter the religion. Marriage is hard.

"If you want to get married, y'know, go for it.

"Black and white adds a little complexity to the thing, but it's still the same basic things: Do we love each other? Do we trust each other? Can I rely on you? Those things."

I left it at that. That was the end of that.

We won both games in Cincinnati.

Now we're on the flight home. It's a charter flight. It's very special and very nice... great food. Great everything. Those are the only times in my life — going to Detroit, and then Detroit to Cincinnati, and then Cincinnati back to Oakland — the only time that I've ever been on a charter. It's *sweet*.

They had — I dunno... "You guys wanna play cards? Dave, here's a table for you"... you deal the cards... you raise your hand... the gal comes, and guy — they come, they give you drinks, *things*, snacks, food, regular dinner... it's just ongoing. You want regular seats? Got it — no problem. You want this? Whatever you need. Everyone's taken care of. Coaches want to be together? Good — you're in front. It doesn't matter. I mean, it was just fabulous.

So we're on the way home. I was walking from one place to

another – when Reggie Jackson encounters me. He holds his hand up. He was on a crutch. He had broken his leg, or whatever, against Detroit, I think, even scoring the winning run – the go-ahead run – in the ninth inning, maybe? I forget. But he was on a crutch. He had crutches.

He puts his hand out so that I couldn't move any further in the aisle. There was Blue Moon Odom, and his wife. Blue Moon Odom is black. His wife is white.

So right away, I knew – it's funny. You know, you come from Pittsburg, California, you better have your antennas up at all times. "Please remain alert at all times." That's the announcement that was made by the public address announcers at the Coliseum. It's advice that I follow absolutely to the "T": *please remain alert at all times.*

I knew something was up, and it wasn't good. I knew it referred to black and white. I knew it referred to the dinner. I knew Mary Barry was involved. The only question I'm asking myself is, do I fire on him now, before he fires on me? And that means *punch.*

I didn't care necessarily about what Mr. Finley thought – it doesn't matter. I'm not trying to test the limits of how far Mr. Finley would allow me to go.

But we got a problem here when the man puts his hand up, then says to Blue Moon Odom, "Blue Moon, this guy here doesn't believe in black and white marriages..." which is the furthest from the truth. Doesn't matter. Doesn't matter.

We've got a major problem on our hands... right now. My heart is thumpin'. My wife now, who had come to Cincinnati, she's seen this all taking place. She was worried – as she should be.

Blue Moon says to Reggie, "Calm down, Reggie. The man's entitled to his opinion."

I said, "That's not – that's the furthest from the truth."

The wife, even, said, "Take it easy, Reggie. There's no

problem here."

So I said, "Are we done?"

And he mumbled something — doesn't matter.

I went back to my seat.

Now remember, my heart is pounding, jumping out of my chest. I feel it's like leaping four to five inches out of the chest, although it's physically impossible. My stomach was in knots.

This was not resolved. This is not over.

All right, so we land. My wife and I gather our things at the carousel. We're about ready to start to walk towards the buses that are waiting for us at the airport in Oakland.

Right behind us is Reggie Jackson, talking to two friends — I guess — that maybe came to pick him up. I'm not sure.

He nodded towards me and my wife as we began to exit the carousel.

I took one look over my shoulder to my left. They were now following me and my wife.

Wow! Now we got a problem. And the problem is real big.

But even in my own lessons, I realize I have very little control over the situation. Do they have guns? Are they going to pistol-whip us? Are they going to run us down on the freeway? How far is this going?

As we exited, now I'm in a rage, because it's unresolved. But I realize: you're in East Oakland, pal. This is not your hometown. You carry no weapon, and there's two… young… strong… black men… tailing me — courtesy of Mr. Jackson.

So, I took my wife four or five steps over to the right. There, was a security guard.

"These two men are trailing me. My wife and I are scared for our lives."

"C'mere a minute." We walked over a little bit to the side.

"You're going to go through this door back here. This door here. You're going to then turn left and then right and it'll take you out to where the buses are, for the Oakland A's. I'll detain them. Don't worry. Don't look back."

And we didn't.

They never reached us. When we got on the buses, they weren't there – because they were not part of the entourage. I assumed they'd be waiting for us in the parking lot. I didn't see 'em.

So, that was my encounter with Reggie Jackson. It's the only time that we ever talked, face-to-face.

Obviously, then, I'm not going to the '73 and '74 World Series, though Mr. Finley called me – every night. Sometimes twice.

In September, of '73…

"Ace! How come you didn't ask to go? Well, you came last time… we want you on board… You're our lucky charm…" All of it.

"I can't go. Mr. Finley."

Then I kind of fudged the truth.

"You know, I'm way behind on my work at school. I pride myself on being a complete teacher. I can't just take a week or two off to go to these events and fly back and forth – as though I have no responsibilities. I can't."

He'd call back again.

"Ace! Have you changed your mind? C'mon! We're going to have a great time! We're gonna, y'know –"

"Mr. Finley. I've made up my mind. I will not."

<Sigh> And that was too bad.

Was it ever resolved? No.

Do you intend to hunt him down? No.

I don't expect it to get resolved in my lifetime.

But… it could. It should.

But it's so far past at this point, it's just another chapter… in my autobiography.

Chapter 30

BEHIND-THE-SCENES GOLF TOURNAMENT

In the early 1980s, after the Haas family had purchased the A's from Charlie Finley, I started a golf tournament for the A's. It was called "Behind-the-Scenes", which means: no ballplayers, no announcers, no one that might be on radio or TV. Everyone behind the scenes.

These people included: Alan Ledford, Andy Dolich, Steve Page — president of, used to be called, "Infineon Raceway"; I think now it's called "Raceway of Sonoma"... A bunch of people who have gone on to be very successful, who were working for the A's at the time — participated in the golf tournament.

Roy Steele played, I played... We tried to get anyone and everyone behind the scenes to participate. As it turns out, we had about 144, for each of the three golf tournaments.

The first golf tournament was held at Franklin Canyon. The Franklin Canyon Golf Course is around fifteen miles from Oakland. Pretty accessible for everyone. That was our first foray into a golf tournament.

It was a spectacular day: clear, no wind. We had lots of fun. Then, of course, we had a nice catered dinner afterwards. This was all for around twenty-five, or forty dollars. Very cheap. We wanted everyone to play. We just wanted to break even. That's it. Whatever the expenses were, we kinda divided it up. Then that's what we charged. No big deal.

The first one at Franklin Canyon was quite a success. So I said, "Well, let's try it again."

The following year, we did it at Tilden Park, in the Oakland/Berkeley Hills. Tilden Park is a gorgeous little golf course, nice and green and lush. The problem was, though… we couldn't tee-off until, like, around eleven o'clock. We were going to start, like, at nine in the morning. The reason was, it was fogged-in. That'll happen from time to time at Tilden Park. So, we waited til you could actually see some fairway, and you could actually see people out there. It was kind of dangerous at first, but the fog lifted within the first couple, three hours. It was a gorgeous day for the rest of the day. We had a catered dinner at Tilden. It was very nice.

Then, the final year — I think, around 1984, but we did three of them — we held the tournament at Boundary Oaks. What I did was, I had everyone over my house on Shuey Avenue, in Walnut Creek. My house had a very private, long driveway leading into the garage. Nicely paved. So, I rented tables, I rented chairs, I rented barbecue pits. Whatever was necessary. We had New York steaks. You cooked your own.

"I'm not going to cook for you. We get 'em started, you go ahead. This is your steak. Any way you want it. You want it real well done? Go ahead."

A great time was had by all. We had all kinds of prizes, and t-shirts, and *things*, and all like that.

We had a big open bar. My daughter, Debbie, even served. She got drunk that day. Probably the only time she's been drunk. She never wants to get drunk again. I can't blame her. But she was only around — I dunno — seventeen or eighteen… I'm not sure.

These tournaments were the precursor to the "sponsor" golf tournament that the A's put on for many, many years. Now, whether or not the current A's ownership continues to have a golf tournament for their sponsors? I don't know. But I do know that the seed for all of these tournaments started with… Behind-the-Scenes.

Additionally, Larry Goldman went ahead and ordered a bunch of golf balls. They were labeled "Behind-the-Scenes." We had tees — special tees. We had everything. We tried to do it as first-class as we possibly could. Everyone got tee-prizes. It was a full-blown tournament, all three years. Full-blown. As generous as we could possibly be. A great time was had by all.

Chapter 31

Eye in the Sky

A lot of people have asked me over the years, "You've watched a lot of games. Fifty-plus years. Do you ever have an input into the team? Suggestions, comments, that type of thing?"

Really, I shy away from those kind of things.

First of all, just a couple of comments. Most all major league scouts have their radar guns — unnecessary these days; the ballparks display the speed. Oh, you don't trust the speed? They're all plus or minus one mile an hour, throughout the majors. It's pretty accurate — when they flash it on the board — that he threw a ninety mile an hour sinker or an eighty-two mile an hour slider. There it is. I mean, you know.

They're often behind home plate — real nice seats — lousy view of the game. In my opinion, where I sit — above the second level and before the third level, kinda where the skyboxes are — is a fabulous view. The view is of the entire field. The entire *everything*. Nothing close-up. No, no. Back away. Take a look.

Okay, in this situation, the guy's supposed to hit to right field. Does he hit to right field? Can he hit to right field? You see that so well from up above. You could see what they're trying to do. You could see what the pitcher was trying to do. So I think that all scouts should be sitting up in the press area, where I sit. Watch the game properly.

"But, Chet! I wanna get a close-up view of —"

Of what? You don't need to see the muscles, whether he has a beard, or — Eh! Just... relax. Second, third deck level, where the press sits... check it out. What does he look like to you? Does he look like a hitter? Does he know what he's doing? You see so many things that you can't see behind home plate. It's unbelievable.

I went to a game once at the Sacramento River Cats, okay, when they were the A's affiliate up in Sacramento. Wonderful at Raley Field — just a wonderful field. Alan Ledford — a former boss of mine and good friend — gave me, and Ray Lucas, and Lynn Harmon, seats right behind home plate. We were sitting where the scouts were. They had their little radar guns. The service was excellent. If you needed anything — you buzzed, you raise your — it all got taken care of.

But, the seats were terrible! You can't really see. When the ball is hit, you don't know if it's going to the second baseman, whether it's going to right-center, all the way to the wall… I mean, how do you even… how do these scouts even analyze what they're seeing? I think it's ridiculous.

But, nonetheless, we had gorgeous seats. But you cannot scout a game properly, in my opinion, behind home plate.

With that in mind, I've only talked to a couple of ballplayers — general manager — whatever. I'll tell you the two stories.

It's tempting to wanna. If I did that for everything that I saw — for example, right now, Jurickson Profar is having a rough time at second base. He can't throw anymore. He can't — it's gone. When you're a second baseman — I play second base — when you're a second baseman, and you can't fire the ball to second base… you can't complete the double play? You can't play. You can't play for a high school team… let alone, a college team… let alone, the pros. It can't be done. When a play needs to be made, it needs to be made. Ground ball to second, he should just throw it to first, get the runner out. Let's throw the ball around… one down. Here we go.

No! It's an adventure. That kind of thing.

But I don't go down there and make those comments. I don't want to… I just… They are professionals. These people have been in Major League Baseball for years. They see the same thing

I see. You can't tell me they don't. They see exactly what I see. They try to deal with it… as best they can. Find a fix. You can't keep losing games, based on your defense.

Isn't it funny how baseball is considered an offensive game and yet it's the defense that wins you championships. It's the defense that wins you a close game, in the end. Oh sure, the pitching's very important. All of that. I'm not arguing — you know, we could go into — we could argue this for days.

But, you got to have your defense. It's gotta be solid. When the pitcher throws a pitch, and it's a ground ball to short, he gets to relax, knowing that the ball is going to go from short to first, one out, and let's move on. If that play isn't made… my gosh!… then everything is made more difficult.

Only twice have I ever done this.

First one was 1989, I think? Our championship year. It may not have been. It may have been the year after, I think. It was. The year after: 1990.

I sit up where the press sits. Great view. What was I observing with Dave Stewart? Well, Dave Stewart threw a split-fingered fastball. In order to lodge the ball in your hand as a pitcher — between the index finger and the middle finger, so that you could throw it like a fastball, but it's just going to drop off the Earth — it takes a while to get that ball in position in your hand, to deliver it to the plate for a strike. Or at least one that appears as a strike, before it dives out of the strike zone.

What was Dave Stewart doing?

Well, let me tell you the whole story. I'm observing what he's doing. I'm not happy about it at all. It's a change from what he did.

The next day, I'm down eating dinner. Sandy Alderson — who was the general manager at the time, around 1990 — he was sitting at a table with some scouts. I go over to the table.

"Sandy, I have something to talk to you about, about Dave Stewart's delivery."

He stood up. "Not here."

So, Sandy and I walked out. We went into the elevator. Kinda went between floor number one and two and kinda stopped it.

"Now, what have you observed?"

"When Dave Stewart throws a fastball, when he's going to throw a fastball, he puts his hand in the glove, grabs the ball and *throws*. His-hand-in-the-glove-throws-the-ball… that's all. Over and over. How long does it take? I don't know. Half a second, a second, to get his fingers on there, on the ball and then release it.

"Now, when he throws a split-finger, it's three, four seconds of getting ready at the top there — at the top of your wind up. Getting that grip. My! Split-finger's coming!"

He would throw — there was a split-finger. He would throw — there's a split-finger. You assume that everyone sees this kind of thing.

And yet, when I told Sandy, he said, "Thank you."

I got off and went to work on the third floor. He went back down and talked to Dave Stewart. The problem was quickly corrected.

The way we did it — or they did it — was that you take the same amount of time — three or four seconds — to throw the fastball, even though your hand is on the ball and you're ready to throw. But, the batter doesn't know. He goes, "Oh-oh. It's taking three, four seconds. It's probably a split-finger."

Well, *every* approach was three or four seconds after the conversation between Sandy Alderson and Dave Stewart. Then you could not tell whether a breaking ball was coming, whether it's going to be the split-finger, a fastball… not at all. That problem was taken care of.

The second one I saw, it was like, 19 — not 1992. That was Dennis Eckersley's Cy Young year, I think. Just wonderful. This is more like 1994.

What am I observing from Dennis Eckersley? If any of you

have ever watched Dennis Eckersley pitch: he puts his foot on the rubber. Here we go. He's ready to go. He's staring you down. Get in the box. Boom! Pitch! Here we go. Get the ball back. Foot on the rubber. Staring you down. Boom! Next pitch! *Et cetera. Et cetera.* A very uncomfortable setting for a hitter.

I don't care if you're a hitter and you love quick rhythm. It's just — wait a minute, now. I haven't even caught my breath. Wait a minute. I haven't had a chance to think that last pitch through. Eckersley gave you no time to think about any of it. Here it comes. Here it comes. Here it comes. Slider. Slider. Spot the fastball. Slider… and so forth.

What was he doing that caught my eye? I don't know. He'd throw a pitch, get the ball back from the catcher… and he'd walk around the mound a little bit. Well, what is that? One pitch. Strike or ball, doesn't matter. He's walking around the mound! Then he puts his foot on the rubber. He's not at the same pace…

It was like… It was all… it was confusing to my eyes, even.

So I said to myself, "Self? Here we go."

This was my second — and I hope last, ever — going down and talking to a player. Why didn't I go to Sandy Alderson? One, I don't know if he was still with us in '94. I think he was. But this was, like, even more personal. Which is, I love Dennis Eckersley. But he was doing things all wrong… bad. I'll just go take care of it myself.

I go down to the clubhouse — I have the credentials — but you can't just walk in the clubhouse. So, I asked for Steve Vucinich. Steve is the clubhouse manager. This is his fifty-second year.

"Steve, I need to talk to Dennis Eckersley… if he has a moment."

"What about?"

Usually, Steve doesn't do that. He just goes, "No, you can't. He's doing this…" or "Yeah, I'll get him."

"His delivery… It's all off right now."

"Oh! You're going to talk to him about pitching?"

"Yeah."

"Just a minute."

So, a couple minutes later, out comes Dennis Eckersley. I introduced myself to him as the scoreboard operator. I start with, "I've seen every pitch that you've ever thrown at the Oakland Coliseum."

Now, that has some cachet. Which is, it's coming from… the senior, tenured scoreboard operator in the major leagues… I'm making a personal observation. Even major leaguers listen up.

"Dennis, what are you doing walking around the mound? I don't know. You look… You're not even *Dennis* anymore."

"You know, it's funny you said that, Chester. My wife's been telling me that for a week!"

"Why don't you listen to her?"

"Well, I — she's not in baseball and I just —"

"C'mon, Dennis. Stare 'em down. Get on the mound. Get ready. All of that is intimidating. All right, maybe your slider isn't as good as it used to be. Maybe the fastball isn't snapping like you'd like it to be. But nonetheless, you have to give the impression to the hitter, that you're *Dennis Eckersley*… and you're comin' after 'em."

"You know, you're right. I know my wife is right. Walk around. I don't… I don't…"

"Well, get out of that habit! It's just a show."

In other words, people think that these things are done for a lot of different purposes. Nah, nah, nah, nah. It's just show. You're trying to show the batter that you're ready. That you're eager. That you're comin' after 'em. That's the persona that you wanna give off. I mean, that's the one that Dennis Eckersley wanted to give off. Some have a great persona, like they don't care about anything. And yet, they pitch a four-hitter, and win 8-1, on an ongoing basis. You don't have to have that kind of intensity that Dennis had, but for him, he had to have it back. And he got it back. He settled down.

That's my history of scouting and helping the A's.

Chapter 32

THE 1989 EARTHQUAKE

In 1989, the A's were in the World Series, and their opponent was the San Francisco Giants.

Had Chicago won that playoff series – against the Giants – to get into the World Series, I would have been able to go on a trip to Chicago with the team for the World Series. However, because the Giants won, there was no airplane, no... nothing special.

We took a ferry from the Oakland side to San Francisco. The trip was about a half an hour – maybe forty-five minutes. We went slowly. It was all the food and drink that you could possibly enjoy. No one's driving.

We were located as guests of the Giants – we were located in the left field bleachers. Maybe around twelve, fourteen rows up. The seats were fine. I can't see too well, but I never expected to be right behind home plate, and I was not.

But it was very festive – the A's had already won the first two games of the World Series. We were up 2-0; we were now going to Candlestick Park. See what we could do.

It was around a quarter to five – maybe ten to five – I'm looking around and I see... some balloons, that have a little metal on these balloons, a little bit of aluminum. They were tangled in the light standard. I saw a guy going up the light standard. I said, "Woo! That's pretty high. Wow."

On the light standards, they have a ladder – not a ladder, but they have these steps – actually just steel bars, where you step on. You climb up, and so forth. I don't know – I guess he was safe.

It was very festive. It was loud. The anticipation was — you could cut it with a knife. It was a gorgeous day.

But, before we got there, while we were on the ferry, I noticed something kind of… weird. When we left port to come to San Francisco — the wind was blowing maybe ten miles an hour? Kind of, as per usual… and it was a normal day on the Bay.

Then about halfway there, I look back at the flags, on the back of the boat — back of the ferry — and I see they were draped. They were limp. There was no wind.

So I commented at the time… I said, "Whoa! Feels like earthquake weather."

But you know, it's funny. I feel there's earthquake weather a lot of times and then there's no earthquake.

Now it's around seven minutes to five in the afternoon. The game is to start — I imagine — at 5:05, 5:07, I guess, so the East Coast could see it at eight o'clock, you know?

Everything was fine.

And then… everything started to roll. There was like a jolt, but a lot of rolling. Everything was moving.

Ay, ay, yai! We're in the middle of an earthquake.

The power pole that the man was climbing, to free up the balloon that had aluminum on 'em, he was sideways twelve to fifteen feet right — Ay! — all the way back, ten to fifteen left. Ah! I felt sorry for him. I thought, "Oh my gosh, what's going on?"

Just then, someone had a little portable transistor radio. KCBS comes on and says, "The bridge has fallen. The Bay Bridge is closed. It has collapsed."

Yikes! Collapsed! The whole Bay Bridge? Ay, ay, yai!

It turns out that there was a section of the bridge that had collapsed. But it was closed temporarily. We had to drive around in through San Jose on the way home.

After the earthquake, the players and their wives were all assembled in the middle of the field, to get away from the buildings and stuff and light standards that might fall during this earthquake.

It was very scary.

The bridge — remember — has collapsed. Is this Armageddon or something? I don't even know what this is all about. But I knew it was an earthquake.

It finally settled down.

The people were very good as we got instructions to leave slowly. That's it. Get out of here. Take your time and do it in an orderly fashion.

And we did. So now we're out on the parking lot. We're just waiting around. We waited for about three hours, doing nothing except trying to figure out what we're going to do, in the middle of this earthquake.

Finally, we got on the buses and started a long trip from Candlestick Park, through San Jose, back up the freeway, to Oakland.

We got to Oakland after a long trip — in which I was a pain in the neck.

"Are we there yet? C'mon on people, are we there yet?"

"Oh, no. Chet! Shut up! We're tired!"

"Eh… whatever."

They were talking. I don't think there were very many cell phones back then. Pretty sure there were none. Maybe there were, but only a few had 'em, I guess? I don't know. I don't own one — still don't.

So there's no one for me to call, and tell 'em I'm all right, and so forth. Just, you know, that's kind of how the way it was.

But nonetheless, once we got back to Oakland, after going through San Jose and up the freeway, then the only thing that was there were some… three-quarter inch videotapes that had tipped over slightly from being nice and neat — a nice stack of maybe twenty tapes, now there were all leaning over. That was the entire impact that we could find at the Oakland Coliseum.

Very little damage — or none — to the Oakland Coliseum.

Really, not a lot of damage to Candlestick.

But, the freeway accesses were blocked. Things were delayed. I think we delayed about ten days, before we restarted the World Series. And of course, as you know, the Oakland A's went on to win… in a sweep.

That's my earthquake story, and I'm sticking with it.

Chapter 33

Flint's Ribs

Many, many years ago, in the mid-'70s to late-'70s, all the way through the 80's, there was a barbecue joint that I discovered. It was funny. I drove right past it, almost every day going to the Oakland Coliseum. It was just up the street.

It was a little dive joint. Very small. Had a nice barbecue pit. The food was just delicious. The prices were very fair.

So I became a regular. By that, I mean, I would call ahead, talk to the owner, Margaret Flintroy.

"Margaret, this is Chester, scoreboard operator for the A's. Could you cut me up four slabs of ribs with medium sauce, put them in an aluminum pan…?"

I would bring them to the Coliseum, put them in my Crock-Pot and we'd have ribs in between the first game and the second game of a doubleheader.

It was very popular. Bob Uecker, baseball analyst and announcer — also TV star, I guess, all of that — he was a regular. He was the announcer for the Milwaukee Brewers. Milwaukee used to be in the American League.

It wasn't just Bob Uecker. It was just about anybody who was — the visiting broadcasters…

"You're welcome to come on down to DiamondVision where I work…"

We had links, we had ribs, we had potato salad, sauce…it was simmering in the Crock-Pot… smelled and was delicious. Fantastic.

Margaret and I… got a little closer, I guess. I was calling so regular, I'd always —

By the way, I want to tell you something: Margaret never prepared the ribs ahead of time for me, for about four years. I would call ahead. I'd order it. She'd wait until I came, then her people would chop it up, and fill the order. It took years before she would actually pre-prepare it for me. She was kind of a tough nut to crack, which is Margaret. I mean, when I call, I'm going to come with my credit card. I'm going to pay, and everything is good. But she was a little leery. In a way, I can't blame her.

One thing led to another. She approached me one day.

"You know, you really seem to enjoy this barbecue…"

"I do."

"… and you say you enjoy barbecuing?"

"At home. All the time."

"You oughta open a Flint's Ribs, in Walnut Creek."

Wow! Now, wait a minute. To open a Flint's in Walnut Creek? I'm a teacher. I'm a high school teacher. What do I know about real estate and building pits and sausage-making and…?

"I'll teach it all to you. Then we'll open a store together. We'll go 50/50."

She would supply the sausage-making machines. She would supply the personnel to chop the meats and cook them — at the Walnut Creek location.

"But, however, before we can do that, you need to come in and work, for about a week. Your wife, too, 'cause she's going to be involved. To keep it nice and safe, and because you have children, we'll have your wife work in the late morning through the afternoon, then go home to the kids. You'll come in in late afternoon till we close. And… you'll learn."

Boy, did I learn. They'd do twenty, twenty-five racks of ribs, at a time. They're on the upper shelf, they're in the medium shelf, they're on the lower shelf. They're cooking off the lower shelf. They're slow-cooking the upper shelf, and so forth. Margaret, when she tested the food: no sauce. Straight meat. It better be delicious. The sauce, then, will make it even better. Lots of people, they kind of cover up the meat that's not so good, wasn't cooked so well — whatever!

By the way, Margaret always used 2-3's, which means each slab weighed between two and three pounds.

The Hick'ry Pit, here in Walnut Creek — all kinds of places — they use 3-4's and 4-5's, the bigger ribs. She insisted on staying with the smaller ribs, because they're tastier, they're more tender, and they're just delicious.

I worked for an entire week. I worked the pit. You're turning these things over, and they're guiding you, and they're showing you, and they're going, "This one's been in the pit kind of long; bring it down," or "put this guy back up..." So you learn to do the proper rotation. People are chopping away...

Please understand. On any given night — a Monday, a Tuesday, a Sunday — ... *jammed*. People coming out of the business, and down the block. Orders were taken while you were in line.

"What are you going to have?" and so forth, trying to move the process along.

The money being generated was — I never counted it — but it was huge.

I was looking forward to a change of career. It's funny. I loved teaching. But... I also loved the barbecue — especially Flint's ribs, especially with a business opportunity.

Twenty years in Walnut Creek, for example, I'd be set for life. So would my partner, Milo Baskar, who was a metal shop/drafting teacher at Monte Vista High School, who loved barbecue, loved barbecuing, and was my partner in this venture.

We found a place on North Main here, in Walnut Creek, by a gun shop/ammo shop. It was by a big hamburger place. I'm not sure what the name of it was. The rent was right. We got the place. We kind of locked it up. We were all excited.

There was only one thing left for us to do for the Walnut

Creek location: get the Fire Department to approve our pit.

A gentleman named "Mr. Dixon" was their premier pit-builder for the Oakland/San Francisco area. Mr. Dixon was going to build my pit.

The Fire Department kept delaying and — I don't know. I'd call and…

So finally, I decided: let's go down and find out if they're going to let us build a pit, or not. So I go down to the Fire Department.

"Oh, you're the guy that's going to bring Flint's ribs to Walnut Creek."

"Yes."

"And you got Dixon, I see. He's a good pit-builder."

"The best. The very, very best."

"Eh… lemme find those plans."

So he went in the back, and here come out my plans.

"All approved, right there."

"Here we go!"

"Are you kidding me? Fire Department loves ribs, links… everything. We want chicken. All of that. Are you kidding me? This place is going to be a hit!"

I thanked 'em.

Then I went to a very, very important meeting, in some offices in the Berkeley Marina. We went to meet with her lawyer, to finalize the approval of this deal.

They met for about an hour and a half. I waited outside in the office. I wasn't even invited in to talk. Then, the meeting was over. She said, "I'll call you tomorrow."

I went, "Whoa! All right!" I didn't know what was going on.

Well, it turns out that the lawyer had convinced her that she had obligations to family, maybe — or whatever… friends — far exceeding anything she should do for me. She should do it first for family and friends.

Margaret called me on — this was on a Friday — Margaret

called me Saturday morning; woke me up, 'bout 8:30 in the morning.

"Chester, I'm sorry. The deal is off. I can't go into details. I feel so embarrassed, but that's the way it has to be."

I didn't open a Flint's Ribs, even though I had the permits for the pit. I had a place… rented, leased, ready to go.

What was wonderful was that everyone accepted — you know, the landlord of the business where I was going to rent — everyone said, "Fine. We understand. No extra money is needed to change hands. It's as though it never even happened."

But I was close… to owning and operating… a Flint's Ribs.

Chapter 34

DANCES WITH WOLVES

In the late 1980's, on a Friday night — I can't remember any closer than that — I walked into the booth where I worked at the A's. There's three sets of rows: front row, second row, back row. Everyone was down in the front row where I sit, at the window, with binoculars, looking down towards the A's dugout.

"What's going on?"

"Eh... Chet, we don't need your help right now."

They always kind of told me that, and still do if I come in early and I'm talkative, and I might actually be interfering with the pregame show. I was brushed aside.

"Eh... We don't need your help."

"All right. What are you looking for?"

"We're looking for an author, Chet. You don't read anyway, so you don't know any authors. You can't help us."

"All right."

It's true; I don't read a lot of books. I probably don't know this author. You know, why would I know an author?

"Who's this guy that you're looking for?"

"Chet, this is the guy who wrote *Dances With Wolves*."

"Oh, you mean Michael Blake?"

"Wow! We're surprised! You knew who the author was. He's been on TV lately, so you probably saw it, and..."

"No, I know Michael Blake. I've known him for — I don't know — the past fifteen years."

Michael Blake used to be in our recording studios at Wally Heiders' all the time, in San Francisco. We'd be there on the weekends — Gray O'Dell was engineering. We got comp time. I can't believe it, how well we were treated by Gray O'Dell, and Wally Heiders in general. It was just great. We'd slip in on Saturday morning, Sunday morning. Not much recording going on those days. It was fantastic.

This guy used to sit in the corner. All I knew him as, was "Michael." He'd be in the corner of the recording studio, in the control room – not the actual studio; the control room – sitting against a back wall, usually on the floor. He'd just be writing.

Every once in a while, I'd go by and say, "Michael, what are you up to?"

"Oh, just writing."

He liked to write things about the western United States and horseys, and cows, and animals...He just wrote whatever he thought. I didn't know what he was doing, this guy Michael. I didn't know.

But he was a nice guy. He was a friend of our lead singer, John Coinman, who was from New Mexico; John Coinman, in the band "Appaloosa", "Blackjack", "Deluxe" – it was called all three. So, he'd be there for all the sessions.

It turns out that this guy, "Michael," was Michael Blake. So I know him real well.

I told the people in DiamondVision – Alan Ledford was in charge at the time – that I knew Michael Blake and could go down and identify him for you.

The response was kind of unanimous.

"You don't know Michael Blake. There's no reason in the world for you to know Michael Blake. You don't even read. What do you know about *Dances with Wolves*..."

Wow.

"Listen, really. I know Michael Blake. Where's he supposed to be?"

"He's a guest of Tony La Russa's. Tomorrow night, they're having a big soiree at the Lesher Theater in Walnut Creek, in the big room — holds eight-hundred, the Hoffman Theater — and it was going to be a presentation by Michael Blake, on 'The Wild Horses of Montana, Wyoming'."

Evidently, that was what was in his heart, what he cared about. That's where he wanted to see all the money that came from the book. He wanted them to go to these horses, to feed them, and keep them safe.

"Let me go down. I'll give him a hug. When you see that, I'll make him face you — the whole thing. You'll see: my arm will be around him and all that."

"Yeah, Chet, *whatever*."

"Heh, heh... All right."

I left the booth, asking someone to take over for me temporarily, for balls and strikes. The game hadn't started yet, but it looked like I might not make it back for the start of the game, if he came in a little late. He came, maybe five minutes before game time. I couldn't quite go down there and return for the first pitch, so somebody had to cover for me.

"Where's he supposed to sit?"

"Front row, right behind the A's dugout."

"All right."

I went down to the front row. There were about four to six people in the front row. None of them were Michael Blake. I sat there and I waited a while. After a few minutes, in comes this entourage of four or five people, I think all gentlemen. In the lead was Michael Blake.

"Chester! Oh! I'm so happy to — oh, this is wonderful!"

We hugged and embraced and reminisced a bit... I congratulated him on his success with *Dances with Wolves* — that I couldn't believe this kid, in the corner, at Wally Heiders' recording Studio D... created this masterpiece. It was wonderful.

We embraced. Then I had him turn around and wave. He did. Then, I went back to work.

Of course, all they could say was, "Can't believe you knew Michael Blake..."

That's my *Dances with Wolves* story and I'm sticking with it.

Chapter 35

Prediction for the A's: April, 2019

I've been the computerized scoreboard operator for the Oakland A's since 1969. During that time, I had an opportunity to watch success in 1971 through '75. We were in the playoffs in '71, but lost — we didn't go to the World Series. We went to — and won — the World Series in 1972, '3, and '4. In '75, we went to the playoffs, but lost. So that was kind of an era all by itself: three World Series in a row is — boy, pretty rare.

Then again, in 1988, '89 and '90, was another era that was very notable, in which we went to the World Series in '88... that was the Bob Gibson home run off of Eckersley. Then we won in '89 — that was the earthquake... we swept the Giants. Then we went to Cincinnati and we lost in the World Series, the following year.

But nonetheless, we were right there in the World Series, three times in a row. We were 1-2, of course, one win two losses, in the World Series, but still, it was a stand-alone era — if you will — of success.

Well, what I see this year is the same thing. I started seeing it for good, last year. I said, "This team is going to be very, very good."

Khris Davis just signed an extension — I think it's thirty-five million, something like that — for a total of two years. He's worth thirty-five million a year... now. Best power hitter in baseball... period.

This team reminds me of either one of those eras that you'd like. This is more like '88, '89, '90, in that... the home run power. Remember, we had Canseco, we had McGwire... just some prolific hitters.

Those '70s teams… we had some power that was really good — surprising power at times. Gene Tenace in the World Series: Wow! Where'd we get that from? But basically, the '70s teams were known for great defense, wonderful pitching, super relief — you know — with Rollie Fingers. Just super relief.

For those of you who have forgotten, it was very often I'd watch Rollie come in with two outs in the seventh. The score would be 3-2, A's. We'd win, like, 3-2. He'd pitch a third of an inning, then a full inning, then a full inning. That isn't normal for closers. Rollie Fingers was the exception. Five-out saves: very common. One out in the eighth: the guy gets in a jam and you relieve 'em. The closer pitches — if you have the lead. Then your closer comes in and tries to close it out for five outs. That was more normal then.

Now, it's very specialized. You got a sixth-inning guy, you got *another* sixth-inning guy in case the other sixth — you got a seventh-inning guy, someone to cover *him*… you got an eighth-inning guy, ninth-inning guy…

The Oakland A's of today. Take a look at what we have. Trevino, Treinen… Treinen: the best reliever in all of baseball last year. Khris Davis: just re-signed — he loves Oakland. He loves the A's. When's the last time someone sacrificed millions — and I'm telling you, he could go out on the market — he could have gone out in the market today. He could have been the first five-hundred million ballplayer.

Problem is, he's already thirty-one going on thirty-two. People don't have much faith. I have faith in him, that he'll do this kind of thing for the next ten years… easily. He doesn't try to steal bases. He doesn't play the field. It kind of broke his spirit a little bit, then, when he was asked to be this everyday DH. The reason is, he's a liability in left field.

See, there are a lot of people who play "okay" left field. All right. But at least they get to the balls they could read — they catch the balls they reach. They can throw and hit the cutoff man… you know, on the fly. They could fire to second base, and throw out a guy trying to stretch a double. Something hit down the third base line… not right on the line, but let's say ten feet inside the line. Left fielder challenges, grabs the ball on two hops… runner runs. A good outfielder has the ball on the bag — no relay man. Then, it's a matter of who beats who: does the runner beat you to the bag, or does the throw beat you to the bag?

Khris Davis would call it — throw… five hops… it would reach second base. He can't even reach the cut-off man. He bounces it into the cut-off man. There is something wrong with his shoulder — or, *whatever* — that has been since birth, probably. Or he had an accident or an injury or something. But, he can't throw; he's shot; no good.

But in the American League, the DH does not have to play a defensive position. He's not a base stealer. So the chances of him getting injured are far slimmer than for any other position player — any other person on the bench. The DH who doesn't steal bases is not going to get injured, unless maybe he gets hit by a pitch. Of course, that's a everyday danger for every pitch. Absolutely.

Beyond Khris Davis, we've got Matt Chapman, and Matt Olson, and Piscotty, and Laureano in center field. We've got Canha, Pinder, backups. We've got people all over the place.

Profar? The jury's still out for me on Profar. The reason is, he's got a scatter arm. Just the other night: ground ball to Profar, A's three outs! He threw it… I don't know *where*! Into the dugout or somethin'!

I used to play — I still do — slow pitch softball. I play second base.

He throws like me. I can't throw anymore. After the operations and stuff, I can't throw right now like I used to. But I'm working on it. It'll come. I'll be able to make that throw from second base to first base without a two-hop bounce.

"Gee, Chet, eh... did you *ever* have a strong arm?"

"Very strong, when I was younger. As I got older, it got weak-er."

"Okay, that's fine. But you could certainly make a throw from second base, shortstop — deep shortstop — especially..."

"Eh-uh. Can't do it. But second base? Sure."

Profar — you know — I like his bat. But then he's only battin' one-something. I don't know. So the jury's still out for me on him.

But, our pitching is, like, struggling. We have some starters who are — a lot of young. We have pitchers getting injured. All these Tommy John[1] cases. But they're all going to come back. They're going to come back stronger than before. Some of them are going to come back mid-year to help bolster our pitching staff.

We re-signed Edwin Jackson recently. Very good. Every clubhouse needs an Edwin Jackson. He's good in the clubhouse; great attitude. Everybody loves him. Very confident. No fear. No fear. Now, Edwin used to be able to bring the ball pretty good: ninety-four, ninety-five. No more. Don't need it. He spots ninety-one or -two occasionally. Breaking balls, location, location, location. He pitches to contact.

It's funny. It's like a miracle happens when you pitch-to-contact.

"Chester, I'm readin' this thing, and I don't understand. What's 'pitch-to-contact'?"

You throw the ball and try to hit the outside corner down low. If he makes contact, it won't be *his* contact. It'll be *your* contact. That's where you wanted him to swing, down there, because he doesn't put much on it. Fairly easy out.

Inside and low: Oh! Handcuffed! Handle hit. Slow roller to Chapman at third. You're *out*.

---

[1] Pitching elbow reconstruction surgery.

He's money. What a gun for an arm. He's money.

So, the A's are in pretty good shape to make a real decent run. We may be a year away from making the playoffs again. It may happen again. But I think we're going to do it again. We're going to get in the playoffs and have more success. And maybe like 1972, win it all. 1988: win it all. But, I do believe we'll make the playoffs.

We've started this run now. Our record right now is hovering five-hundred.

But, I had surgery last year. I had to miss the first thirty games. I didn't come back till June 7th. That ten-game homestand, we won the last two against Houston, but our record was 5-5 on that homestand. The two games that we won against Houston — the last two — started us on our real red-hot streak. But at that point, we were barely over five-hundred. Might even have been sub-five-hundred, I don't know. But not too good.

That's as of, like, June 17th — ten days later. That's not the midway of the year, but certainly, passed the one-third mark. We were just hovering five-hundred last year. We're going to be doing better this year, I predict, than we did last year, at that time. We'll not be just hovering around five-hundred this year by June 17th, but we should be ten games over, by then.

It takes a lot to get thirty, thirty-five games over five-hundred. Formula for that is: win two-thirds of the games at home, half of them on the road. We weren't doing that early last year.

So, I see the A's for the next couple of years — maybe even three — in this playoff run, "we're goin' to the World Series" attitude.

And I'm looking forward to the future — right now.

Chapter 36

Al Davis and Me

As you know, 1969 was when the first computerized scoreboards in the world — fully computerized — were built in Oakland, California, at the Oakland-Alameda County Coliseum. I've been working it since then.

But there's one little story that I'll share with you, that's kinda interesting. This happened in 1969. It was the very first year of the scoreboards. This was all new to all of us. We didn't know exactly how everything would evolve.

I can tell you now, that the software that we ran that was written by a company called Information Concepts, Incorporated, in New York — two guys, one who worked on messages, and one who worked on baseball scoring. They wrote a great software program for the IBM 1131.

I was learning a lot. By the end of the year, boy, I was really rollin' pretty good. I could get the audience fired up. Ray Crawford, who was my partner for about five years, was more conservative. He didn't like "working" the crowd. He was just more of a straight man, which is fine.

If he was working a given day — 'cause, we'd alternate — he'd run it. I'd set up all the messages for him that he needed to enter, the lineups, and so forth. Or if I was working it, then he would set it up for me, read it off to me as I'm typing it in. It can be done by one. It's three times faster with two.

So, I get a phone call at my house. I think it's… maybe July, I'm not sure, of 1969. It was a gal on the phone

"Is this Chester Farrow?"

"Yes."

"Al Davis wants to meet with you."

"Al Davis… Al Dav —… Yeah! The owner of the Raiders. Oh, oh. Okay, what's he got in mind?"

"He'd like you to be their scoreboard operator."

"Well, uh… when does he wanna meet?"

"Well, he's opened this time —"

Eh! We arranged for a time. I went to his office at the Coliseum, at the time. I don't think they had off-Coliseum-site facilities for their offices, at the time. I'm pretty sure it was all done at the Coliseum.

I know how to get to the Coliseum. I'm ready to go. No problem. We arranged for a time.

I walk in. He's behind his desk. He stands up. I go over to greet him, we shake hands, and everything is hunky-dory… to start.

"Sit down. We'll chat… Listen, I know you're the scoreboard operator for the Oakland A's."

Now, why he wasn't talking to Ray Crawford, I don't know. *He's* a scoreboard operator, Oakland A's. But I guess he wanted… I dunno. Maybe he wanted what I had to offer, you know, kinda like, "have a lot of fun," and so forth. I'm always into havin' fun.

But you gotta realize a football game is an all-day affair.

<Al Davis speaking> "Chet, kick-off is one o'clock. They're done by four."

Really? Call time is like, 8 AM. You've got to load that computer up with all the messages you have, all the different groups that you have, all the different advertising that you want to have, and so forth. It's not that easy. It changes week-to-week. Some things stay constant; many change.

Working a football game is not like working a baseball game.

Baseball games? Nice catered meal. Football game? You get sandwiches. Really? All right, but I was used to… first cabin, you know, a couple of different meats at carving stations, those things.

There's a lot of things that aren't appealing about doing a football game, not to mention the rowdy crowd. It's kind of tough, just getting through to park. They kick your car. They hit — I dunno.

It's like, semi-scary, working a football game — for me. Some people find it exhilarating. I found it combative.

The Raider Organization has always been... combative. Knee-jerk reactions. Ay, ay, yai!

But I figured I could work within that system. I'll make it work.

<Al Davis continues> "Chester, I understand you're making twenty-five dollars an hour for the Oakland A's."

"Yeah, that won't last long, because we did it our first year. We're going up next year, so..."

"I want you to work for *me*, for the Oakland Raiders."

"I can't work for twenty-five dollars an hour."

(Long pause...)

"Get the F- outta here! You're either *with* us, or you're *against* us!"

I went, "Whoa! This man wants to punch!"

Now, at that age — 1969... eh, 43... I don't know, I'm 26 years old? This man's around 46, in good shape, and he's got like... the veins were popping out of the top of his head.

"You'll *never* work for the Oakland Raiders!"

Ay! He went on and on. Like I was an enemy.

But we did get a chance to negotiate, just a hair. It kinda went like this.

"Mr. Davis, I'll take the twenty-five dollars a game... just for this year. But I would need four season tickets, so that I could give to family and friends, to come watch the Raiders."

I also added — and he didn't take too kindly to it — I said, "Mr. Finley taught me: empty seats are valueless. The A's have a lot of empty seats. 'You want tickets? You got 'em!'... as part of the negotiating process. This should be easy. You're averaging — " and I told him, "Mr. Davis, you're averaging thirty-five, thirty-six thousand, I'm seein' in the paper. The place holds forty-somethin'. It shouldn't be a problem."

And again, he used the F-word. "Get outta here!"

That was my experience with Al Davis.

That's my story and I'm sticking with it.

Chapter 37

USFL Oakland Invaders

In 1969, I was offered the job to work for the Oakland Raiders.

Of course, I turned it down; it wasn't enough money. Al Davis said, "Get outta here..." and so forth, and there you go. So I've never done football, up until 1982.

I didn't do any of the Raider games. I ended up doing one Raider game, in my life. It was when they were down in Los Angeles. They came up to the Coliseum — it was scheduled, I guess... they played a game against Houston, at the Coliseum. I substituted for somebody who was ill.

It was all right; it's a long day. They don't pay enough money. It's crazy. But I filled in just the one time. So I actually did work for Al Davis, although I don't think he knew who was running the board.

I didn't really do any football. Then, in 1982, the United States Football League was created: the USFL. It was created with the idea that it was going to compete with the NFL — in a way.

The schedule was more summer-ish, though, than winter-ish. I guess they were trying to give fans a fix. They found a little niche, and it worked for a few years. They signed Steve Young to a giant contract.

By the way, I just want to mention, the day that Steve Young signed on, his team was playing the *Invaders* — the Oakland *Invaders*. In the press lounge, he was giving an interview about having just signed a multi-million dollar contract.

I remember, he was kinda a big guy. I mean, I'm five-ten, five-eleven, I forget now. I'm kind of shorter as I bend over. But, anyway, he was like, six-two, six-three… and two-hundred and ten pounds, maybe, or *somethin'*… I dunno, two-fifteen? He looked solid. He was quite the player – especially in the USFL. Then he went on to stardom and, I think, to the Hall of Fame – for the NFL.

That was my little impression of Steve Young. There was a lot of press around, and he seemed like a genuinely nice guy.

That's all I have to judge on Steve Young – he seemed to be very nice, he seemed to be a very good person, and he was a big guy, for me.

I thought about playing football, one time, in college. I went down, and I saw a practice. Eh! Too big! They hit hard! In other words, in high school… sometimes – I mean, not always, not often, but – the quarterback could be bigger than your guard. 'Specially back in the '60s, in the late '50s. Five-nine, hundred and sixty-five-pound guard – that was kinda common.

When I played football, we had a big, big center. That was nice. Guy named Phil Lacosta; still remember him. Always snapped the ball well. I always had like, a lot of room, because he took up a lot of room. He was a big guy. But anyway. I digress.

So anyway, I get hired by the Invaders. They hired me specifically not to be able to do down and distance, but to work the message board, to get the crowd fired up, to let the crowd have a good time. My, gosh! That's what I do best. To be turned loose like that! I said, "Listen – any limitations?"

"No foul language."

No foul language. Okay. I got it. Any others?

"You know, well, don't try to denigrate any religion, or whatever."

"No, no. All right. But I mean, I could go… 'C'mon! Turn it up!… Let's get going here!… I can't hear you! – those kinds of things?"

"Any time you want."

Wow!

Then they said, "How much money do you require?"

"For what you want, three hundred dollars a game. It's a long day, football. And that's it."

That was more than what I was making at the time. It was a nice raise. I get to have fun and fire up the crowd.

Our average attendance during those three years was right around twenty-five, or twenty-six thousand. Occasionally, we'd get thirty... sometimes as low as twenty-two.

It was always pretty nice weather for the USFL. I thought they had a chance.

Many of the people from the USFL — well, Steve Young — went on to the NFL. Every time they start these new leagues, that's another showcase for someone to show what they could do. In that respect, I think it's good for football. If you like football, then have another league. Why not? We've tried all kinds of different leagues, and we're going to try more, probably, in the future.

The reason is... they don't think they've reached a saturation point. That there are still people out there who still want to see football in March, April, May, June, July.

I had a great time. I'd work the crowds. My personality came through strong. Everyone wondering, "Who is that guy, or gal?"

It was almost — let's go like this. It was a bit more rowdy with the USFL than it was for working the A's, at that time, which were now owned by the Haas family.

The Haas family wanted to kinda calm things down. They didn't want me to go all out. They kinda saw what I did.

"Well... we'd like a little softer, a little... *whatever*. Maybe take some of the personality *out*."

That was kinda the start of the downfall in terms of what I could do on the scoreboard, in terms of firing up a crowd. I could work a crowd of twenty-, fifty-thousand — it doesn't matter — all... day... long. We'd have fun. People would laugh.

But, it's kind of a lost art now. Doesn't happen anymore. By the way, these days, if you wanted to create a message real quick, like, "C'mon! I can't hear you!" — can't do it. You've got to type it *pre-* — you gotta do it ahead of time. Then you gotta dedicate a slot in the computer for it. Then you gotta press that button to make it happen… Eh! All right. Can't do it on the fly.

Systems right now are not meant for you to be… *spontaneous.* Systems are meant for you to… think it through… store the message… use it as needed… where appropriate.

For three years, I had complete reign over the entire game. That whole thing, "Shhhhhhh! Offense at Work!"… Come on! Did that years ago! C'mon, now!

It's funny, people pick up on other things. If you do it in your stadium, they pick it up fast. Way fast. So I like being creative. I loved it when they said, "Ay, they're doing that in Houston. Ay, they're doing that in Cincinnati." Perfect. Thataboy. Keep it up.

They paid me well, they fed me well… all kinds of comp tickets… everything. I have no qualms about the USFL. It was just a wonderful experience. Got a chance to work the crowd. We all had a nice time together.

Then it folded after the '84 season. I'm pretty sure that my years are correct.

But it was fun. And I'm always lookin' to have fun.

Chapter 38

Genghis Blues

Circa 1999, 2000, I called one of my former students, Ian Williamson, to talk about something that was going on, probably to arrange for him to do, maybe, the recital or something. I'm not sure, as to why I called him. Then, as we are chatting, he was telling me that he was working on a new project. This project was a full-length documentary, called "Genghis Blues."

The documentary was about a musician from San Francisco who was blind. Name was Paul Peña. He was quite the musician. But he was also an aficionado of shortwave radio. On the shortwave radio, in the Ukraine... Mongolia — I'm not exactly sure where — he was listening to a throat singing contest. It's a very guttural sound. I don't know how to reproduce it myself.

For some reason he wanted to — you know, I guess if you lose your sight, your hearing becomes even more acute — he felt that he replicated as well — maybe even better — than the top contestants. It's not singing *per se* at all, but it is emotional. You'd have to watch the movie to fully understand it — and we'll get to that in a minute.

<Chester> "Oh, wow. It sounds interesting. They went over there, and they filmed it?"

<Ian explains> "Yeah! They went over. He entered the contest — he wins the contest. All kinds of troubles along the way. They filmed it all. We got great footage. The fans who are all just — local Mongolians, I guess — just erupted in applause, that this American from San Francisco would win this award."

It's a wonderful movie. A full-length documentary. But, I'm getting ahead of myself.

"Wow! You're doing the editing?"

He said they entered the Mill Valley Film Festival a couple of years back, and were rejected. So they re-edited and maybe they tried a second time? I forget. If they tried a second time, it was rejected a second time.

Now, exactly how the brothers Roko and Adrian Belic, the filmmakers, and Ian connected — but they got along so well — I don't know. But it's funny. You're out there freelancing. You do a lot of things. You meet a lot of people. You take a lot of chances. Ian did. He committed to this movie. I don't think they had much money to pay him, if anything.

They were using their credit cards for everything. They were in debt, trying to make ends meet, to make this movie.

Ian came on board.

Ian Williamson was one of my former students. He graduated in 1993. At the Monterey Aquarium, he was the one who did the videos for about five to six years there. You press the button, it comes on and it shows you what the animals are like in nature, I guess. I'm not sure. But, he made good money then. He keeps working on projects that are successful.

He's got success written all over him.

All you gotta do is lay the project in front of him; if he believes in it, he's going to improve it. A lot of editors don't really add much. Ian is quite different.

So anyway, he worked on the film... To make a long story short, they entered the Mill Valley Film Festival the following year. They won Best in Show, for full-length documentary. Best of all of the ones they watched.

So, spurred on by that, they entered it into the Sundance Film Festival... Park City, Utah.

I forget who the actor is, who was in charge. Oh! Redford? Robert Redford. I guess that was his festival. Maybe it still is — maybe he's still part of it — but he was very active. I saw him in Park — eh, it doesn't matter. But I'll tell you about it.

So we go to the Sundance Film Festival. I mean, we were entered into the Sundance Film Fest — "we," I mean, Ian and his crew. They're accepted.

So, I told Ian, "I wanna go. Pay my own way, the whole thing — doesn't matter — I'm gonna go with my friend, Doc Siino."

He was from Pittsburg, but he wasn't in good shape to actually make the trip. So I asked Roy Steele.

"Roy, listen. I got a condo already in Park City, Utah. I got flight tickets. Just change the name through the airport. Cost you... ten dollars, I don't know — name change. I'm not sure. We'll go to Utah."

"Yeah, let's go."

So, off we went.

They had rented a nice home there. After the show was over, we had a place to go and have some drinks, play pool, and chat with all these creative people. It was wonderful. I've never been in the movie business arena before. It was invigorating. It's different.

I'm more pragmatic — get things done, problem-solved. These people are more, "Well, what about this?" They dream it up and talk about it and dissect it and... eh! too much for me, sometimes. But, y'know, each to his own.

Leading up to it then, Roy and I, we got our little condo, and we got settled in. He didn't want the bedroom. So I took the bedroom. He likes the couch so he could watch TV. Everything was spacious and nice... and snowing.

Y'know... I'm not a snow person. I'm not a cold person, even though... Alaska! You want to go to Alaska? Why? It's cold there. Why you wanna go where it's cold? Why you wanna go to the Ukraine? Why you wanna go... anywhere where it's cold? Montana? What do you want to do in Canada? Wha? What's in Canada? Too cold for me.

Bay Area's just perfect. Not too hot, but it gets hot sometimes. Not too cold, but it gets cold sometimes. But, pretty nice. I lived in The City[1] for about six years: long sleeve shirt and a nice light sweater over the top — couldn't go wrong. Work all day, play all night. Other way around? Doesn't matter. You're ready to go.

San Francisco has this allure, too. But I like Walnut Creek. It's just, really nice. Anyway, I digress.

So now comes the night of the show. Roy and I are all excited. We take a taxi. It's all we did, take taxis. Taxi service made a lot of money. They didn't have a Lyft and Uber in those days…"in those days" that's only, less than twenty years ago. But, they didn't have it. The taxi service in Park City, Utah, was excellent.

So we go to the show now.

The producers, the two brothers, they come out on stage ahead of time. They tell you a little bit about the show that you're about to see. I guess they do this for each movie. I only went to see one: "Genghis Blues."

"You mean, Chet! You were there, and all these wonderful films are being done by all these creative people…"

Nah, nah, nah… I just went for "Genghis Blues."

It's like when I go shop at the store. I got a list of five things? I buy five things. My eyes don't wander, left or right. I don't go, like, "Well, let's see… while I'm here, I think —"

No. Shopping is a chore for me. Therefore I handle it quickly, and to the point. And that's it. I get in the car and come back home. Done.

"But you could've, while you were there, picked up —"

Eh! It wasn't on the list.

"Yeah, but 'member we talked about it last week, you cudda —"

Nah. Wasn't on the list.

So I did my job. That's it. I'm done for today. Boom, you know, whatever. That's how I do.

So I went to see one film. It was a great film, great film. But —

---

[1] San Francisco, that is.

Here we go. The movie's over now. They go ahead and they come out, the director, the two writers, two brothers. Little question and answer period. "Where'd you, how'd you afford that? You flew all the way over… How many in your entourage? What gave you the idea to make it a documentary?" And so forth. All those standard-type things.

We went out to eat that night, Roy and I. Then we took a cab over to the house where there was Paul Peña, the star — so to speak, the focus — of the documentary, and the brothers, and Ian of course, and girlfriends, and *whatever*, and other friends… a houseful, about sixteen, twenty people, something, maybe more earlier.

Roy was having time of his life, Roy Steele. Played some pool, have a drink, chat a while, another game of pool, ping-pong, whatever they had going. It was a very fun evening. It was great.

Then we find out, later on — I'm not sure when we found out — but it was voted Best in Show at the Sundance Film Festival, for full-length documentary.

Emboldened by that, they apply to the Academy of Arts and Sciences for an Oscar, in full-length documentary.

Then they're told they have to convert it to thirty-five millimeter. You no longer have to do that; I didn't understand why you had to do it then. Why go through this expense? Well, cinema's different. Yeah. It's got a different look, a different depth; I understand. But for thirty-five thousand dollars, to convert to thirty-five millimeter? Get outta my face! How does a creative person get the money in order to afford that? I didn't like it then and I'm glad they don't do it now.

Because, eh… I'm kinda creative. Maybe I'd like to make a film. Maybe I'd like to — y'know, who knows? I wasn't into film, but I'm just saying… maybe I would get hooked one day. And you're going to limit me by saying thirty-five thou — where am I going to get thirty-five thousand? The bank would laugh at me, like, slap me in the face, get outta my face. Got no money for you to make a film… take a chance… y'know. It's all a chance.

So they converted to thirty-five millimeter like they had to. I don't know where you get these sponsors, these angels, that pay for these things, but it was wonderful. And now they entered.

Now, I go to the Academy Awards. Want to see how they're doing. Very exciting time, but I couldn't get in. Doesn't matter.

They were favored going in.

At the last minute, a movie was allowed to enter, that I think was against the rules, but I won't argue with Robert Redford. But it was a very late entrant. Past the deadline. <Chet, pointedly tapping on the table…> They were not on the official first list, coming out.

It was a documentary about the Holocaust.

Can I tell you now? You can't beat… the Holocaust… in a documentary. You got stock footage there, people being massacred and such, pulling at your heartstrings. Somebody tried, like, a Schindler's List, trying to help and so forth… you know, c'mon.

Ya can't beat… the Holocaust. You could… but you'd have to concentrate on the babies. Show the babies being murdered, and so forth. *That* would beat the normal, seeing the adults being… Show the dogs, whatever pets they owned, the cats — being gassed and such. *That* would win. Always does. Most common denominator. Makes you sick. Makes you win.

We got upset. I mean, we got beat. That's it. I think the producer and all those people were heavy Hollywood-connected, whispers of, "We could have it… and, give us a little time, we'll be — we're ready, we're right there…"

I think — I still think it was unfair.

But nonetheless, what an experience: to see a film that was rejected two, three times… then win Best of Show, Mill Valley… Best of Show at Sundance Film Festival… nominated for Academy Award… favored for the Academy Award… lost to the Holocaust movie.

If you'd like to see the movie, I think it's still on the Sundance Channel. It's called "Genghis Blues."

It'll be absolutely worth your time.

Chapter 39

Bombs Away: 1996 Olympics in Atlanta

Sometime early on in 1996 — probably the first homestand of the Oakland A's, in early April — I found out that, not one, but two of my former students were going to "work" the Olympics, one being Michael Baird, and one being John Moore.

"Hey! I gotta go."

Just like my student who was in the Sundance Film Festival, and the movie went ahead and was nominated for an Academy Award — Ian Williamson was the editor, my former student — I need to be there when those special — very special — moments occur.

So, I booked a flight for Wendi[1] and me. This was early on in our relationship. She wasn't really ready for all that would come… in that, there were really no rooms, in Atlanta. You had to go to someplace called "Buckeye", or Buck-*somethin'* — I dunno — in Georgia… you had to be way away from all the action.

It turned out that my former student, John Moore, was working for NBC, I guess. I might have that wrong, but I think it was NBC. Basically they had the entire hotel. All the rooms. There was nothing available, of course. John said that we could stay in his room. We put another bed in. It was wonderful.

The main reason that I went, was just to take them out to dinner… to raise a toast to them… to tell them how proud of them, I was. That's all I intended to do.

The first night that we were there — I think it was the first night — we went out to dinner with John Moore and Michael

---

[1] My longtime companion, Wendi.

Baird and Wendi and I. It was a wonderful time, possibly the only point in the trip in which Wendi really enjoyed herself, as things became more confusing as the vacation went on. Anyway, that was a wonderful dinner we had. We all hugged...

Next morning — you know, we're in John's room. He's up at six-thirty, out the door by seven. Probably comes back around eleven o'clock at night. We really don't see him during the day. So, Wendi and I decide, the next day, that we were gonna go to the Olympic Village.

The Olympic Village, they said, was quite commercial. As I looked around... it was. It was so commercial, it was almost garish. Here we are, Americans hosting the world's Olympics, and it's very tacky. There was not a lot of forethought put into the Olympics. A lot of advertising signs. I don't know. It didn't seem like a "world event" to me.

Nonetheless, we went to the Olympic Village. One of the things I wanted to see was the stage, where bands play.We walked around and we found it. Probably had seating — portable seating — for about, maybe as many as a thousand. They were prepared for a fairly large crowd.

In the daytime, when Wendi and I went and visited the Village, there were bands that were playing during the afternoon. The number in the audience — at that time — was maybe twenty... fifteen of us. I really wasn't in the audience; I was back near where the mixing console was. I wanted to see what kind of equipment he had, what kind of monitor system he was using, and so forth. We chatted, and all like that. It was a nice afternoon. Very nice.

I walked up to where the stage was, and checked it all out. Seemed very spacious for the performers. Very sturdy. Well-built...

We returned to the hotel room. We went out later that night. Very nice. We retired about — I don't know — ten, ten-thirty?

Gets very warm and muggy in Atlanta. We were kinda worn out.

We may have gone and seen a baseball game, in the Olympics — with the Americans — that day. If it wasn't that day, it was the following day. But anyway…

We're sleeping. It's around eleven o'clock, I'm pretty sure.

Sirens from the fire engine house that was right across from our room were — it was crazy! One fire truck after another fire truck… sirens all through the night! Unbelievable! Unbelievable.

The sirens raged all night, starting at around eleven o'clock. I don't think it stopped till three or four in the morning… maybe five. I don't know, but something was going wrong… somewhere.

As it turns out, there was an explosive device… set right near the stage where I was, earlier in the day. Set off the explosion and… oh, my! It was just horrific! Just horrific! We heard about that in the morning… at least we had answers as to what was going on.

We heard that there was something called a "lockdown" at the hotel. I didn't really understand what "lockdown" meant until I went down to the lobby to go outside, to buy a newspaper, to kinda see what's going on.

As I exited the hotel… as I tried to exit the hotel, they went, "Oh, no, sir. No, you can't go outside. We're on lockdown."

"How long does this go on?"

"Well, heh… until we're sure that everything is safe. Everything is locked down."

"I just want to get a newspaper, right? It's right there."

"Give me the money. I'll get it for you."

Very nice! He went, and got me a paper and gave it to me.

"Now, stay in the hotel."

And we did.

I'm not sure, I don't remember how much damage was done or injuries or somethin'. But, such a scary blast… here in

America. Truly, those in attendance — as well as myself and Wendi — were shaken to the core.

Bombs in America. Wow.

Chapter 40

Traditions

When I was growing up in Pittsburg, California, my aunts and uncles all lived right around me. We'd have Christmas dinner over at my grandmother's house on Fourth Street: raviolis, meat, sausage, all of those things. I learned traditions…

Thanksgiving. Thanksgiving was held at our own house. We didn't all do it together, all the aunts and uncles. No, no, no. New Year's Eve, we'd all get together: aunts and uncles, play cards… eat… tamales was the tradition for New Year's.

A lady lived behind my grandmother on Fourth Street. Her name was Rose Salazar. My grandmother helped her with her ravioli. Then, Rose Salazar taught my grandmother how to make delicious Mexican tamales.

So to have them on New Year's Eve, before you play cards, and all like that at night — we were a card playing family. Not everyone, but I'm just saying, we did play cards in the family.

That's a wonderful tradition. I'd like to speak a little bit about traditions… and we'll see where it leads us.

Y'know, everything we do in life could be tagged to the word "traditional." You might call it "habitual." Whatever you want to call it.

If you meet with a friend at Starbucks on Tuesdays at eleven, is that not a tradition that is taking place? Is "tradition" too heavy of a name? If you have a situation in which every Tuesday, at Starbucks, at a certain time, you're going to meet your friend — and you do — that's a wonderful little tradition.

Maybe you only chat for a half-hour… twenty minutes. And you both move on with your lives. That becomes a special moment in your life. One of those… happy-smile-about moments.

Let's say your tradition is going to the donut shop. In the donut shop, are five, six people, that you used to go to high school with. What a wonderful thing that is.

"Well, Chet! Maybe the wives want to get 'em out of the house. Maybe the husband is one —"

I don't know. It doesn't matter to me. What matters is that they are — in fact — getting together, that they are — in fact — socializing. That's healthy.

Now, do they also gossip a little? Why, sure. I mean, people do that. But, nonetheless, it's a wonderful little thing.

Now, let's talk about a bigger tradition. Especially, if you were ever a student, or ever a teacher. Meeting every day with a second period class, which goes from eight twenty-five to nine fifteen, or something of that nature… every day, all year long, Monday through Friday… is a tradition. You have guests in your home, your classroom.

They're learning to not speak when you speak. Maybe, you're learning to not speak, when they speak — you listen. Just like you would in your home.

So, to me, it was a wonderful thing. Second period. Every class has its own personality. If you're not a teacher, and don't know that, it's a fact. Second period is unlike third which is unlike fourth which is unlike fifth which is unlike sixth which is unlike seventh… and so forth.

This one's sharper. This one's sleepier. This one's funnier. This one's more serious.

But I loved them all.

It's a tradition. I looked forward to it.

I didn't look at the clock and go, "Oh, wow. Another class."

Don't forget, I taught four of the exact same subjects, for over thirty years. Electronics I. Second period, third period, fourth period, fifth period. Then we had lunch. Then, it was my recording and television production classes that took over the entire afternoon and into the evening.

But nonetheless, I looked forward to that personality of that class. I looked forward to seeing some of the individuals in that class. This one's funny. This one's intuitive. This one's goofy. Eh, whatever.

So our lives are encompassed, entwined with… traditions.

Now, if it's not a good tradition… you're getting tired of the people that you're seeing at Starbucks. You don't like their snide comments. It's getting a little uncomfortable for you. Well, then end that tradition. That's all.

"But, Chet! It's hard… 'cause I still like some of the people —"

It's gotta go. It's a cold hard call. But now all you're doing is *semi*-participating and really feel like you'd like to be somewhere else.

When you get that "somewhere else" feeling… get out. Whether it's a relationship or whatever… get out.

"Chet! I'm married for 20 years. I can't get out."

Well, then… deal with it. Talk it over.

But, a tradition to me is just wonderful. It belongs in all of our lives.

Let me give you some simple examples.

I live here in Walnut Creek. I have a big deck out back that overlooks a creek that goes by. It's a gorgeous little setting. I've got geese on the hillside with their baby over there and geese over here and ducks and everything… egrets… great blue herons… river otters. I'm just encircled by wonderment.

I have this big deck back here. It's shaded. It's very nice. So, every Friday, when the gardener finishes his work, around four-thirty or five… Wayne comes over, next-door neighbor — Art — comes over. Wendi's[1] here. I'm here. We chat. We snack. We recap the week, in a way.

---

[1] My long term companion.

It started about four or five years ago, maybe further — I don't know. It just happened. I think Wayne got off work.

"Wayne, you wanna beer?"

"Oh, yeah. That'd be great."

He sat down, and one thing led to another.

We got a neighbor, Art. He comes over, and all… wonderful.

And yet, Art hasn't been coming by lately. It concerns all of us. Which is… Gee, a tradition of many years, and there's no Art on Friday now. We miss him.

How much control do I have over Art's life? Answer: none. Then what are my expectations about Art coming over? I have none. If he's here, he's here. If he's not, he's not. The trend, lately, has been "not."

These little things… you don't think much of it. It could be going to the soccer field with your son or daughter, sitting with another parent. Each time your daughter or son is playing soccer, that lady or man or whatever is there. You chat. It's a little bit of a tradition.

"But, Chet! That tradition will go away when the children… separate into different activities, the following year."

Sure.

But while it's happening, enjoy it. It's good. It's healthy for you.

You have wonderful things to look forward to. And, by the way — as I said earlier — if you don't look forward to it, end it.

I'm a big "traditions guy". Everything I do, is part of a tradition.

Chapter 41

Making a Change: Teachers

A lot of people don't realize this, but teachers spend more of their waking hours in their classroom and the school campus than they do at home.

Let's say you're on your way to school at seven — seven-thirty — whatever time you leave, and let's say you arrive home at three or four. That's eight or nine hours.

Let's say you sleep eight hours. I know some of you can get by on four or five, and less — and that's wonderful. It's probably very good for you.

I always needed a full eight. Didn't often get it, especially working a second job with the A's and you get home late at night and it takes you a couple hours to unwind and all like that.

Since you spend more time — more of your waking hours — in your classroom, shouldn't that really be your second home? I believe it should.

You spend more hours there in that atmosphere, than you do at home, while you're awake. Why shouldn't you surround yourself with what you like? It's your classroom. Why do all the walls have to be — in every classroom in the United States — if it's not, like, re-sawn redwood and all like that Monte Vista had — but just regular sheetrock? There's nothing wrong with sheetrock. But why does it have to be painted off-white — all the way to the dark of light beige? That's it. You go to Illinois, you go to San Francisco, you go to... anywhere: same thing. Colleges: same thing. Junior High: same thing.

Wait a minute. Let's go down to the elementary. Ah! a little bit of lively. However, the problem is that the walls are still: off white to light beige.

Why shouldn't they be the color you want? What I'm saying here in this chapter is, I'm going to tell you some things that maybe you thought were impossible to have. Like, "How do we do this?"

Many of us don't want to pull money out of our own pocket, but we do anyway.

The school was like a second child to me. I put probably a hundred and fifty to three-hundred a month into the school. You send a kid on an errand, to do this and that and tell him to get a hamburger for himself and do whatever, and gas and thank you very much. Thanks. That's it. You get reimbursed? No.

But it was important to have this errand run. It was important to bring this back now. Life goes on. We make progress. Can't let a little money stand in your way. Many of you who are teachers out there know exactly what I mean, at all levels. Money out of your own pocket. Many teachers — not many, some — teachers pride themselves on, "I haven't paid a nickel. Whatever they have, they have... I order these things, I use my budget and..."

Okay, Good. Good. Good, good.

But for a lot of us, we want more. Sometimes we don't know we want more, especially when you don't think you can get more.

So, this chapter is about things that I think teachers need. The following chapter is addressed to the administrators to provide those things you need.

So! Let's start on what I think we need.

Do you have noisy neighbors? I mean, you don't have to be a teacher. In your house, your condo, your apartment, wherever you are.

"Yeah, the neighbors to my right — boy! They get loud, and this and that."

I don't care if I rent the apartment. Gonna put sheetrock on that wall. Oh, yeah, right over the sheet rock that's there. Oh, yeah, knock a few holes down real low with a little nail… find where one stud is. Then all the rest are usually sixteen inches on center from there. Oh, yeah, draw a line all the way up and down the wall. Don't matter. You're going to cover it with sheetrock.

I took one size of a classroom. My classroom wasn't this big. But all the additional room — my lab that I had — the edit suites and what-have-you. Wow! I had five edit suites. I had a full control room studio. I had a work area that could handle fifty kids, plus my classroom that was used as the studio, if necessary, for television production and recordings.

I had a *kingdom*. I had a lot of area I had to cover. Not the typical one I'm going to cover here. I covered it with the carpet squares. It all started with just doing a rainbow over the top of the wall there, above the chalkboard that I had. I liked it. The kids liked it, "Ay… far out!"

"Eh… why'd you use a rainbow?"

"I dunno. Cuz we're going to call this 'Rainbow Studio.'"

Initially, we had called it "Zap City." What we did, our little club: electronics, TV production people, you know, studio recording people — like that. Then it was called "Crapé:" Concert Recording and Production Enterprises, is what it stood for. Then, around 1974 — something like that, '73 — when we finally moved from the science room to what's called the "Industrial Arts" area, I had woodshop on one side of me, and I had metal shop on the other side of me. Noise was a problem.

First thing I did was have a wall installed between me and the woodshop. Then we recovered it again with a couple more sheets of sheetrock. Can't hear a pin drop.

Had a neighbor right here. I live in a condo in Walnut Creek. They were meth people. They did it, they sold it, they — the whole thing. Arguments in the morning early, loud music in the morning, loud music at night, the whole thing.

I went over there one time. They almost punched me in the face.

"Get outta here. We'll do what we want, old man. Go away."

I went, "All right!"

I immediately went and bought sheetrock... put that in, and... Heh! Can't hear 'em! Two sheets of sheetrock per wall. That's what you need. Not *one* half-inch sheet of four-by-eight sheetrock; *two* sheets of half-inch, four-by-eight sheetrock — staggered, meaning the seams don't meet each other when you put the second layer, but you go about halfway.

<Student> "Oh, I have to cut one of these to get started then, halfway —"

"Yeah, there you go!"

Halfway, then a full one, a full one, a full one... and then the other half goes down at the other end — whatever. It's easy to do.

The cost of covering a room — you know the size of your room. Maybe you have not the exact dimensions, but you have an idea. I chose a room twenty feet by twenty-four.[1]

Now my classroom wasn't that big. All my other facilities — added in — were much larger. But the actual where-I-taught-class, where the chalkboard was, that's where I taught.

So, to put sheetrock on the wall for four-hundred and eighty square feet, is $330, and that's it. $13.83 a sheet, current prices, Dolan's Lumber in Concord.

$330 plus labor, and you shut out — not one wall. I've priced in two walls: someone to your left, and someone to your right. Usually, then against the back wall or something is outside, and the other one with the door and everything is like a hallway.

Usually you have neighbors for your left and right. If you'd like to take care of the neighbors left and right, okay, the current price is three-thirty, plus labor. Now I'm not going to mention, gee, how much it might cost for labor. Maybe for sheetrock if you had to pay someone to come in, just nailing up sheetrock, and doing a seam — put seam tape on them, where the seams

---

[1] Under $750 INSTALLED... much less if you can do it yourself.

are. He does some sanding a couple of days and he comes back and he's all done. Then you paint it.

"How much for his time?"

I don't know.

"Can't you do it? Can't your students help you? Can't the parents help you?"

If everyone were to roll up their sleeves and help teachers — just like in my classroom...

We had to move chairs for the concert. First class of my day: move the chairs. Second class of the day: vacuum the theater. Third class of day: stacked all the chairs in the *thing*, very nice and neat, eh. Next period: we're finished — last minute touches everything — Ah! Now the truck arrives. Fifth period: helps unload it, you know, the PA system, the guitars and everything, for the band and such. Can't do it alone.

If — one of the themes in this book — if I could get it through to everyone: you can't do it alone. You gotta ask for help.

I asked my students all the time, "I need some help. I need to bring in twenty sheets of sheetrock. They're kind of heavy."

<Student> "Uh, Chet! You were going to cover *this* today..."

"Yeah, we'll get to it. But I need some help. It may be too heavy for some of you, but I need help. Can some of you guys, please — girls? Help me out. Get out of the classroom, get some air and... bring in some sheetrock."

And they did.

Who painted everywhere, all my studios and control rooms, edit suites — those things? Well, we did. Then we carpeted 'em. We didn't have to do anything after that.

<Student> "Chet! Does the school allow you to put carpet on the wall?"

Well, I didn't ask at first. But it turned out that they said, "Well, we have to fireproof all this."

"How do you do that?"

"Well, someone from the district is going to come in with a

canister. It's going to spray. It's just fireproofing. It takes a couple days to dry, so don't try to touch it. We'll come in on a Friday. When you're done with your last class, spray it. We'll do that, twice a year, the fire department wanted."

Your carpet is as fireproof as sheetrock, almost. It's gotta reach certain standards — fire protection and so forth. So your carpet is good — carpet samples.

<Student, again> "Where'd you get all these carpet samples, Chet?"

Any carpet store. I just went to a local Danville store and said, "Here's what I need."

I had a little pickup truck. He gave me maybe… seven books of carpet samples, to get started. I used them all up. Went back to him.

"Do you have any…?"

<Carpet Guy, smiling> "Come on, Chet."

So we go back. He went into a big store room. He said, "See all this? Take it all. Discontinued, shag carpet, fill in the blank — out of here! Old stuff. Been trying to peddle this stuff… one little thing… yeah, people, they don't come in for that. Occasionally they do. You just need a few. I kept too many. Get rid of them."

So a gal in one of my classes had a big giant van — I've never seen one — all enclosed — like a big Dodge, big van thing. She said, "I'll get my van. I'll bring it. We'll do it."

Drove down there, loaded that thing up, all the way to the top. All the way to the top. Ones I didn't like, just tossed 'em. They go in the dumpster. The shag carpet — eh, neh, neh, neh. Not going to use this one.

So we had every kind of nap, every kind of *thing*, long nap, short nap, this nap… tried to coordinate the colors so that they didn't shock each other as they stood out. Deep green was always the one that caught my eye. I placed them myself. So when I walked in the room, I could just — "Look — I love deep, rich, freshly vacuumed and cleaned deep green carpet."

Yeah, it's funny. One of my favorite colors; orange is one of my favorite colors, too.

But anyway, I digress.

"Okay, what else are we going to do in your room?"

"We're going to paint this room."

"What would you like? Oh, you want an accent wall?"

"Yes…"

"And whatever —"

"Yes…"

"Eh, no problem. C'mon!"

"You know, I'd like to do a wood wall."

Laminate! A buck a foot. All day long. Less than that; go to Home Depot; go *wherever* — Lumber Liquidators… whatever. They all have inexpensive laminates and stuff. Looks great on the wall. Put it horizontally.

In one of my homes in Concord, I had — and by "one of my homes," I never owned two at a time. I had a home in Concord. I made an *accent wall*, so as soon as you walked in the door: there it was, looking right at you. It was made from what are now flooring. Six inch wide pieces, different lengths, so I had four different kinds of wood — all laminated, you know, the plywood — quarter-inch thick. One would be birch, one would be oak, one would be — *whatever*. I used four different stains: four different stains and four different woods are sixteen different combinations. Those are all gorgeous. These were in the browns and golds. Looked marvelous. Wha! Comes pre-made now. They even got it where they have the adhesive on it. Take off the tape and put it on. C'mon, now! We're talking cheap.[2]

All right. The paint. What does it cost to paint this room — four-hundred eighty square feet — that we were talking about? Well, let's talk about the paint first: one of the problems with all the paint in all the schools in the United States, is they use

---

[2] Paint and/or laminate for accent under $400.

interior paint.

Interior paint is for like, people are going to be in this room. We've got to use an interior paint.

Eh, it washes all right. After a year or two, you can't really get out some of these smudges and things. Things begin to look old faster than you can blink an eye. Immediately everyone in the United States involved in painting their schools, should shift over to exterior paint. Oh, yeah! Wash it. Bump it. Hit it. Kick it. Do whatever you want.

<Administrator, again> "Chet! Exterior paint is for exterior — Exterior paint is meant for the exterior."

Shut. Up.

Put the exterior paint on the inside; it dries nice and quick — probably takes a little longer to really dry all the way. Probably a good thing to do the painting on the weekend, which you'd probably do anyway. Leave a window or two open so we get some ventilation, while the alarm is on. Tell the alarm company that this window is going to be open and get a little cross breeze going. Or don't. Only open the window while you're there painting.

Come the next day, open the window and let it air out a little bit while you're doing something else. Paint's already dry. You'll be so happy with the exterior paint. It's unbelievable. You should do that in your home.

Now somebody's — some chemist — is going to read this someday and say, "You're crazy. You can't use that because you're going to — "

Eh, I dunno.

Read the label on exterior paint. It does not say cancer-causing. Latex paint. Sorry. I see no harm there. Been doing it for years. Recommending it for years. Now I'm putting in writing. That's all. I'm just putting it down.

What does it cost to paint that four-hundred and eighty square-foot room — that twenty-four by twenty room that you're talking about? I don't know. Maximum would be five gallons. Maximum. That's paint and everything. Thirty bucks a gallon — going price — exterior paint. Not bad. I got a hundred and fifty dollars, plus labor.

Who's going to do the labor? I don't know. People are going to help. Your students are going to help, because we're going to revitalize your classroom and we're going to do it as a school. We're going to raise money for the school. So the teachers can have these things, without putting money out of their own pocket.

Now, if you have carpet in your classroom, which a lot of people do… I'm gonna ask you something: how often do they clean that carpet?

<Administrator> "Uh, Chet, they vacuum every day. The custodian comes in…"

"Oh. Okay."

You've got probably four-hundred and eighty square feet in where you live. Maybe you have four-hundred and eighty square feet or more of carpeting somewhere. It's not much. You vacuum it every day. How many people walking on your carpet? Couple of kids? Husband and wife? Doggy?

How often are your classroom carpets steam cleaned?

Let me tell you something. I don't care if you could do your carpets once a year. It's not enough for a classroom. Yeah, at your house, you got ten, twelve little feet running around. In a classroom of thirty-five, plus a teacher… OK, what do you got, seventy-two feet going? All dirty shoes, rain, dust, wind — you name it. On and on.

Elementary School: head lice problems, other things that come from the carpet… Every school should own two or three steam machines — good ones, powerful ones, with the engines that really do a job. Talk to any manufacturer of carpeting and they will tell you: they recommend for your home — every 6 months — that it be steam cleaned.

When they say it's a thirty-year carpet, they mean it, if you'll steam clean it every six months and keep it up.

There you go! Always looking nice. Carpets… get filthy – if I may use that word – filthy in school. Disease-carrying? You bet. Irritant-providing? Huh! Guaranteed. That musty little smell the vacuum doesn't quite get all of it – that vacuum can't get all of it? You need a powerful steam clean. Suction. That's what cleans carpets. The manufacturers recommend it. We don't do it in the schools enough.

Once a year if you're lucky, if they can get to it, during the summer. Maybe they can catch your room at Christmas vacation time. I don't know.[3]

How about blinds for the windows you have? Window coverings? Mini-blinds? California blinds? Something!

Think about that. Put that on your list.[4]

You don't have fluorescent lighting at home. All the schools have fluorescent lighting, throughout the United States. Go anywhere: same thing. One school looks like the other school.

By the way, did you know in California, there's about four or five models of schools. They change them every so many years. They go like this, "You're going to build a new school? Here's the model we're building."

No re-sawn redwood. None of those things. Too expensive.

So they all kind of look cookie-cutter, if you will.

I won't teach in a cookie-cutter setting. I would never be an administrator in a cookie-cutter setting. I'd change that. We're going to landscape this; we're gonna paint that. Oh, yeah, we're going to have a garden area. We're going to have a – *whatever.*

---

[3] $175 would do most classrooms professionally.

[4] How about a lamp or two in your classroom? A picture wall of the kids… curtains… let your mind wander. A small garden. Fresh flowers. Everything that we've talked about, for your room, would cost about $1500. Who's going to pay for all this? READ THE NEXT CHAPTER.

<Administrator, skeptical> "Yeah, Chet, the kids will just drive by and spin out on your roses, bushes..."

"Eh! Rebuild. Hunt them down somehow. Kids always talk; they can't shut up."

One of the things about a school, as you know — I can only speak for a high school. That's only where I taught. Everybody talks. I don't know why. Where I came from — Pittsburg, California — no one talked.

<Pittsburg, California, Administrator> "Who did that?"

"I don't know."

"You were right here."

"I wasn't — I wasn't even looking that way. I well — I dunno..."

But for some reason, in Danville, California, they talk. Maybe in your area, they don't. Maybe the guys will come by and do donuts again. I don't know. Maybe you have to put up some kind of fencing, kind of low fencing. Tasteful. Two-inch by two-inch thick walled steel. There you go! Concreted deep into the ground. Welded across; couple of nice pieces, going across. Maybe the height is three feet or something, four feet. Doesn't block the view. Paint it whatever your school colors are — whatever — flat black, whatever you like. I don't care. There is a way to solve every problem. Only thing is, we don't do it at schools anymore. We just come, we go, and we leave — it's crazy.

I mentioned lamps. Maybe one by your desk, someplace else, something nice. Wall hangings? How about little wall hangings and stuff? Posters, and *things*, are kind of things they put on every wall. I'm not saying you shouldn't put a poster on a wall. I'm just saying, try to think outside the box.

What would you do at your home? How about this: better yet, what would you do at your home, if it was just you? The kids aren't there; your children are not there. They're at school somewhere, or at home, or wherever, with the babysitter. Your husband's not there; your wife's not there. Just you. What do you want for your classroom? That's what you should do. That's what's important. That's what'll bring out your personality. That's what'll make it a home. That will make kids want to come to your classroom.

Ah!

Got a photo wall of students? Activities going on? Got a phone? Take some pictures! Print 'em out. Change 'em. Add to 'em daily. Whatever! Whatever you like to do. Please remember: it's your home.

Now last: I want to mention something about the arrangement of desks in your classroom.

If you have a rectangular room, make sure that you're standing where you're looking out at only about four rows of desks. Maybe it's nine across in each row. In mine, I had four rows, going from left to right — you know — deep. Four rows deep. In the first and second row: four chairs. These are desk-chairs that folded up, on each side of the aisle.

So four, four; that's eight. Four, four… that's sixteen. So I've got sixteen, so far, out of two rows. The last two rows had five each. Five each, plus the very last row had one more, for the center. So, because there's no more rows — nothing — we could have a chair right at the end of my aisle, so that I could pace up and down the classroom. Short walk for me. It's very easy. Easier to be heard, if you're speaking to only about four rows deep, maybe five.

If you had forty chairs in the classroom, you'd want to do four deep, ten wide. Five on each side of an aisle. You don't want to do ten deep, four wide: you lose attention past the fifth row. Kids are fooling around, and, eh — no good. No good.

<Administrator, questioning Chet again> "Uh, Chet! It's always been this way."

"Well, then, change it!"

"But, Chet! The chalk board's here…"

"Then, move it! What do you think, it's in stone? It's screws! Unscrew it! Move it!"

"Chet! This wall, now, is this off-beige…"

"Paint it!"

Now. You've got your desk arranged correctly. You got your chalkboard or whiteboard or whatever you're using, in the right location. Now you're teaching. Now, you're teaching.

<Another teacher> "Chet! I already have it that way."

Good for you.

<Yet another teacher> "Chet! I need to change mine."

Change it.

In the next chapter, we'll talk about how we pay for this.

Chapter 42

MAKING A CHANGE: ADMINISTRATION

Any change in a school system or school itself usually comes top-down. We're used to that in education. What do they want to do now, and so forth?

We've got millions of teachers in this United States that maybe didn't realize things could be better, things didn't have to be the same. They could make their classroom their home, their home away from home. Their waking hours are more at school than at home with their husband, their wife, their children. It's just a fact.

We do it in these drab, banal — if you will, I don't know — classrooms, that are all the same. It's all the same. Same color, same everything, same carpeting throughout... Same. Everything: same.

When you go home to your own home, maybe on the weekend, — you and your husband, wife — you do things around the house. You make a few changes. You add a new lampshade.

We have teachers now that understand that there can be a change, and it's achievable, and it's not too expensive. In other words, to make teachers really happy, every teacher wants to go to their room on the first day of school. They want to get organized. They want to get ready. They want to put up a new poster. They want to do *whatever*.

When you have your first meeting of the school year, whether you're the principal of many years there or you're brand new, doesn't matter.

"Hi, I'm Nancy. I'm Bob. I'm your principal. We've got coffee over here. Tea, water, pastries, everything! Enjoy, mingle about..."

Send them to their classrooms immediately, to start work on their design for their home away from home. They don't want to hear all the — I mean, I know the first day of school, meeting only an hour — keep it brief. Jump right to the thing — the heart of the matter — Day One of school.

We're going to erect a big sign out front with a $100,000 goal. Oh, yeah! We're going to do this every year — but we're starting this year. Hundred thousand. It's for the classrooms, for the kids, and the teachers. You'll make your teachers happier. They will be in their — quote-unquote — "own space," unique space, accented differently, painted differently. And they want to do it now.

Send them to their room. Let him start designing. They'll work in teams. Some people aren't very good. I'm all right at designing. Actually, pretty good. But I mean, I'm just saying, I'm — I could do it. But, there are people that are just easier with the eye, which is, "Gee, if you just paint this wall this color, or this color — either one is really good — like in this tone. That'll just offset this and make it just — really make it look nice."

Don't forget: in the end, it's just paint. They'll be glad to start doing their design, but they'll want to know, "When does this get done?"

Well, tell 'em.

"During Christmas vacation, Easter vacation, and summer, this calendar year, stretching into the next calendar year, we're going to start. We're going to have a drawing. It's going to be a lottery. We're not going to do by seniority. We're going to do straight lottery: Who gets their rooms done first?"

How much money are we talking about here?[1]

How you gonna offset these labor costs, Mr. Administrator,

---

[1] $1500 per classroom, if the teacher opts to do this. No one should feel they must change.

Mrs. Administrator? Whatcha gonna do?

I'm gonna help you here. You're going to get ideas from this. You're going to go, "Huh! I have even better ideas..." Do those.

Make sure their teachers give all your input. You want the teachers involved in this. You want the kids being happy. You see — Mr., Mrs., Ms. Administrator — it's all about the teachers. Without the teachers, none of this happens. None of this education takes place. All you are is a facilitator. You're just their advocate.

What do you need? Help you out.

Some of us need a lot of help. We're needy. Some of us are not. I don't happen to be needy. I kind of do my own thing. I always ask for forgiveness *later*. But I always go like, "Well, I'm thinking of painting the room *this*. I'm going to do *this*." This is before I put the carpet.

The administrator goes, "Well, let's see... your schedule is four years from now they'll be coming to our school, to repaint."

"No. No, I'm thinking about this weekend. I'm going to paint this. I'm thinking about — you know, I'm thinking about it."

"Well, uh... you know, they have people that come —"

"Yeah! Every four years or five years, they come. I want it now."

"Well, —"

Then we don't solve anything. Very good. The weekend would come. I would go, buy the paint, come on down and paint it.

I had a mural on my room — in my room, where I taught, before I put the carpeting. The gorgeous little mural — I asked somebody from the art department, I asked the art teacher who's really good at murals. They said, "this gal is really good. So they could work together."

I paid 'em a hundred dollars to paint me a mural — on the wall — of a creek flowing by, with the redwoods... and all like that, because that's where I love. That's where I live — now —

right by the creek.

Then the administrator came in.

"Whoa! That looks nice! Who did that?"

But first they said, "Who said you could do that?"

That's always the first question from an administrator. Why it is you people have to do that, I don't know. Why you don't just say, "Wow! That looks good! Great!" The first question was, "Who said you could do it?"

So I went, "Well, I was talking about it and there didn't seem to be much of a reaction, and, uh... I don't know. I just wanted it and I did it."

"Well in the future, Chet, let us know what you're going to do, because..."

Because what? Because what? Because you don't think maybe it's okay? It's okay! Let yourself be an administrator! Help your teachers!

If you take care of your teachers, and you make your teachers happy, everything will fall into place. If you aren't aware of that now, then learn it... now. Teachers first. They'll take care of the kids. Give them the environment that they so desire. They didn't know they desired it. They didn't know it was possible. Now they know.

Changes should be made... right away. Put that sign up: hundred thousand dollars. That's what we're gonna raise this year.

"Gee, Chet, how're we going to raise all this money, to pay for this?... $1500 per classroom?"

Administrators: here's what I'm saying. Roughly, you're talking fifteen-hundred dollars a classroom. How many classrooms do you have at your school? Fifty? Thirty? Twenty? Seventy-five? I don't know the number and I don't care.

You put that sign out and all of a sudden the school becomes one. Why?

"We're doing it for the teachers, who then will be teaching

your children, in a more satisfying manner, a more complete manner. Home. It's unbelievable the changes that we're going to make. Unbelievable."

So, what do we do to fundraise? How do we raise this hundred thousand? Don't forget, you're going to raise a hundred thousand, you're going to have this lottery, and you're going to knock out as many as you possibly can at Christmas. We've raised enough to do four classrooms. Four! Do 'em! They become the model.

"Come check out the English Room Five! Come check out Math Room Seven! Whatever! Check out what they did. Notice, there's no noise in those rooms from either side. The teacher can't hear the other teacher. Nobody hears nobody. Oh, look at the colors! Boy, nice! Yeah. I know. I'm not fond of that green myself, but it was done nicely and you know, trimmed out nice... boy, the windows are clean, carpets are freshly steamed cleaned. We're happy here. It's a good thing."

"Gee, what kind of labor do we have to pay for painting?"

I don't know! Have the parents help! Have the kids help! It's called painting. We're going to be working over the Christmas holiday. Can you donate a day? Can you do anything? Whatever! By the way, it doesn't have to be then — you can do it on a weekend. You know, nothing says you have to do it by Christmas. Heck! Try to knock out the first one, the first fifteen-hundred you get: do it! Nothing wrong with that. That's your model. Let 'em come in and look at it. Get some ideas.

"So, to raise some money how're we going to do this?"

I don't know. How about a bingo night every week on a Wednesday? Pick a Wednesday. It's a nothing day... hump day. Every night, in the cafeteria, and I mean — each night in the cafeteria, those things raise thousands of dollars for a school's program.

Pittsburg High School was running — their bingo thing was run by a cousin of mine, Al Bonanno. They made bank. They put more money into that school... it was unbelievable.

"How is that possible, Chester?"

People like to gamble. Indian reservations that have casinos are a far drive. Tahoe and Reno, even further. All they want to do is take their twenty dollars, go sit down, have a coffee, look at the numbers, chat a little bit, mumble about losing... kabbish about – whatever... gossip, or whatever they do. They usually come in groups of twos and threes and fours and they're usually elderly. That's not fair. You get all age groups, but you get a large group of people that are, like, retired and whatever, on a fixed income. They've got their little budget and they like to – they'd love to come, every week. That's eighty dollars a month. That could be their gambling budget. They'd like to do it at your school, where it's convenient to park, where they feel safe... where, when they drive in, there's a rent-a-cop waiting for 'em.

<Rent-a-cop> "Welcome. Are you coming to bingo? Good! Just park right—"

You know, that type of thing. There you go!

<Skeptical Administrator> "Chet! We don't want to pay a rent-a-cop."

Good! Then you do it.

"Welcome to bingo night. Glad you made it to – *fill in the blank* – School. We're so glad you're supporting the teachers of our school."

Everybody's on board! Kids want the teachers to be happy. Kids want the teachers to have a nice room.

And what do you want, Administrator?

The same thing!

Then do it.

Fashion show and dance! C'mon. I did it. They work great. Have it off-campus. C'mon! Casino night! Off-campus. Crab feed! Off-campus. Live auction with silent auctions! C'mon! You could have that on campus or off. It's better off because you could serve drinks. When you serve drinks, people loosen up the pocket. You don't want people drinking on your campus — I get it. So have it off-campus.

Have fun. Make a lot of money on drinks! Costs you a buck or two to make a drink; charge ten. C'mon! It's a fundraiser!

All of these things.

You could have a big garage sale at the school. School-wide! Kids could have donations, parents, businesses. C'mon! Maybe you do it twice a year. Maybe you do it three times a year. Garage sale. Sell stuff! People donated, you sell it, you thank 'em. Whatever! It's pretty straightforward. Not that complicated. Where are you going to hold this thing? I don't know — gym or cafeteria. Either one. You need a big space.

<Administrator, a downer> "People… we don't want them walking on our gym floor."

That was a big thing in the past. Not so much anymore. I don't think anything is made of wood anymore. I know when I go bowling, the alleys aren't wood anymore. It's just… plastic. Do you remember the old days, maybe, that when you went bowling and if you lofted the ball, that they wouldn't let you bowl?

<Bowling proprietor> "You can't bowl if you're going to throw the ball out there: it dents the wood…"

Pfffft! It's like steel now. You dent nothing. The only thing that makes the lanes dangerous is the oil. Put no oil on it: better floor than you got in your house. Nothing will destroy it.

But, they're not really going to harm your gym floor anymore, you know. People walk on it all the time — tennis shoes get dirty, too. Wear tennies all the time. I don't know why, but at least it won't make black marks. I understand.

But, c'mon! People gotta open — gotta loosen up a little bit for this fundraiser. This is a two-, three-, four-year project. This is roll-up-your-sleeves and go to work.

This is a happy time, something that's never happened at your school. Never. Now it's going to happen. It's going to be a reality. You're going to do it. The reason is, it needs to be done.

<Administrator, questioning> "How do we get better teachers, Chet?"

I don't know! Make 'em happier.

Some people are outgoing teachers, some are quieter… they're all pretty good. They all try their best. They've all been trained, you know.

You could hold marathons, you know, the 5K run, 10K run, those kind of things… plus all the normal fundraisers, that kids can help with: car washes, cookie sales — I don't know. Candy sale… I don't know.

"Chet! The choir — they sell candy in November and…"

I don't care! Let 'em sell their candy in November! Raise money so they could go on a trip to — wherever they go sing. I don't care. There's no conflict of interest.

Roll up your sleeves. We're all competing for people's bucks.

"Chet, I live in a poor district."

Well, then it's going to take you a little longer to raise the money. But you can still knock out a few every year.

Come on! You can let the parents come in. You could have an open house. You know, on back-to-school night: making sure they stop by Room 101 — if that one's been done. Let 'em look at it.

"This is the future of what we're going to do. This is Miss Davis'. This is Mr. Smith's room. Check it out. Here's where we're going."

You've got to get the parents on board. They're the only ones with money. You got to tap into 'em.

"Chet, we already do, uh, you know in order for us to have supplies and all like this, eh, we asked for seven hundred and eighty dollars. We asked for over a thousand…"

I don't care. So what! This is "in addition to."

You do your thing. We'll do our thing. We're all doing a good thing. There's no conflict here. It's just, we're going to do a little more fundraising. But it's going to be different — and I'll tell you why. You're going to have the support of parents. That's important. You're going to have the support of students. That's important. Most importantly, you're going to have the support and appreciation of your teachers.

That's going to make an improvement in your school — just attitude adjustment.

We're not asking you to go back to school and do a better job. No, we want to make you happier. How can we do that in your classroom? The answer is, you now know, make some changes.

Read the chapter that I wrote for teachers, and all those changes that are going to be made. Help them make the change! Support them in every way. Do not have a doubt.

When they say, "Gee, do you think they'd mind if we put a third lamp here?"

No! They won't mind. It's a regular lamp that you bought at Macy's, cost you twenty-three dollars and it's cute? Plug it in. All of our electrical outlets are proper. We're a school. We trust the school.

"Chet, I'm an administrator and I don't know if I trust —"

Well then get a pro out there and inspect every plug! Make sure the ground is intact. Make sure nothing is loose in any of the wiring. We don't want overheating. We don't want sparks. That's your job. Make the room safe.

If you feel you need to do something before this work is done — inspection-wise — do it.

Check for leakage of the windows. Maybe those single-pane windows are now leaking and double-pane is called for. Then let's suck it up and replace it.

Make it safe. Make it warm. Make it quiet.

Make it a home.

Chapter 43

Valuable Lessons

I taught at Monte Vista High School for thirty-two years. Worked very closely with large numbers of students. Whether it be electronics in the Open Lab, showing 'em how to solder… these are all great little lessons that you could carry on in life. Maybe you use it later. Maybe you might even use it in a job, maybe not.

I taught two lessons to all the students that I had over the years, having nothing to do with whether I was teaching electronics or TV productions or studio recording or physics or pre-algebra. I did teach a few other classes throughout the years but…

First one is called "Breaking Away," and the second one is "etc".

So let's talk about "Breaking Away" first. Oh — and by the way…

"Chester, why are you even telling us about this? Who cares about these silly little lessons that you taught in a classroom?"

Well, let's think about it.

"Breaking Away" has to do with what it costs to leave home. In the '80s — '70s and '80s, the costs were very minimal. The kids were very anxious to get going… with life. Not so much today.

One of the important things they needed to know was how much do I have to *net* per hour in order to just… make ends meet… pay the rent… pay for the food, the laundry, the *whatever*? Whatever expenses there are in life?

"Etc" has to do with… controlling your emotions.

People say, "Don't get too high, too low." Well, I think we

need a little guidance on that. I'll provide that in this chapter, in that section... on "etc".

Let's get on with "Breaking Away."

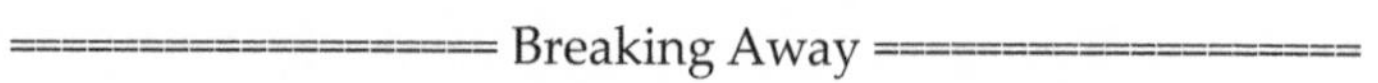

Breaking Away

I had four classes of electronics at Monte Vista. They were year-long classes. We got to know each other. So, this was usually done in the springtime. You don't want to introduce this subject — if you're going to teach it — too early... it's a downer. You know, reality sucks. We're going to address reality here.

So, I let each class, and each student in the class, make their own sheet. We did this in one day.

I'd say, "Okay. What do we need?"

"I gotta pay rent."

"Oh!" We'd write "rent" on the board.

Then we'd go like, "What are we gonna do? One-bedroom, two-bedroom?"

"No. No... I'm gonna be with a roommate. We're going to share the one-bedroom."

"Oh! So what are one-bedrooms going for now? Do you want to live in this area?"

They'd usually say, "Well, I can't afford to live *here*."

"Okay, what area you want?"

"Uh... Concord." So we'd look it up in the newspaper: what is a Concord one-bedroom going for?... Write it down.

Then someone else in the same class would go, "Nah, I gotta have two bedrooms. I want a roommate, but I gotta have my room. He or she could have her room."

All right. What does a two-bedroom cost? Where you wanna live?

"Uh... I wanna live in... Alamo."

Ay, ay, yai! All right. What are these two-bedrooms going for an Alamo? Maybe in those days was twelve-hundred. I don't know… one bedroom: six-, seven-hundred. I'm just guessing. I forget what the numbers were.

So you'd write all this down. Then you'd start incurring all the other expenses that it takes to live. Paying rent don't cut it. That's a nice start. Don't forget: you got to have first month, last month… maybe a deposit… gotta have some cash.

Most kids said, "No, my parents would pay for that to get me on my own."

Wow! Very nice. I never had that kind of opportunity, but that's a wonderful thing. You find these things from time to time in an upscale neighborhood like Danville, California, where I taught. The parents were generally successful.

I got sad sometimes when kids had to buy kits. Maybe they wanted to buy a kit. The mother writes a check for the kits. The check bounces. Then you go like, "What, can you tell your mom that it bounced?"

"Well, my dad and my mom are separated now, and uh…"

Oh, man. From a nice idyllic upbringing — Mommy, Daddy… you… maybe a sister or brother — to now, the house is broken apart. Eh!

So, we'd cover for that kid or have them bring — or her — have 'em bring in something to repair… something so you're staying active and on target for what we'd like to accomplish… though there are sad times in your house.

But, I digress.

So anyway, we'd look at the list of everything: food… I dunno… washing clothes… I don't know. What does it cost to have an apartment? You're out on your own. How about gas money? How about a car payment, maybe? Lot of the kids, "No, my parents bought me a car."

Oh, good. There's still gas. So: PG&E… Comcast… water bill… garbage bill…

All these things. Some are included in some apartments; some are not. Generally, electricity is broken out separately. You gotta pay separately. So if it's cold at your apartment in Concord then… putting on a couple layers of thermal underwear isn't doing it for you? Well, then… turn up the heat. Cost you money, at the end of the month.

So the kids would do all of these things. Some would say, "Well, gee, wait a minute: you forgot snacks."

All right, let's write down "snacks." Some people snack, some don't.

"How many people here snack on potato chips, or something like that nature?" Well, almost everyone raised their hand.

By the way, one of the nice things about being a teacher: you get instant feedback. You know, they talk about this Internet stuff, they tabulate things… it's real easy to tabulate in a classroom. Y'know, "How many of you do snacks?" All but two. There's thirty-seven, thirty-five kids; thirty-five out of thirty-seven said they snack.

"Uh… What do *you* do? You don't snack, at all?" Maybe I would ask, you know, like…

"Well, no. I eat celery and I eat… carrots. I love raw potatoes."

"Okay. Are you growing your own or you go —"

"Nah! I'll go to the store."

"Well, are we going to put that down? Come on now? That's a snack."

"Yeah, but it's not very expensive, Chet."

Eh! Not very expensive. Is it eleven cents… or closer to five dollars, ten dollars a month… twenty dollars a month? If you do this daily, maybe it's eighty dollars a month. You'd be surprised.

"Chet! I gotta have my Pepsi!"

"Well, huh… add it up."

"Chet! I eat half-pound of bacon in the morning."

Add it up.

When you'd get to the end, each class — I'll summarize, you

know, just to make it easier — essentially was varied by class. Usually the first class of the day: semi-sleepy. They're not really thinking it through. Their totals were like $11.45, net, per hour, to make ends meet.

That was in — let's say — in the '80s. Then, it crawled its way up. It's getting even more expensive now. I know, minimum wage is around seven, eight bucks — something like that — and the states or cities are trying to bump it up twelve-fifty, fifteen... they have to. Who could live on — you know — eight bucks an hour? Y'know: ay, ay, yai! You'd have to do two or three eight-dollar-an-hour jobs — there are people who do.

But, around $11.45 was the cheapest, net, per-hour that I really came across. The average was more like fourteen, and a quarter. If you inflate those numbers a little bit to help cover for — because I haven't taught since 1999 — then you'll find that the numbers are a bit higher. For example, the apartments in my condo — when I first came here — okay... this was converted apartments. Now they're condos. People trying to sell their one-bedroom condo: fifty-thousand in 1999 was common. Fifty-thousand! Cudda bought 'em all! Thought 'bout buying 'em all — the ones that face the creek, like mine. I'd be wealthy today. *Wealthy*. Why? They're all going three-, four-hundred thousand. There we go.

See... fifty in, four-hundred thousand out. I don't know. That's pretty good jump.

But... anyway, you get the drift. It's all expensive these days to live. Especially if you want to live well. You know, these kids weren't talking about exclusive nice apartment complex with — you know — a guard at the gate, and so forth. Maybe it has a pool. Kind of looks like a motel. But, nothing wrong with that. It's home. But it costs.

After we did all this, in the early days — let's say, late '70s, '80s... like that — kids were anxious to leave. Parents were glad to throw 'em out. "Get outta here. Get going. Go do sumthin'."

In Danville, it was generally, "Go to college. Get yourself an education so that you could get yourself a decent job." Makes a lot of sense.

The kids would go, like, "Yeah, my parents would give me a coupla grand to help me get settled – just to, eh… because I'm a pain in the neck to them…"

"Well, good!"

Now, fast forward to the '90s. I could feel it comin'. How'd I feel it comin'? My son, John, came home to live with me. In other words, I got a home, and my son is coming to live with me. Times are tough in between jobs.

Then you hear of others who bring in their sons or daughters. You hear of others that don't leave at all. They didn't come back; they just won't leave. Where they gonna go? How they gonna afford it?

Let's round off to today's numbers. Gotta clear fifteen dollars an hour! In order to clear fifteen dollars an hour, you gotta make eighteen. Yikes! Eighteen dollars an hour!

"Chet! I can get by on, uh, eight dollars an hour, and four of us stay in a place –"

All right. All right. Yeah. There's all kinds of exceptions. Live in your car. Maybe your parents will love you – let you live in the backyard. I don't know.

But, today, as we speak – eh, what is this… April? No… May? No. April 26th, 2019 – the kids don't want to leave. They're rackin' up college expenses, student loans – can't believe it.

I'll tell you something about the student loan process, real quick.

Student loans. They started that when I was in college. It was like a breakthrough. Money for a kid going to college. What was the highest loan they had in those days? Twenty-five hundred. What did it cost you to go to school for a year? I don't know. I saved up seven hundred dollars during the summer, working at Fibreboard Paper Products. That's seven-hundred, plus — my mother would give me twenty dollars if I came home on the weekend — and then she'd make me spaghetti sauce and sausage in order to take back to school to share with my roommates.

Maybe... maybe fifteen-hundred, to get through the year. Rents were about a $105, for the month.

A couple of years later, get married, now, got a place in the Haight: $105. Nice big, one bedroom apartment. It was nice! Good size kitchen, dining area, good sized — Oh! You could get a lot for a $105 bucks.

So it was comparatively cheap in those days.

Then all of a sudden, the cost of school starts skyrocketing. There's no more Prop. 13 where a lot of money was going into education. Not anymore. So, there you go. With all these extensions... costs a lot of money.

Kids are kind of scared to move away. I wouldn't move away. I think my mother — I'm almost positive — if I would have just stayed home — went to college, whatever, doesn't matter — if I would have just ended up with her, she would have been thrilled.

She'll cook for me every night, make something for me every day... Ah! spoil me to death. I'd have to take her to the racetrack every once in a while, even though I only go a couple times a year, but... that's a different story.

But, y'know... it wasn't for me... What I'm saying is: if times were tough enough, sure, I'd live with Mom. Pffft! All day long. That's kind of what's happening now.

But, getting back to the lesson about "Breaking Away." It's an eye opener. Now, those who don't wanna believe the numbers — I mean students in the classroom...

"You don't have to pay six-hundred a month for an apartment."

"Well, all right! Where's it cheaper?"

"My brother and his friend. They got a place — they only pay, eh, four-fifty!"

"Wow! Where's that?"

"Chico, California."

"Wow! Awful *north*. Is that where you want to live? If you live there, yeah, it's a little cheaper. Four-fifty's a lot cheaper than six-hundred."

And so forth. But if you want to live kind of within a certain circumference of your friends and family — you were born and raised in Danville, California — one way is… you can go out to Dublin. Another way, you go out towards Concord. Another way, you go out towards Lafayette/Moraga.

Pick a way you want to go. Stay within the area: costs. But if you move… hey: *Yountville*! It's a nice place. I'll bet you could find some place to live for three-hundred… in Yountville. Question: got work? I don't know. I don't think there's much industry in Yountville. Probably some wonderful restaurants and such, but…

Anyway, "Breaking Away" was a wonderful lesson. Do it with your children! Sit around the table —

"Hey! You want to leave home?"

First response would be, "No!" I think these days.

So you have to do more hypothetical, which is, "If you wanted to go out on your own, do you think you'd go with a roommate or not?"

Now, it's not appropriate with — necessarily — for a four- or five-year old child, but I do believe — everything that's educational is appropriate for anybody at any time. Got a two-year-old that understands what you're talking about? Pfffft! Talk to him about it. Got an eleven-year-old that kind of understands what you're talking about? Talk to her or him about it.

But generally, I know it's successful at the high school level. Junior high, they're not quite thinking about breaking away — with some, some are. Some boys, some girls, are a little more advanced socially, whatever... already looking towards the future. Okay, but certainly appropriate for high school and above.

So, I hope that helps you and your children and get a grip on what things cost. Make your own thing, with your family, you know, just like I did in class. Write 'em down as they come.

"Oh, yeah... forgot about snacks."

"Oh, yeah, I forgot about laundry."

"Oh, yeah, I forgot about —"

What? I dunno. Gas. PG&E. Garbage. All of that. Oh, yeah. I mean write it down. Just be realistic. Don't inflate anything. Reality is stark enough.

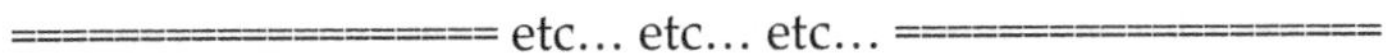

I came across this acronym — I'm not exactly sure what you call it — but it seemed to work out — where I use the letters E-T-C, meaning *et cetera, et cetera, et cetera*... to explain three human emotions.

E stands for "expectations."

T stands for "temperament."

C stands for "control."

Notice the "t" in "etc" is a little taller than normal, than the other two letters. Okay. That's what we're trying to address: your temperament, your attitude, with this lesson.

Let's start with "*expectation*."

You know, it's funny. You go out to your car every morning, you get in, it starts, and you drive away.

Until one day, you go out there, it's a flat tire, or it won't start. Now you're angry. Now you're befuddled. Now you're... *whatever*!

"This car always starts. I trust this car. It's never failed me."

Well, it did today.

My expectation, when I go out and start the car, is: hope it turns over.

I got a nice little Honda, too. 2007… CRV. Nice and clean inside. Doesn't even have a hundred thousand miles — ninety-eight- or ninety-nine-thousand… goes nice. Should it start every time? Sure. Do I expect it to start every time? Nope.

When it does, I smile. Right away, my day is better, by something so simple.

"Ah! The car started. Ay! And it sounds pretty good. Eh! And it goes into reverse as I back out of my parking spot. Eh! And it goes forward, and the tickers work and… Wow!"

The rest is up to me now. Drive safely… get to where you need to be, and all like that.

"Chester! That sounds so silly, so banal, so… basic."

Well, I think all lessons should be kept basic, until we begin to delve into the particulars. Then it's not very basic. Then these things become very important.

So let's start easy. Expectation could be… how 'bout this: Let's take a girl at Monte Vista High School, fifteen years old. She's a sophomore. Maybe she meets a junior. When she meets a junior… her heart goes a little flutter. All right. They chat for a few minutes. Very nice.

Maybe they exchange phone numbers. He says, "I'll call you."

She goes, "That'd be great."

She goes home. Kinda real light on her feet. Kind of excited. I'd be. Y'know… in those early days? Wow! Don't get that much excited anymore, but I could understand her excitement.

But he never calls. He doesn't call that night. He doesn't call the next day. In fact, you don't see him again for a week.

Well, if she had *no* expectations — at all — that he would call… if she would lower those expectations…

People say, "I'm going to call you…" They don't.

People say, "I'll come by…" They don't. Eh… just, casual, maybe.

But now, she's unhappy for an entire week. She's wondering, "Do I confront him? Do I — what do I do next?"

"Well, he didn't promise you."

"Yeah, but he said he would."

"Yeah, but it —"

Oh, my.

Now let's shift real quickly over to the letter "c"... meaning "*control*."

In that situation, for that fifteen year-old sophomore girl...

Question: Does she have control over the situation, namely that he will call her... and probably tonight?

None! Absolutely none.

Ah! That normally would make it a lot easier. Sure does for me.

What, did you tell me you're going to call me? I'll believe it when the phone rings. I'm not waiting for your call. I'm not going to call you on it. I'm not gonna challenge you.

You said, "Chet! Call you tomorrow."

Good! If the phone rings, and it's you, good! If the phone doesn't ring and it's not you, good!

Both the same. Wanna call? Call. Don't wanna call? Don't. Whatever makes you happy. I have no control over you calling me. Thus, I have no "e" — or *expectation* — that the call is going to be made.

Ah!

Take a look at my "t," in the middle. "*Temperament*." Tall. I'm happy.

Yeah. Nothing ruins my day. Not like that.

I had no *expectation*, and I certainly had no *control*.

"Chet, I can't help myself from having expectations."

I got that. Please realize you have absolutely no control over whether or not another human being phones you today, tomorrow or ever.

That will help lower your expectation, realizing you have no control. A lot of people think they have control of the room, control of the — eh! eh! Careful what you think.

You can barely control yourself, most people. You certainly can't control someone else.

A lot of human beings are not in control. They've got one substance abuse or another, an attitude problem or another. I mean it goes on and on.

You know, it's funny. This world is very simple.

Keep your expectations down. Realize you have no control — especially like weather — people talk about weath—?

"This isn't right. We've had too much rain. It's about time we get some sun and have —"

Whatever. White noise. White noise. That's all that is: background garbage.

It's a beautiful day. We need the rain, deh, dah, deh... and let it go!

To sit, to pontificate, to conject, as to what it means, and then this and that — eh, c'mon! It's got some rain. It's raining.

Don't make it any more complicated than that.

So, to understand — like, even in a marriage. Let's try — I've never tried this before. Let's just think about it, right now.

Husband and wife. Couple of kids. Here we go.

Husband says, "We're out of milk. We're out of... *whatever*."

Wife says, —-

Nah, let's not make it milk; that's more of a daily thing. Whatever.

"We're out of celery. I feel like a celery stick, and that would be fun."

She says, "I'll go to the store tomorrow. I'm going to pick up some other things. I'll add you to the list."

The next day, you come back with the groceries, wherever you shop. You set the groceries down. Maybe the husband helps you carry 'em in. Why is he helping you carry 'em in? Eh, probably wants to see his celery.

"Oh, son of a gun! You forgot the celery!"

Husband makes some kind of a snide comment, which is…

"We just talked about this yesterday. You said, you told me you were going to go to the store and you'd pick up some celery."

She says, "In all honesty, I forgot."

He goes, "Forgot?"

Let's stop right there. I don't know where this is going to go.

But in my life it goes, "No, we're good."

Now, we got to talk about *your* word, versus *my* word. Now, we got to talk about promises broken. Oh, my gosh! Promises broken.

"But you said…"

"Uh, yes, I did. But I forgot."

"What a cavalier attitude you have! You just forgot!? What about that list? You didn't write it down on your list!?" — and so forth.

I'm going to stop right there. I hate arguments. I don't allow arguments. We never argue in the classroom. I never once had an argument in the classroom… *ever.*

I don't allow arguments here, at my home. We could be outside, you're drinking a little too much, you're getting loud and argumentative… I throw you out. Time to go home. We're done here.

Not going to argue about politics or whatever. You're drunk. Get outta here.

I don't like arguments. There's no reason for arguments. Arguments are just a mental exercise that people wanna… grind into other people. I don't know. Maybe they're angry at other people. Maybe they resent.

Marriages, like we were talking about — kinda complicated, in its own right. You're with someone essentially… all the time. Maybe you both have separate places to be during the day. She works. He stays home, vice versa, both work. I dunno. But you do share a lot of time.

If we could just remember: keep the expectations low.

Somebody gave your word? Don't go that high and mighty. Give me your word. They're just a passing thing. Yeah, I'll call you. Then they forgot or whatever or didn't want to. Sometimes people do that just to be nice, then they don't follow through. Who cares? It doesn't matter. Keep the expectations low.

Realize: you have no control over another human being, what they're going to do. You might barely have control over what *you're* gonna do. Not all of us do.

Got a drug problem? Got a alcohol problem? Got a anger problem? Got a gambling problem? C'mon, the list is endless. Those people have no control. Think they do. No control.

"Chet, I've got a lot of self-control."

Good! Apply that self-control idea to the idea that you have no control over another human being and what they're going to do. *None.*

"Yeah, but Chet! It's my mother!"

Mothers make mistakes. Mothers forget.

Lovers make mistakes. Lovers forget.

C'mon, high and mighty. Broke your word.

It's just a common thing that happens all the time. If you have high expectations, based on comments just as casual as, "I'll call you," you're in the wrong direction, in the wrong direction. You know, like they say in Missouri — I dunno... — "show me?"

So, I don't even wait for "show me." If it happens, it happens. If it don't, it don't. That's all.

"Chet! Wouldn't you be happier if they called?"

Maybe. Depends what they called about.

There are certain people that aren't very uplifting.

Think they got control, and they don't. Have high expectations, and they shouldn't. I don't know if I want to talk to this person today. That's a lot of work.

I'm done.

Chapter 44

THE CREEK

When my wife passed away in 1992, I put the house up for sale. We had purchased the house on Shuey Avenue many years earlier. It was 'bout a hundred and thirty-five thousand, I paid. We sold it for around two thirty-five. We made a nice little profit, for those days, but not like the money they're making today. My gosh. That same house right now is going for one-point-two million, on Shuey Avenue. My, my, my… what an investment if I had held on. But, I wanted to get out, didn't want to be in the house anymore. Leave those memories behind.

My realtor found me a place here, in Walnut Creek.

I told him I wanted to look at three places. We looked at one in Danville — it was nice. I told him I wanted an end unit, and a minimum of two bedrooms, two baths.

He found a nice end-unit in a place in Danville — it was kinda nice, but it was right next to the sound wall on Highway 680. Not the view that I wanted. Then we looked at another place — it was just between Alamo… Danville — I'm not sure. No, didn't quite do it. Then he took me to this one… which is on Creekside Drive, in Walnut Creek — the south end of Walnut Creek.

It doesn't look like much from the outside. Looks like a motel kind of apartments. Nothin' special. Built in the '60s.

But when you come in… it's very spacious. Got three bedrooms, two baths… it's like mid-century modern: tall windows, lotta light coming in.

As I looked, I went, "Eh, it's all right… I dunno — Let's take a look at the view."

The realtor opened the sliding glass door. There was an Asian family that was living there, husband and wife, and at least two, maybe three kids.

"You could feed the raccoons!" they told me.

I went, "Oh, all right!"

We walked out. It had, like, a little cement patio, then cyclone fence. It's cyclone fenced-in. But at least it's an area like around fifteen or twenty feet, by fourteen feet. There was some room to do something.

I went up to the cyclone fence, looked down, and there was... *San Ramon Creek*. San Ramon Creek is a controlled creek. It runs 24/7, 365. There are seven agencies involved here: East Bay MUD[1], Army Corps of Engineers, Department of Wildlife — it used to be called "Fish and Game." Now it's called something else. There's the City of Walnut Creek. There's Flood Control. There's the County of Contra Costa. There's the State of California. All the agencies were involved in this.

When I wanted to make little changes, or *things*, over the years... you called one agency, they referred you to another, which referred you over to somebody else. It was crazy.

But I fell in love with it right away. It's all natural sandstone, for the creek. A lot of trees. Wonderful setting.

But, there were several problems. One: the cyclone fence had to go. So on my first day of ownership, I took it down.

Well, it's funny. I get a letter right away at my door: "This is a condominium. We have CC&R's. You can't be taking down that fence."

I said, "I looked at the CC&R's. Didn't say anything about not being able to take down the fence."

"Well, what do you intend to do?"

"I'm buildin' a deck, but I'm gonna build it fast. I see the property actually goes out beyond this. It's just that it's kind of steep right here, 'bout a 45 degree angle going down to the

---

[1] Municipal Utilities District

water. We're about 25 feet above it. But there's additional space out there.

"So I'm gonna make a big deck. It's going to go from this end, to that end... fifty-five feet long." It ended up being seven hundred and sixty square feet, all redwood.

Then I had to tell them what I was going to do, why I was doing it, that I didn't mean — they said it had to do with insurance purposes. Well, it's just so much easier just to walk into our complex from any of two or three areas... just walk right in... break a window, steal what you want? I don't know. Why are you going to go down the creek and then climb this hillside? It's treacherous, I mean, to make it up to where I am. You think a crook is going to go through all that? I'm not worried. I feel very safe back here; he ain't comin'. They never did.

But anyway, the first thing I did was build this big deck. How long did it take me? I bought the house in May of '93. I got my lumber and everything together by August. Steve Settle, former student of mine, really helped me out with this, as he provided very inexpensive prices for me to buy wood from *Piedmont Lumber*.

So anyway, we built the deck. Then my eyes turned to the creek, which I had been ignoring since I moved in.

What was on the hillsides? I don't know, you name it: mattresses... complete motor... a couple transmissions... all kinds of beer bottles... heavy things. A lot of steel, a lot of metal... just... *things*... it was terrible. Things at the bottom of the creek. Things everywhere. Like, no one ever paid attention.

I called the City of Walnut Creek.

"I am paying attention to this, and I don't like it."

They came out, took a look.

"Yeah, it's a mess. That happens. Nobody ever comes down here much, though."

I dunno.

So, I hired some kids from Monte Vista High School. They

came out on weekends. We filled three dumpsters full of… *stuff,* heavy stuff, waterlogged stuff, all kinds of stuff.

Pretty soon — took a while — but pretty soon, it was clean.

Then we started to — I started to address the hillside across from where I live. I watered over there, took out the weeds, added lawn seed and such. What was just a bottle-strewn area… dog poop everywhere… just… human poop…

Ay, ay, yai! All clean. Now regrowing. Wow! Very nice.

I turned my attention to the trees. All the suckers going up these gorgeous trees. They looked like they had been abandoned for years. No one had pruned these dead things… nothing. So that took another couple weeks — pruned it all. All the suckers going up the trunks? Gone. Dead limbs? Gone. Sagging limbs that are about ready to go in the water? Outta here.

Then, I turned my attention to what was a small little waterfall — and by "small," I mean, maybe four feet high — that someone had installed. You could tell it was hand done. But it was *something*. I increased that to a full eight, ten feet, whatever the level of the water would be. You took gunny sacks and filled them with sixty pounds of your concrete. Then you tied it off at the end with a zip tie. You rolled it in the water, first on one side, then on the other, kind of mixing it in the bag. Then you put it in place. You start building your dam that way. The weight of the bags — put 'em two-deep, where necessary — can just about restrict any kind of water flow you wanted, on this creek. All I did was even it out.

I took what was like "ugly, but it had potential" to now being a very nice waterfall, that you can enjoy.

By the way, the water here is only about five inches deep. There are certain pools that go as deep as six or seven feet. It all used to be fully deep with water… twelve feet deep… nine. I had my measuring poles… ten feet right below me; now five inches.

What happened? Well, the Army Corps of Engineers from

Washington, they came out and did this project. They created a dam — I mean, a *limiting system,* to where the water coming down could only go so high, only so wide, in this opening that's up the creek. We call 'em "The Grates." That's where the water comes from, up above, and down.

Feeding into this is East Bay MUD water. This is not run-off that just comes — this is East Bay MUD water... keepin' it flowing. It's all good.

But the thing is, when the Army Corps of Engineers built these forty- or fifty-feet, twenty-feet high big walls, that are going to contain all this water — because this area used to almost flood, and occasionally actually flood, prior to 1993 when I moved in — but when they finished the project, it was a controlled creek...

They left all their construction debris there. All the stuff they did for the digging, save a lot of money: just dump it in the creek. Let it come down the creek.

When I called Army Corps of Engineers on it a couple years later, like, "Uh... Aey, your stuff filled the creek. I reported you to Fish & Game" — now, it's called something else.

He said, "*They're* state, we're *federal.* We don't answer to them. Yeah, we didn't take out all the stuff. Right. But the budget was limited. So, where'd the dirt go? Down in the creek. But where'd the water go, too?" He said, "It's flowing, isn't it?"

"Yeah, but it's only about five inches..."

"Well, that's somebody else's job to remove the dirt. Not mine."

And he hung up. Least he answered. Pretty good.

So I tried my best to try to stay ahead of it, clean it, keep it deep. I did that for a few years. That was crazy. So I built some little inlets that look really sharp coming in, making a nice deeper pool for the fish. We got a family of river otters here, and so forth.

It cost me a lot of money over the years — I pay two-hundred and fifty a month just to maintain… blow off the leaves, just kind of pick up trash and branches that have fallen … those kind of things.

You can also tell it's my work — you'll see that five to eight feet along all the edges makes it totally walkable. No poison ivy. All gone. It's all, like… *bank*. You could walk on it — the kids walk on it. Dogs come. People are very nice now.

My friend — name is Doc Siino, of Pittsburg, California — he was over here. Always a paranoid guy. He was heavy into… well, anyway — always paranoid.

"What are you doing over there and stuff? It's like, it was way better before."

"What do you mean?"

"Well now, anybody can come. Before… just the punks and the drunks."

"Doc. I want the grandma and the granddaughter and the doggie and the — to come down and have fun and not feel threatened by the drunks and the druggies. So I'm making it very nice. Maybe you call it a gamble. I think it's a solution."

And it was.

Very rarely, do you have a little dog doo-doo anywhere in this area.

But, I have to say: women generally pickup better than men. I've got a good twenty-six years of observation. I promise you: the women, the girls, are more responsible than the guys.

In fact, there's a guy, now, that I'm kinda dealing with. I will; I'll address it. He has a big, giant dog. He's a family man… married, a couple of kids. Everything's ideal. The animal's about a hundred and twenty five, a hundred and fifty pounds. Big animal. Love dogs. Love. It looks like a big lab, but it's, like, got to have something else in it because… it's *big*. Well, then the excrement is also big. The guy's always on his phone. Doesn't pay attention. When he leaves that area: big hump of poo-poo.

Does he have a bag in his hand? No.

Did he come prepared to clean up after the dog? No.

That's not the kind of people we want around here. I'll bring it up to him when I see him.

This is the general reply: "It wasn't *me*. I pick up. Look!" He'll reach in, and he'll go, "Look, I gotta bag!"

"Really?"

"Yeah! It ain't *my* dog!"

Oh, good.

So what do you have to do? Catch him in the act. So, I will… which is, dog will take a poo-poo there, and I'm gonna watch 'em. I'll give 'em about eight seconds, ten seconds to pick it up. If he doesn't, I'm gonna point it out to him. He will. With something… not a bag, because they didn't bring it. His wife brings a bag. The kids are too small to be responsible.

These are the kind of things that I deal with now, which are so small, compared to what I had to deal with before. If all you gotta do is straighten someone out a little bit about — "C'mon! Pick up what you bring in here, including your dog poo-poo." That's it?

On most days, you can look all the way up — it's about a hundred yards to my left, the creek that I could see, three hundred yards to my right — not a drop of paper. No poo-poo.

But, on a bad day, when people get a little carried away: some papers, plastic bottle or two, maybe some dog poo-poo. I used to go clean that up all the time. I can't do it anymore. So my… the gardener, Wayne, he'll take care of it, when he works for me on Fridays. He'd kinda clean it up, blow it away or whatever and just — especially the trash, he picks up. Try to keep it clean.

It's like Heaven on Earth.

I'm so lucky in this respect, too: my favorite camping site ever — I caught pneumonia there — was Pfeiffer State Park. I think it's called Pfeiffer. Big Sur?

One of the people that I taught with in the school district — I taught at a high school, he taught at a junior high — he was a ranger. He made arrangements for me. I made reservations through him and, you know, pay the park.

But he gave me the prime site: Number 21… same as mine here on Creekside Drive. Number 21.

The water was streaming right by Number 21 at Big Sur… just like it is here. It was meant to be.[2]

[2] If you'd like to come enjoy the creek, come to Walnut Creek, California, take South Main to Creekside Drive to Near Court, turn right. Come halfway down the block, park on your right. Take the little path down to the creek.

Afterword

Writing an autobiography puts life in perspective. It's very easy. You just have to decide what you're going to relate to your readers — that's the hardest part — and start.

Because the stories of your life are real, everything flows. It took me eight days to write the book, doing five to six stories (chapters) a day.

The harder parts were selecting which newspaper stories to use, the photos to use, the type set, the cover art, and especially editing.

But I hope this book was a fun read and/or an enjoyable listen — because we have it on digital format for everyone.

Either way that you enjoy it, I had fun. I love and miss you all!

Chester
I'm done.

"Journey is on the way—gotta clean back stage!"
Photo by Stu Shader

ABOOKS

ALIVE Book Publishing and ALIVE Publishing Group
are imprints of Advanced Publishing LLC,
3200 A Danville Blvd., Suite 204, Alamo, California 94507

Telephone: 925.837.7303
alivebookpublishing.com

CPSIA information can be obtained
at www.ICGtesting.com
Printed in the USA
LVHW090814040720
659412LV00005BB/41/J